LIBERAL'S PROGRESS

Edward A. Filene on his return from Europe in 1926

Liberal's Progress

BY GERALD W. JOHNSON

> Wherefore, Simmias, seeing all these things, what
> ought not we to do that we may obtain virtue and wis-
> dom in this life? Fair is the prize, and the hope great!
> —PHAEDO, *Jowett's translation*

COWARD-McCANN, INC.   NEW YORK

21524

Acknowledgment

To list by name everyone who courteously and patiently assisted the writer in the preparation of this book would be to make practically a complete catalogue of those friends and associates of Edward A. Filene who are still living, so this general word of thanks must do. But three went much further. Percy S. Brown, Esq., Robert Szold, Esq., and Miss B. W. Connors all read the manuscript and by their special knowledge of the subject saved the author from falling into many factual errors. None of them, however, has any responsibility for the interpretation of the facts made by the author, nor do they necessarily agree with it.

CONTENTS

An Explanation

‹‹‹

THIS BOOK deals with an individual, but it is not a conventional biography. The subject did not want a conventional biography, and he was right.

There was a man named Edward A. Filene, who lived seventy-seven years, most of the time in the city of Boston, but about that man's loves, wars, comings, goings, uprisings and downsittings there is not a great deal in this book—only as much as is indispensably necessary to give the reader some idea of what sort of man he was.

The reason for this omission may be expressed in two words, to wit, who cares?

If he had been a man of action, the case would be different. To determine whether the commander of an army corps moved on the fifteenth of the month or the sixteenth and to know whether he moved north or east may be vital to any adequate judgment of his competence as a general. To determine whether a President of the United States delivered a certain address in Wichita, Kansas, or Atlanta, Georgia, may be important, since a politician commonly suits his deliverance to his audience, and to know what he meant it is as important to know to whom he spoke as to know what he said. To judge a businessman accused of, say, embezzlement, it may be crucial to know with whom he dined on the night before the money disappeared.

But Edward A. Filene's importance to this generation rests

not upon his acts but upon his ideas. There were some hundreds of thousands of men living in Boston during the years that he lived there. Many of them were as active as he was, some more active, but of all those multitudes only a handful did anything that has a traceable effect upon the lives of their successors. Still smaller is the number who thought anything that remains important for us to understand.

Edward A. Filene set up two public trusts endowing foundations that are still operative. This is almost the only overt act of his life that still influences the course of events in the way that the winning of a battle or an election influences them long after the occurrence. But he expressed innumerable ideas, some of which have increased in potency since his death and may become dominant in the years to come.

The important thing about him therefore is not that he lived, but that he thought for seventy-seven years, or for as large a proportion of that time as anyone thinks. The development of his thought had an unusual effect in that it made him a liberal, which is not the usual effect upon a man who starts as a poor boy, applies his mind to business, succeeds brilliantly, and becomes rich by his own efforts in an old and conservative city. Here, then, is a case sufficiently out of the ordinary to deserve examination.

But it is his ideas that count, not his activities, nor his associations, nor his experiences except in so far as they had an unmistakable effect upon his thinking. For this reason chronology is of little significance, and small respect is paid to it in the following pages. Even his career in business is treated somewhat cavalierly for two reasons. In the first place, although it was exceptional, it was far from unique, and if its success is to be measured by the money it brought him, many Americans have exceeded it, and some have exceeded it vastly. In the second place, his business success was not achieved exclusively by his own efforts but is attributable in no small measure to the assistance of able associates, notably a brother who also proved to be a business genius.

Incidentally, the record of the Filene business has attracted the attention of economists, sociologists, and business analysts who have published many detailed studies of its operations, which are available to anyone who seeks them in the literature of American business. These activities, therefore, the writer has felt under no compulsion to include here, saying, rather, of the merchant what was said of many of the ancient kings of Israel: "And the rest of the acts of Nadab, and all that he did, are they not written in the books of the chronicles of the kings?"

Filene was well aware that the significance of his life lay in his ideas, not in his acts nor in his personality. As will be explained later, he was skeptical of biographies of businessmen and anxious if ever a book should be written about him that the emphasis should not be misplaced. "Make the book not too biographical," he said with emphasis to one man who contemplated writing about him.

A biography that is not very biographical is an idea unconventional enough to be worthy of Filene, who was frequently startling but whose most startling notions invariably had a hard substratum of common sense. Unquestionably, the successive steps by which this shrewd, forceful, and successful American businessman attained a position that made him the most conspicuous liberal leader in his economic group constitute the interesting and significant elements in his career; but these steps were rarely, if ever, forced by extraneous circumstances. Almost without exception they were developments of his thinking, and extraneous circumstances, even such circumstances as place and time, had little relevance.

Needless to say, Filene's mind did not differ from all other minds by moving in one direction only. Like other people's, his thought proliferated in many directions simultaneously, hence the order in which his ideas are examined must of necessity be more or less arbitrary. The order in which they are presented here cannot be defended as the only correct and logical one.

Nevertheless, a progression there certainly was. The child may have been father of the man, but he was not the man, and some, at least, of the stages of the transition from one to the other are clearly discernible. This book is an effort to present them and to describe as accurately as may be their relation to each other. It is assuredly a book made "not too biographical," as its subject wished. If it has erred in the other direction it is not because the writer lacked appreciation of a salty personality, but because the progress of an acute and vigorous intelligence toward an advanced position on the liberal side seemed vastly more important and interesting than any individual history could be.

GERALD W. JOHNSON

LIBERAL'S PROGRESS

CHAPTER 1

The Man

‹‹‹

I

THE MORNING of May 20, 1888, was exceptionally fine, and Edward Albert Filene walked across Boston Common rejoicing. Young Mr. Filene was not alone in that; all Boston rejoiced with him. The season up to that date had been fitful, not to say spiteful. The withdrawal of winter had been slow and sullen, including repeated Parthian shots that had nipped the ears and noses of the populace and depressed their spirits. Cold seemed destined to last forever.

But on the morning of May 20 everything indicated that it was over. The brilliance of the sunlight, the balminess of the air that still had a sparkle in it, the gay and jocund demeanor of the birds that had returned to the trees of the Common, the misty and tremulous, yet resolute green of the trees themselves —all signs agreed that summer was icumen in and if Mr. Filene did not "lhude sing cuccu," it was not for lack of the impulse to do so but only because in his day up-and-coming young businessmen of Boston did not so express themselves. However, he did the equivalent. He wrote in his journal on that day, "I feel big enough to conquer the world—and know that tomorrow I shall sell pins."

Young Filene was as far as possible from being a mystic, but that entry betrays a moment of prophetic insight. In 1888 he was not yet a big man, and he never became big enough to con-

1

quer the world, but he belonged to a group that has come astonishingly close to doing so, the group that led American business through the final quarter of the nineteenth century and the first quarter of the twentieth. Yet on the morrow and for many morrows thereafter he did sell pins.

In the interest of precision perhaps the dates should be thrust back a decade, extending from the close of the Civil War in 1865 to the outbreak of the First World War in 1914. This was the period in which the American economic empire was built. What that event portended for the world is still obscure and may not be fully understood for generations to come, but nobody from the educational level of Arnold J. Toynbee to that of a bootblack doubts that it was important. The men who accomplished it altered the course of history, and Filene was one of them. The young man was extraordinarily perceptive that May morning.

His position in the hierarchy of American business is still a matter of dispute and is likely to remain so for some time, because if he had any large importance, it was as a prophet. In the nature of the case no one can tell how good a prophet is until enough time has elapsed for his predictions to be either fulfilled or discredited. Edward A. Filene has been dead only a little over ten years, and thus far his predictions have been fulfilled only in part. The next generation will know what this one can do no more than estimate.

Certain minor phases of his career are, however, clear enough. For one thing, he was never one of the great whales of American business. He accumulated between ten and twenty million dollars, which by comparison with the fortunes of certain of his contemporaries—a Rockefeller for instance, or a Carnegie, or a Vanderbilt, not to mention the greatest and latest of the financial colossi, Henry Ford—was really small stuff.

But a man's importance in any group is rarely to be measured by a single factor. If Filene's fortune was never to startle the business world, his ideas were, and if the test of time proves that those ideas were sound, he may yet come to overshadow men with money enough to buy him up a dozen times. In any event, they were not petty ideas. The very fact that a decade has been not nearly enough time in which to test them is evidence of their range.

The central core of his thinking was his profound belief that liberalism in the modern world has no necessary connection with altruism and is definitely antipathetic to sentimentality. He contended that the most completely self-centered business-man, if he is really intelligent, must move into the liberal position, not out of regard for his fellow men but to protect his own interest.

This made him a paradox to his contemporaries, although since the Long Armistice and the Second World War his arguments have become much more comprehensible than they were in, say, the early part of 1914. Yet to this day he is an odd figure. He prided himself on a marked indifference to the ordinary charities, yet he gave away his entire fortune. He contended that selfishness is the basic motive of human activity and stripped himself to improve the lot of mankind. He was a large employer and in many respects an autocratic one who fought consistently for the rights of wage earners. He could be star-tlingly mean in small matters and as startlingly generous when thousands or millions were involved. He was self-contradic-tory in a dozen ways.

Baffled by these contradictions not a few of those who knew him in the flesh have given up any attempt to classify him. They have decided that he had no real place in the evolution of American business but bears the relation to it that a biological sport bears to the evolution of a species. That is to say, he may be disregarded except as an oddity.

If this were so, he would hardly be worth a book-length study. Even his work toward establishing the United States Chamber of Commerce and the International Chamber of Commerce, in endowing the Twentieth Century Fund and the Good Will Fund, and his vigorous championship of the co-operative movement, particularly the credit unions, would constitute merely personal idiosyncrasies worth an essay but not a book.

But if these things actually fit into the unfolding pattern of American business history and are destined to be permanent elements, then the businessman who first apprehended their importance and attempted to adjust the loom to its necessary work was no freak but as integral a part of American commercial history as unusually farsighted statesmen are of its political history.

Economics and politics, never far apart, have merged completely in the larger part of the world and are visibly merging even in the United States, the most conservative country still surviving. The wars and their aftermath have pounded into our heads the urgent need of making our people, especially our young people, familiar with the basic structure of our political government. A thousand errors and follies have been committed because the common man understands so imperfectly how the republic was built and why it was built that way. Schools and colleges have been roundly denounced for ignoring American history—meaning political history—and many of them have hastily revised their courses of study to give the subject more attention.

But we have been slow to realize, or at any rate to admit, that we have been erecting a commercial empire alongside the political republic. Now that they are obviously coalescing, we may have to revise our teaching of history a second time, for the common man's knowledge of how the empire of business came into being is even more vague and scanty than his knowledge of the origin of the Constitution.

Certainly what used to be known as political economy has been studied intensively in this country. Indeed, it has proliferated into a dozen branches, some of which have long ceased to be regarded as tool courses and have risen to the status of intellectual disciplines, overshadowing Greek and Latin in the eyes of college students. But this study has been largely impersonal. It investigates trends, techniques, the interplay of forces, but rarely personalities. Biography has occasionally picked up one of the more conspicuous figures—Nevins' *Rockefeller* is a striking example—but biographers have examined with meticulous care at least twenty Civil War generals all of whom together contributed less to winning the war than was contributed by the civilian, John W. Garrett, a railroad man. Perry, the naval officer who perhaps regrettably opened Japan, is mentioned in every school history, but few even list the names of Whistler and Winans who perhaps even more regrettably opened Russia. Whistler built the railroad from St. Petersburg, now Leningrad, to Moscow, but he survives in history, not for that really first-rate achievement, but only for begetting a son who developed into a second-rate painter.

The abandonment of the great-man theory by historians came pretty much at the same time as the realization of the indivisibility of economics and politics, and this may account in part for the languid interest in chronicling, rather than analyzing, the construction of the empire. We no longer share Carlyle's unclouded faith that Frederick the Great and Cromwell, with their own two hands, molded nations and turned the stream of history. We do not assume that the Standard Oil Company sprang, full armed, from the brow of John D. Rockefeller, Sr., nor the steel trust from that of the elder Morgan. Realization that these men, like the rest of us, did pretty much what they had to do has rubbed the glamor off them. But we are wrong in assuming that when the glamor went the significance went with it.

The most ardent opponent of the great-man theory can hardly deny that, while there may be no great men, there certainly are pivotal men, men who serve as the points on which history turns. This is plain in political history and even plainer in commercial history. Few would deny that Abraham Lincoln, for instance, stands at an angle in American political history, but no rational man will deny that Henry Ford stands at an an-

gle in the history of the automobile industry. The pivot man in
a military formation does not himself change the direction of
the wheeling front, but he is worth watching, because if he
doesn't keep his place he can easily wreck the whole maneuver.
The spectator who keeps an eye on the pivot man can follow
and understand the logic of the most complicated close-order
drill.

If Edward A. Filene was in fact no more than a Boston merchant who, in spite of his commercial success, was full of eccen-
tricities, emotional and intellectual, then his story can be no
more than the mild amusement of an evening, like an account of
any other crank. But there is much evidence to support the theory that he was in reality a pivot man in American business and
that where he seemed to fall out of alignment he was really
doing a half step while the whole line wheeled into a new direction.

This is not yet proved, for the change of direction he indicated is so radical that to effect it will take a long time, probably
marked by a great deal of jamming and wavering and the opening of shocking gaps in the line. It is however the theory on
which this book is offered to the public, for if Filene was in
truth a pivot man, then the line that he took is the line of the
future. He advanced only a few steps along that line, but he
moved far enough to make its prolongation possible and thus to
serve in some degree to foretell the future.

In all probability he would have disliked this presentation.
Prophecy has a touch of the miraculous and one of his firmest
tenets was that there are no miracles. Indeed, he blazed into
fury when someone described him as "a cross between a Jewish
pack peddler and the prophet Isaiah." It was a description sav-
age enough to explain his wrath and yet containing enough
truth to stick to the memory. It is a question, though, which end
of the description infuriated him the more. Doubtless he resented the implication of pettiness associated with the pack

peddler, but he may have resented even more the implication of mysticism associated with the prophet.

Yet he admitted the dualism in his own nature by the entry in his journal. Who does not? The spirit to conquer the world coupled with the destiny to sell pins is not peculiar to Edward A. Filene. Probably every man has felt it at one time or another, although not all are articulate enough to phrase it so sharply. But a pack peddler sells pins and a prophet conquers the world; Edward A. Filene did the first with spectacular success. Whether he did the latter or pointed the way to its accomplishment remains to be seen, but the inquiry is worth while.

II

Edward A. Filene expressed not once but repeatedly and with resounding emphasis his disgust with the sort of biography that is merely an application of whitewash. He regarded it as both repellent and pernicious in a biography of a businessman, yet he was aware that it is very common indeed. He asserted that if ever a book were written about him he wished to be painted, like Cromwell, with his warts. To do that, it is essential to give due attention to the second half of his entry. It was not merely his destiny, in some degree it was his nature, to sell pins.

It was a habit he could never break. Early in life he emerged from behind the counters of William Filene's Sons Company, and in middle life he emerged from the store—indeed, he was thrust from control of it by exasperated associates whom he had tried beyond endurance—into a much larger world. His merchandise then was no longer clothing but ideas, and his customers not Boston housewives but very eminent persons indeed, Woodrow Wilson, Georges Clemenceau, Aristide Briand, Ramsay MacDonald, Nicholas Lenin at least momentarily, and, later, Herbert Hoover, Eduard Benes, Neville Chamberlain, Mohandas K. Gandhi, and Franklin Delano Roosevelt. Yet to the very end he could not stick to traffic in ideas in the grand style but would ever revert to fussy preoccupation with trifles, breaking down his own influence by exhibitions of what seemed pettiness of spirit and enraging people whom he needed by minor and useless irritations. He would be selling pins, and nothing could prevent him.

Thus there were two men walking across Boston Common on the morning of May 20, 1888, although other people there saw but one—a small figure, about five feet, six, spruce, jaunty, almost cocky, with dark hair and keen dark eyes above a large but straight and well-shaped nose. For the rest, his features were indistinguishable, since at twenty-nine he was prodigiously bewhiskered as was the fashion among up-and-coming Boston businessmen in 1888.

He walked. Already he was well established, not perhaps yet in position to maintain a carriage and pair but well able to afford a hansom cab, if he had chosen, emphatically able to pay the fare on one of the horsecars available. But he walked, and for nearly half a century he was to continue to walk to his office. On that fine morning perhaps it was pleasanter to walk than to ride, but he would have walked in any event. He was no Beacon Hill aristocrat, but there was more than a touch of *The Late George Apley* in Mr. Filene. The time was to come when he would throw millions around lavishly, but the time was never to come when he would throw nickels around lavishly. So he proceeded, rejoicing in the burgeoning spring, and those who encountered him saw only a rising young businessman stepping decorously and sedately to his place of business, nor did they suspect that his dapper attire covered a man with a surging impulse to conquer the world and one whose inexorable destiny was to sell pins.

But now that he has been dead ten years and more, the world knows that two Filenes walked across the Common. There was the big man who built up an obscure women's specialty shop into the greatest store of its kind in the world, who played a large part in establishing the United States Chamber of Com-

merce and the International Chamber of Commerce, who apprehended—comprehended is rather too strong a word—the
trend of modern economics long before his contemporaries, who
understood mass distribution before Ford understood mass production, who grasped the principles of the New Deal before
Roosevelt did, who set up two great foundations and became
the counselor of statesmen and potentates all around the earth.

That man deserved the respectful consideration of mankind
and got it.

But there was also the inveterate seller of pins. He quarreled
with his business associates, he quarreled with his relatives, he
underpaid his secretaries and office assistants, he drove them
mercilessly and thanked them rarely, he hunted publicity re-
lentlessly, and he was a master of blistering invective which he
applied ruthlessly to anyone who displeased him.

That man deserved a swift kick—and got it not once but over
and over and from all sides. He got it from business associates,
from friends and relations, from political opponents, and from
mere acquaintances. It is the unanimous testimony of those
who knew him that he was anything but a happy man. Some,
exasperated beyond the capacity to reason about it, declared
that he didn't desire happiness, that he was the complete misanthrope, but those in best position to know are certain that his
incapacity to maintain friendly personal relations with all
around him rankled and that his loneliness was a heavy burden
to him. His arbitrariness and unreasonableness brought their
own punishment, for he was frequently deprived of sympathy
and understanding when he most needed them, and in spite of
his immense capacity and his impressive achievement, his personal life was depressingly gray and barren.

However, the seller of pins is dead and gone while the big
man survives in the ideas he evolved, in the movements he
launched, above all in the vision he inspired in others. It may
seem to the reader ungracious, to say the least, to evoke the unpleasant ghost to dog the footsteps of the philosopher and phi-

lanthropist through these pages. To the tender-minded it may seem better quietly to forget his faults, since they no longer count, and to recite only his merits, which are still active influences in the world.

Edward A. Filene would never have approved. One of his most conspicuous characteristics was his strong belief strongly, even violently, expressed, that nine tenths of the troubles that afflict society stem from the refusal of men to bring all the facts into the light where they can be examined for exactly what they are. He held that businessmen are especially negligent in this respect and in nothing more than in examining their own lives. Over and over he denounced the tendency of biographers to gloss over anything that might seem to detract from the moral perfection of their subjects, which, he asserted, makes most biographies of businessmen worthless from the standpoint of one who seeks to acquire genuine understanding of our times. A decent respect for his wishes therefore requires that this order— for it was nothing less—be executed as well as may be.

But it happens that in this case respect for his wishes is also respect for the truth. He was right in his assumption that a book omitting or glossing over his faults would lose a large part of its value to his successors. For he failed in his larger aims. He was so well aware of it that he thought a book about him ought to bear the title "An Unsuccessful Millionaire." He was aware, too, that the failure was attributable, in part at least, to his own shortcomings, and a book that failed to make this clear would be a stumbling block rather than an aid to any successor who might attempt to complete his unfinished work.

For Filene was not the complete egotist. Egotistical he was, beyond a doubt. Vain he was, with an undeniable tendency to overestimate his own importance in the scheme of things. But his egotism, his vanity, applied to the immediate present. He felt—and frequently he was right—that he was a better man than X, who stood at his elbow, that his mind was quicker and shrewder than that of Y, who nevertheless held authority. Naturally, this infuriated X and Y and betrayed them into considering him a sort of human cockatoo strutting and preening himself without good cause.

Their natural irritation sometimes blinded them to the fact that the element of greatness that they recognized in the man enabled him to look beyond the immediate present and to perceive how infinitesimal was his size in the prodigious sweep of events with which he was presuming to meddle. To this day, half Boston will laugh sardonically at the suggestion that there was any trace of humility in Edward A. Filene. But it was there. One proof of it is the fact that he demanded that the truth be told even at some cost to his own reputation. For he had undertaken a work much too great to be hindered out of consideration for any one man, even if that man were Edward A. Filene. A man who humbles himself before an idea possesses genuine humility no matter how arrogant he may be toward his fellows.

III

But all this was years ahead in 1888. At that time Edward Albert, son of William Filene, was merely a young Boston businessman coming up and coming fast but not yet arrived. He and his brother, named for Abraham Lincoln, were just taking over the business founded by their father, not of their own choice but of necessity. William Filene's health had been failing for some years, and in 1888 he himself decided that the boys must assume responsibility for the conduct of the business, although he did not transfer legal control for three years longer.

It was a decision characteristic of the man. William Filene was mild in his personal and family relations, but in the intellectual and moral realms he was as stern and rock-bound as the New England coast. It was his pride to face the facts, whatever they might be, and nothing aroused his scorn more quickly than a refusal to admit the truth because it seemed to be unpleasant. Knowing that he was a sick man, he did not cherish the delusion that he was nevertheless competent to manage a business growing rapidly and therefore demanding alertness and energy in the highest possible degree.

He was a native of Posen in Prussia, and although he had come to detest the Prussian social and political system, the high value it placed on discipline commanded his grim admiration. But even in this respect he realized that the Prussian system was fatally defective in that it attempted to impose discipline from without, whereas the fact is that it is truly effective only when it is imposed from within.

He was a youth of eighteen when the abortive liberal movement that culminated in 1848 set all Germany by the ears. There is no record that he participated actively in it. He was too young, to begin with, but even in youth he had no taste for that sort of thing. Too many of the liberals were refusing to face the facts and thereby refusing to take the only course by which their movement could succeed. As far as numbers were concerned they had the country with them, but they were confused, irresolute, uncertain of their own direction. So after a few months of wild and startling success their movement lost its cohesive power, and the forces of reaction were able first to divide and then stamp it out.

However, no young man of character and intelligence could live through such stirring times without being impressed and perhaps somewhat unsettled. This was certainly true of a man in the position of William Filene—or Filehne, as the name seems to have been spelled in Germany. He was technically a Prussian, but he was no strutting Brandenburger, or arrogant *Junker*. He was a Jew of Posen, which had been Prussian a scant half century, ripped away from Poland in the partition of 1793.

It is a land drenched with blood and sorrow where Slav and Teuton have looked sullenly on each other for centuries, where men live suspiciously and uneasily even during those periods when they are not at each other's throats. It had been a bitter land for countless generations before William Filene was born there, and in the century and a quarter since it has become far more bitter. Three times within this generation "the red-hot rake of war" has been dragged over Posen, three times it has changed hands by the persuasion of fire and steel, from German to Polish to German to Polish again—Posen in 1914, Poznan in 1919, Posen again in 1940, and Poznan once more in 1945.

Blithe optimists do not emerge from such an environment nor men of equable and reasonable temper. Idealists may spring up in profusion, but they are likely to be fiery and desperate men, handier with the bomb and the torch than with syllogisms, spiritual sons of Savonarola rather than of St. Francis. Posen had them in 1848, and for courage and devotion they were probably equal to the best in all Germany, but for common sense they were not impressive.

The disturbances in Posen took the form of a wild uprising of the Poles, devoted not so much to the ideals of even-handed justice rigorously defending the rights of man as to the restoration of the ancient kingdom of Poland, extinct since 1793, which most of the insurgents saw through a romantic haze. The kingdom of Poland had actually been one of the worst governments in the history of Europe, so rotten, indeed, that the feeble and incompetent imperialism of Russia under Potemkin could knock it over with ease. To an observer not moved by patriotic mythology therefore, its restoration seemed to offer little improvement upon the existent Prussian tyranny.

There is no evidence that William Filene was ever directly involved in the disturbances, as were many of the German immigrants of the time—Carl Schurz for example—who later made distinguished careers in America, but it is clear enough that he was affected. Even a lad in his teens, assuming that he was intelligent and realistic, must have been depressed by the evidence that in eastern Germany the choice lay between despotism on the one hand and folly on the other.

It is probable, however, that a much more powerful factor in his discontent was the death of a beloved brother under depressing circumstances. The boys' father was a dealer in ribbons, which in those days did not bear the connotation of frivolity that the words have now. Throughout the nineteenth century ribbons were a tremendously important part of costume, and a ribbon dealer's shop was no trifling establishment. Today it would be called a specialty shop catering to the luxury trade. The ribbon dealer's financial position was evidently sound, for he aspired to put both his sons into the professional class and to that end sent them to Berlin to study law, an enterprise that would hardly have been undertaken by a petty tradesman making no more than a bare living.

But the outcome was tragic. Before the end of the first year the older boy succumbed to illness, dying apparently with no member of the family present but William. It was a shattering experience for an adolescent, reinforcing the gloom that the political disturbances had already cast over Berlin. Altogether, the situation was too much for William Filene, and he abandoned Berlin and the law definitely, apparently in the face of his father's disapproval. After some time and probably after some struggle he was allowed to go to London to join a relative in business there. There is no record of a family quarrel, but it is a reasonable assumption that his father was somewhat disappointed in William and not disposed to assume further responsibility for his career.

In any event, the London adventure did not turn out any too well. Events were moving toward the climax of 1848 in Europe, and the echoes were loud in England. What other factors may have influenced him we do not know, but after a few months William Filene determined to abandon Europe altogether, and without consultation with his family he took ship for America, landing in 1848 when he was eighteen years old.

He worked first as a merchant tailor in Boston and eventually accumulated enough capital to go into retail merchandising in a small way. He opened his first store in Salem, Massachusetts, in 1856, later removing to Lynn. His life must have been difficult as an immigrant without money or influential friends and forced to contend with the handicap of a new language. But it does not seem to have been inordinately difficult.

In Salem he married, and there on September 3, 1860, his second son was born and named Edward Albert. The name throws an interesting sidelight upon the times. Looking back, we ordinarily attach to the year 1860 one significance only; it was the moment when the American sky was completely overcast by the clouds of war. A combat was impending that was to engage two million men and cost the lives of nearly one fourth of them, a war that was to be, and to remain for fifty years, the bloodiest in modern history. Already the lightning was playing constantly over the heavens, and it is hard to believe that people could have been thinking much of anything else.

But they could and they were. The terrific event of 1860, as the general public saw it at the time, was not the rending of the republic, but the first visit to these shores of British royalty in the person of Albert Edward, Prince of Wales. Society was thrown into paroxysms by the coming of the Prince and even the little people were affected, including the Filenes of Salem. They already had one son, Rudolph, but when a second arrived, along with royalty, it seemed fitting to commemorate the occasion in naming the boy. Why they reversed the names is not clear. Possibly it was a simple mistake. In any event, the child was to bear through life the name of an individual whom he admired with very distinct reservations, for while the energy and astuteness of Edward VII no doubt commanded his respect, the grossness of that monarch could not have appealed to the somewhat fastidious Bostonian.

During the confused war years another son and a daughter were born and were named Bertram and Emma, but by the time the last of the children arrived, on April 5, 1865, America was once more ringing with one great name, one destined to overshadow that of many princes, and the Filenes gave it to their youngest son. He was called Abraham Lincoln.

The mother of these children was Clara Ballin, in some ways

a more salient personality than her husband. She was born in
the little Bavarian town of Segnitz in 1832 and lived to the
extraordinary age of ninety-four years, surviving her husband
by more than a quarter of a century and exercising a strong, if
unobtrusive, influence upon all her children until the last day
of her life.

Among her papers when she died was a short account of her
early days, written in her own hand at the behest of her second
son. It is a document illuminating by more than the facts it
records. The writer was a very old woman at the time, but her
hand was clear and firm and her style as laconic as that of a
Spartan general dictating terms of surrender to a conquered
foe.

When William Filene died in 1901 all the Boston papers carried long obituaries, which without exception slid discreetly
over his New York venture. After a few years in New York he
returned to Boston, said one. He entered the wholesale trade
in New York but after a short time withdrew from it, said another. His wife put it differently. They stayed in New York, she
wrote, "just long enough for Mr. Filene to lose every dollar he
had." There was no nonsense about Clara Ballin Filene. She
could have found excuses. Filene went to New York in 1863 at
the worst moment of a great war. He was caught in the mael-
strom that followed the collapse of the South, when many vastly
bigger houses than his went to the wall. He was induced to sink
money in the iron trade, which he did not know. He collapsed
in 1870 when the country was moving toward the financial catastrophe that followed three years later. But she wasn't looking for excuses. Filene went broke. That was the fact, and she
stated it without equivocation.

This uncompromising determination to face the fact, whatever it might be, and to deal with it on a factual basis was one
of the most prominent characteristics of her second son. That
he inherited it from her, at least in part, is a reasonable assump-

tion; that she approved this characteristic and endeavored to strengthen it is a fact of record in letters, in the memory of her children and her acquaintances, and, above all, in every circumstance of her long life.

That Clara Ballin was an American not by the accident of birth but by deliberate choice is clearer even than that William Filene was. He decided to come to this country on the basis of hearsay evidence obtained in England, and once arrived it would have been difficult to go back. She came as a visitor with the understanding that she was to spend a year with the family of an uncle in New York and then return, but she liked the country so well that, when her uncle went back to Germany, she contrived to transfer to the home of other relatives in Hartford, Connecticut, where she met young Filene.

After that she was still less inclined to return although her people were growing increasingly impatient. Filene was obviously attracted, indeed he was assiduous in his attentions, but he kept shilly-shallying in a way that would have tried any girl's patience. Clara at length decided that nothing would bring him to the point except a threat of departure, so at a particularly imperious summons from her family she yielded and prepared to go, announcing that it would be permanent. Frankly she confesses that she had a bad moment when it seemed that even this desperate measure would fail. Her passage was arranged, her belongings were packed, and she was on the very point of leaving before her hesitant lover screwed up his courage to take the plunge. But he did, so when she arrived in Germany she was able to confront her family with the fact that she was affianced to an American and must needs return.

Parental opposition could not withstand this argument. She came back, and they were married in Salem in 1858.

Skeptics may suspect that there was more common sense than romantic passion in this alliance, but it endured for forty-three years and then was dissolved only by death. If there is a sounder reason for calling a marriage successful, no one has as yet defined it.

It is hardly necessary to point out that the atmosphere of the home created by these two was wholesome from the psychological standpoint. Neither of the parents had any pretensions to brilliance, but they were people of integrity and, above all, of strong sanity, despite William Filene's aberration in believing that he was equipped for the wholesale business. It was a hard blow he was struck in New York, and, considering the effects of the panic of 1873, there must have been some hard years after he returned to Lynn and to retail trade.

There however he achieved a moderate success. He dealt in women's clothing and accessories such as gloves, shoes, parasols, and the pins bitterly mentioned by Edward. The dress shop as the modern world knows it was still far in the future, but Filene's establishment was its ancestor. Even then it was a form of business profoundly affected by changing fashion, calling for quick decisions based on evidence that was usually scanty and always hard to interpret correctly.

William Filene was good enough at it to hold his own without exacting undue exertions from his family, but the business was nevertheless very much part of their lives. His children were kept in school and by no means deprived of all recreation, but the store was nevertheless a distinctly family enterprise. The merchant discussed his problems with his wife in the presence of the children, and he was wise enough to listen patiently when they expressed their opinions. Because they knew what was going on, their interest did not have to be forced, and the boys in particular grew into the business as naturally as they grew in height and weight.

But as the years passed it became increasingly evident that Rudolph, the eldest son, simply was not a merchant. There is no record of any startling clash. He was apparently willing enough and intelligent enough, but he had no flair for that kind of business, and when Edward began to demonstrate a very marked capacity, the older boy apparently was quite content to allow him to take the lead. Long before he reached his majority, it was clear that Edward was the merchant, not Rudolph, and it was Edward who must be prepared to take over in case of his father's disability. This became urgent about 1880 when William Filene's health began to fail definitely; he had to find someone to assume not full responsibility but at least part of the burden that was breaking him down. His choice fell upon his second son.

The point is important, because it interfered with Edward's own plans. He had hoped to go to Harvard the following September, and his father's illness blasted that hope, but the effect upon him cannot be understood unless one understands his attitude toward the business. He never ceased to regret the loss of a college education. In fact he probably regretted it too much, for like most men deprived of the opportunity he tended to overvalue college training. But he was not embittered as some men are. He accounted it as extremely bad luck and bewailed it, but he considered it the sort of bad luck that is always in the cards for a man in his position. He had the idea, and it is a reasonable assumption that it had been instilled in him by William Filene, that the business was something more than simply a means of livelihood; it was a permanent institution, the creation of the Filenes, father and sons, their justification to society for burdening the earth. As the most capable son he was next to his father most responsible for conducting the business, strengthening and expanding it. This responsibility overrode any entirely personal plans. In short it was a sort of dynastic responsibility.

If any other obstacle had blocked off a college career, the effect on him probably would have been much worse. In that case his disappointment would have been equaled by his resentment of what he might have regarded as cosmic injustice. But since it was the good of the business that stood in the way, he was estopped from resenting it. Such a misfortune was one of the risks inseparable from the position of second in command, and since he valued the position, he could not honorably cry out against its risks. Lamentation was permissible, and lament he did, but to permit the iron to enter into his soul was not correct, nor did he permit it.

Yet it was peculiarly hard, for his effort to obtain admission into Harvard had cost him unusual exertions. He was not well prepared. His schooling had been somewhat casual owing to an accident when he was five years old. A careless nurse permitted the child to fall, and he received a permanent injury, a rupture, that throughout his boyhood made violent exercise dangerous and for a long time caused him to walk with a limp. He was, therefore, definitely apart from the other boys, in the crowd but not of it, both at the Cobbett School and afterward at the Lynn high school.

Sometime during the New York interlude his mother developed an idea that did her second son no particular good, however it may have reacted upon the others. During Clara Ballin's girlhood in Segnitz the town boasted a school for boys, the Händels Institut, that had a high reputation and the impression made upon her in youth perhaps overcame her own common sense. She decided that her boys must go there, and when Edward was nine, he, Rudolph, and Bertram were taken to Germany by their mother and left in the school.

Edward learned little and had a wretched time. Perhaps his father's financial difficulties in 1870 were a blessing in disguise since they compelled his return, but it is a practical certainty that the loss of nearly two years put him behind educationally. In any event, he reached the age of eighteen badly prepared to take the Harvard entrance examinations, although he had passed through the local high school. Everyone assured him that he had no chance and advised him against even trying to make up his deficiencies, but he set to work resolutely, and by a year and a half of effort so intense that he all but broke down under the strain he prepared himself and actually passed the examinations. In the spring he was accepted for entrance in the following September, but in the summer his father fell ill, and there was nothing for it but to go into the store, unless he chose to shirk his responsibility.

He went, regretfully but resolutely. His regret lasted all his life, but it was never clouded by doubt that he had done the right thing—yet perhaps that statement is inexact. From his standpoint it was not so much the right thing as it was the only possible thing. Fate, or chance, or whatever you choose to call it had decreed that he was not to go to Harvard, and he was completely helpless in the clutch of circumstance. The one way out simply didn't exist for him. That way would have been to set aside his duty to his father and the rest of the family and pursue his own interests regardless of everything else.

This point deserves careful and detailed analysis, because it explains a great deal about the Filene of later years including some of his apparent contradictions. He was a social being. It is true that he had unsocial traits. He was dictatorial, he was sometimes morose, he was tactless, he was amazingly ignorant of some of the commonest traits of human nature, and thus he developed a downright fabulous capacity for making enemies, which gave him the look of a misanthrope rather than a leader, a Timon rather than an Alcibiades. Yet every one of these social traits is easily traceable to some circumstance more or less fortuitous that tended to warp the man's nature, while every really crucial decision of his life bears testimony to his profound sense of relationship with his fellows.

His dictatorial attitude, for example, was certainly fostered and stimulated by the very nature of his business. Doubtless every man of unusual intellectual vigor tends to become dictatorial, simply because intellectual vigor inevitably brings a sense of power, which is the foundation of dictatorship. But the business in which Filene was engaged, a specialty shop in women's apparel, is one which is at the mercy of veering fashion. In the early days especially, when the resources of the firm were severely limited, a single bad decision could result in serious financial difficulties. Moreover in that particular trade one of the worst of all decisions is a slow decision. In a fashionable dress shop to have the wrong goods is bad but not to have the right goods at the right time is even worse. The wrong goods may have to be disposed of at a financial loss, but failure to supply the right goods when they are wanted will lose the shop its patronage. A financial loss may be recovered, but loss of customers is irretrievable ruin.

So the executive responsible for the conduct of such a business, if he is to be successful, has to think fast, faster than fashion can change, which is very fast indeed, and translate his thought into action instantly. There simply isn't time to explain everything in detail to slower minds. The only safe thing is to issue orders and require their prompt execution, reserving explanations until later. But this is dictatorship.

It is doubly necessary when a business is small and struggling. When it has become great and powerful, a single false step or a single moment of hesitation and irresolution is not likely to do it serious damage, but in the early years one slip may be ruinous. When Edward A. Filene was a young man, his business was small and precarious. By deciding swiftly and acting instantly he built it up into a great one, but inevitably he also built up in his own mind the habit of ordering without explaining, and this habit handicapped him when he moved into fields in which persuasion is more powerful than accurate thinking.

His morose fits, his tactlessness, and his inability to understand others' points of view are likewise susceptible of explanation without assuming that they were born in him. All of them could have been generated and certainly were exacerbated by experiences in childhood and adolescence.

The physical disability that handicapped him in school has already been described. The result was that he developed into

a lonely child who grew into a lonely man. This, in one who
was essentially a social being, was bound to result in an inner
conflict increasing in intensity during adolescence. In Filene
it seems to have risen to such a pitch as to produce physical
effects. About the age of puberty he developed an eczema that
baffled the dermatologists. It was plainly psychological, at
least in part, for it reached an acute stage whenever he was
subjected to emotional tension. Fear, anger, disappointment,
and above all embarrassment invariably brought it on.

A more distressing condition for a shy and sensitive boy can
hardly be imagined. It is a reasonable assumption that this
was one of the main factors that kept him a bachelor to the
end of his life. A certain emotional tension in the boy who is
making his first approaches to girls is normal, and in a shy and
sensitive boy the tension is greater than average. Consider the
state, then, of such a boy who whenever he approached a girl
was almost sure to break out in spots! The more his embarrassment increased the more the eczema flamed, and the more it
flamed the more embarrassed he became. The result was that
he avoided feminine society just at the age when he should
have been learning to appreciate it.

In the course of time the affliction subsided and disappeared,
as such things frequently do, but before it had vanished Filene
was a grown man, well up in the twenties, with no experience
of girls behind him. The golden moment had passed, and, once
passed, it is hardly ever to be recovered. Certainly vast numbers of men marry after thirty, but equally certainly not many
men ever marry if they have approached thirty with no romantic experience whatever. Adolescence is the natural time
for any human being, man or woman, to discover the enchant-
ment of love, and once discovered, it is not forgotten even
though its fulfillment may be delayed; but the original discovery is difficult indeed for one who has attained voting age
without it.

There is, in fact, a story that in his middle thirties he made what were then called his advances to a young woman, and the affair reached the level of "an understanding," if not a formal engagement. But there it stuck. Filene was assiduous in his attentions, remarkably so considering that the business was then just reaching the point at which great success seemed within his grasp. But the young woman noted, without enthusiasm, that he was not disposed to leave his business at a critical juncture in order to go off on a honeymoon. The crisis continued. The business hung on the verge of really great success and could not quite be pushed over, yet Filene was always convinced that only a little more effort would do it—as, indeed, it did at last.

But in the meantime the critical weeks stretched into months and the months into a matter of two years. Eventually one night when he and his ladylove were returning from the theater—a trip involving a thirty-minute car ride—a man whom Filene had been vainly seeking all day on a deal of importance entered the car and sat down near the other end. Filene excused himself and approached the man. At the end of half an hour three things were completed—the car ride, the business deal, and his engagement. The young woman, not unnaturally, decided that she was regarded as an impediment in the way of business and promptly removed that impediment. She informed Filene that he need not trouble himself further about her.

Perhaps it was a blow, but he survived it easily enough and in later years recounted the incident with more humor than distress. One suspects that secretly he regarded it as in the nature of an escape rather than a defeat, yet it may have been a heavier blow than he ever realized. The girl plainly had some force of character or she would not have acted as resolutely and decisively as she did, and marriage to a sensible and resolute woman would have knocked a great deal of nonsense out of his head. His most conspicuous weakness was his social incompetence, through which he constantly made enemies unnecessarily, but a tactful wife can retrieve innumerable social blunders made by her husband and smooth out difficulties that otherwise may hamper him seriously.

However, since this is supposition, one must take into account the opposite possibility. The American is certainly the most uxorious man in the modern world, and the American Jew is conspicuous for that trait even among other Americans. One cannot deny the possibility that, if Filene had married, he might have become so absorbed in family affairs as never to develop the broader social outlook that made him what he was. "He travels fastest who travels alone," even along the path of concern for the common welfare, for concentration upon a wife and children may easily enough obscure one's vision of mankind.

All the rest of William Filene's children married and left descendants, so it is clear that Edward's celibacy was a strictly personal idiosyncrasy. Furthermore, the luxuriant beard that he wore until about 1910, when he reduced it to a mustache, close-cropped but with a tendency to bristle, is only one of many evidences that he was 100-per-cent masculine. It is, therefore, a reasonable assumption that his avoidance of domestic ties is attributable to his social inadequacy in early youth rather than to any congenital abnormality, psychic or physical.

III

One intellectual attitude, however, he owed directly to his father. This was his rationalism. William Filene has hitherto been described as a Jew, but the word was used in the loose popular sense in which it is applied to any person of Hebraic ancestry, as Saint Paul described himself as "a Jew of Tarsus" although he had abandoned Judaism.

Adherents of that particular religion are Jews, whether they are Hebrews or not, and by the same token a Hebrew who has abandoned it is no longer in the strict sense a Jew. Long be-

fore he left Germany, William Filene had become convinced
that the faith of his fathers was so riddled with superstition as
to be no longer worthy of credence and had renounced it.

Here is another word that may be misleading. He renounced
it formally, that is, not by means of a prescribed ceremony but
in form. The truth is, he never renounced it in fact. To the day
of his death, although he railed against synagogues and rabbis,
he adhered to the basic principles of Jewish morality. Above
all, he abhorred the idolatry of things and instilled in his children a profound distrust of the corrupting influence of luxury.

Incidentally, this is also one of the basic principles of Puri-
tanism, and the moral climate of Beacon Hill was remarkably
similar to that of the Filene household. In both the acquisition
of wealth and the procreation of the race were admitted to be
prime social duties, but the frank enjoyment of either was regarded as scandalous. William Filene was gratified by the
prosperity of his sons, but anything even suggesting luxury in
their way of life he denounced with the rigor of an Old Testament prophet, and even things that most men regard as rather
modest comforts, he looked upon with the uneasiness that
filled George Apley's soul when his son bought him a parlor-car
seat for the journey from New York to Boston.

It was a sort of antique Roman virtue that would have delighted Cato, but its effect upon his eldest son was not of the
happiest. None of the Filene children was guilty of silly ostentation; to that extent the influence of their father controlled them
all. But those who married came, doubtless through the exigencies of family life, to think it no shame to enjoy such amenities
of civilization as were well within their means. Edward, the
celibate, on the contrary never came to that point. Even after
he possessed millions he had to indulge in complicated and
absurd rationalizing to convince himself that it was proper for
him to purchase superior accommodations on a train or steamship. His entertaining, unless his secretaries and associates
watched it, was likely to be inappropriately meager. Again and

again he practiced petty and useless economies in unfortunate circumstances where they gave a false impression of his character and damaged his influence.

However, if the austerity of William Filene's philosophy was something of a handicap as applied to material things, it was a tremendous liberating force in other ways. This emphatic repudiator of Judaism held as firmly as ever the author of Deuteronomy did to the doctrine that "man doth not live by bread only," which is the central pillar and support of Judaism and every other spiritual faith. Honor, integrity, duty were in his opinion as essential as bread and breath to anything fit to be called life, and this view he was remarkably successful in imposing upon his children.

To some extent, probably to a large extent, this influence was responsible for Edward A. Filene's restless, incessant searching for something that would give significance to his life, significance that passed beyond the individual. His brothers and sister might find it where most people do, in family life and the rearing of children. But that was not for him, yet the son of William Filene could not be content with an existence that had no meaning beyond mere personal success.

From the very beginning he realized that financial success was but a means. His real problem was to find a worthy end to which to apply the means. His was too active and dominant a spirit to be content with a life of contemplation and reflection; he was a philosopher, indeed, but a peripatetic in the original sense—he had to be up and about, bustling about if you choose, not meditating in some remote hermitage.

Thus he was driven first to examine his own occupation, not solely as a means of livelihood but as a way of life. Was it in truth the whole aim and end of a merchant's existence to sell pins? He could not admit it. His whole nature revolted, and the revolt was supported and reinforced by his father's stern contempt for the life that is maintained by bread only. To sell pins and sell them at a profit was obviously necessary to insure the merchant's continued existence as a merchant. But a financial profit is bread only; he was persuaded that something more is not only possible but necessary.

This search for the increment beyond and above the financial profit is apparent even in his early writings, but it becomes increasingly urgent with the passage of time. It could hardly be otherwise when one considers that as his prosperity increased the struggle for mere bread became less and less exigent. By early middle age he was assured, as far as the mutability of human affairs permits anyone to be assured of anything, of bread and raiment for the rest of his life, which only unmasked the other necessity and made it dominant.

Naturally he was misunderstood. This does not imply that morally he towered above all his associates, but simply that his need was different from theirs. They had wives; they had families; they had interests of many kinds that supplied them with spiritual satisfactions not to be found in trading for a profit. For them, therefore, it was enough for business to be a means of livelihood and nothing more. Most certainly they did not live by bread only, but if business would supply them with bread they were content, for they could find elsewhere what else they needed.

Eventually Edward A. Filene discovered other resources too, but in the early years the business necessarily bounded his horizon, and he resented the boundaries. He paced up and down behind them, as restlessly as a caged tiger. "I ought to be happy, very happy, for there is no real cause of worry, but my ambition is so restless, so unsatisfied, that it takes all my philosophy not to 'kick over the traces,'" he wrote in 1888 when the business was beginning to open up possibilities of large success. Again, two years later, when he was head of the store in all but name, "I cannot think fast enough or logically enough to satisfy myself and allow myself to rest."

Wild dreams went through his head. He thought of a novel

"showing the effects of nationalism" to be written in about ten years. He joined the Liberal Club and followed the discussions at its meetings with avid interest, frequently sitting up after he returned home to make a digest of what had been said. In 1890 at one of these meetings a young professor from the Middle West showed up and impressed Filene greatly, although he confessed that he couldn't see exactly where the man's ideas were leading. His name was John Dewey.

The demand for the eight-hour day was just beginning to pick up strength at the time, and Filene's comment on it is curious. In principle he disapproved it as being too conservative; the three-hour day he regarded as being nearer the long-time objective. But in practice, and under conditions obtaining in 1890, he regarded it as premature, and he added, nearly sixty years beforehand, the substance of Prime Minister Attlee's prayer in 1947: "Oh, for power and eloquence to show working men that any curtailing of the world's product means so much less for each one of us, no matter how much pay we get in money."

But he was caged by the business, and all his restless prowling behind his bars did not alter the fact. He was not embittered beyond reason. He was too rational not to be aware that every man is caged by something, and it is no great matter whether it be behind a counter, or at a desk, or within a classroom, or merely by refractory language that will not be bent to follow the sinuosities of thought. All who have the power of coherent thought are imprisoned; all are aware of vast reaches that they cannot attain, and whether the barrier be of steel, or of circumstance, or of the prisoner's own intellectual weakness, a barrier it remains.

Knowing his fate to be no quirk of spiteful destiny but the common lot of intelligent men, Filene was never in serious danger of sinking into hopeless apathy. He did, indeed, suffer fits of depression coming dangerously close to melancholia, but they were always attributable to a recognizable cause—illness, or prolonged and excessive fatigue, or some series of mischances —and with the removal of the cause he recovered.

Instead of benumbing him, his spiritual malaise drove him to thrust against the bars of his cage, and he found that, although he could not break them, they would give. The business itself he made the means of entry into a realm extending far beyond the bounds of trade, and up to a point the business itself profited. Selling pins he knew to be necessary to his own survival, but gradually he began to conceive it as a contribution to the social order. A retail store must make a profit in order to exist; so much must be known to any merchant who survives, but the ordinary merchant assumes that when the store has made a profit it has justified its existence. This Filene eventually came to deny. He held that really to justify its existence as a social institution—which it is of necessity—the store must not merely make a profit but make it by expediting the satisfaction of human wants.

Part of this has come to be understood by all, or nearly all, American businessmen. The fact that the largest attainable total income is derived from a small unit profit on a large volume of business is the theoretical basis of mass production. But Filene meant more. He included institutional permanence as an indispensable element of true business success, and permanence rests upon the intangible factor called good will. So does profit but to a smaller extent. As long as there was no comparable bargain on the market, Jews continued to buy Ford cars, even though Ford's magazine was denouncing them. Good will had nothing to do with that. Filene constantly bedeviled his employees with the question, "Why does a customer go by other stores to buy in Filene's?" and he was not satisfied with price as an answer. He did not think that was the sufficient answer.

This matter will come up again in later consideration of Filene as a merchant. For the moment let it rest; the point em-

phasized here is that the man undertook to transform his
business from a cage into an avenue to a larger life, and within
limits the effect on the business was astonishingly stimulating.
The idea of the automatic bargain basement, for example, was
primarily a method of moving into the hands of consumers certain classes of goods that had been impediments to the flow
of trade, that is to say, it was a social service. But it turned out
to be fabulously profitable, so the world paid little or no heed
to its social significance. People simply said that that wizard
Filene had struck another gold mine and admired his shrewdness without ever suspecting the range of his thought.

Even his close associates, although they knew better what
was in his mind, were not altogether convinced. Not all of his
notions were equally successful, financially or otherwise. One
in particular, by which he set great store, failed dismally. This
was his scheme to have the business taken over eventually by
its employees. The rock on which it split was the average human
being's fierce objection to assuming responsibility, a trait that
Filene simply could not understand, and to which therefore
he never accorded sufficient weight.

Filene could study an idea with a rapidity that amazed
and confused most of those who dealt with him. Yet it was anything but a superficial study; no German scientist examined
hypotheses with more scrupulous care to look at their every
aspect, yet this merchant's mind for all its thoroughness acted
with bewildering speed.

But when it came to studying a man, he was utterly lost. All
that he left to his brother, Lincoln (the Abraham was dropped
in later life), who was as good at it as Edward A. Filene
was with ideas. Lincoln accordingly became the administrator,
dealing with personnel problems that demanded an understanding of human nature, while Edward A. worked out the
merchandising ideas. Together they were unbeatable, and
the store marched from triumph to triumph until it became
the greatest in the world of its particular kind and had made

its proprietors rich men with every prospect of becoming immensely rich.

Lincoln Filene was satisfied. After all, the store occupied only a part of his life. He had a wife and family to whose affairs he could devote his surplus energy, and through whom he could hope to attain that extension of the personality that is every man's desire. It cannot be said that he lacked sympathy with his brother's aspirations. On the contrary, for many years he followed Edward faithfully even when he was not convinced, and his counsel and energy helped make a resounding practical success of more than one idea that tradition-bound businessmen regarded as insane. But Lincoln Filene was not driven as his brother was to regard the store as more than a business, as the sole avenue to the attainment of his heart's desire. He had alternatives while Edward had none, and this led to catastrophe.

In time the store developed from an adventurous experiment into a solidly established institution, and inevitably the minds of its responsible heads began to put the problem of consolidating their position ahead of the problem of seeking out new territory to occupy. This was true especially of the minority stockholders, Frost and Kirstein, who had always been less sympathetic to Edward than his brother was. Gradually Lincoln himself shifted over to their position. He was a man of middle age by that time, and without doubt the prospects of his children were beginning to interest him more than his own. To hand over to them intact a valuable property may have seemed to him more important than further efforts to demonstrate the possibilities of mass distribution.

The crisis came over a question of affiliation with a group of comparable stores in other cities. To three of the four it seemed a straight business proposition, promising increased profits but also promising vastly increased stability. But to Edward A. Filene it meant voluntarily donning a strait jacket. As a minor factor in a huge organization what earthly chance would he have to try out the new ideas that were constantly bubbling into his mind? He would have to conform to the judgment of others, and conforming was to him intellectual death.

A blazing row developed, but Lincoln Filene could be pushed no further. He stood with the other two, and among them they were able to exclude Edward A. Filene from active control of his own business. The battle he put up was Homeric. Litigation piled on litigation and dragged on for years to the annoyance and expense of everyone concerned, but Filene never regained control.

This may have been in the end a public benefit since his emergence from the field of private business left him free to devote all his energies to public service. But whatever its public aspect, it was a private misfortune since it poisoned his personal relations and embittered the last ten years of his life. To the end he felt that he had had in his hands the key to accomplishing in distribution what Henry Ford accomplished in manufacturing, and he had dropped the key. This was his main reason for asserting that his biography should be entitled "The Story of an Unsuccessful Millionaire."

His last years were devoted to absorbed scrutiny of the gigantic experiment in politics and economics known as the New Deal. Naturally he was for it, as he had always been for striking off the shackles of tradition and boldly testing any hypothesis that seemed based on logical reasoning. This was the biggest and boldest experiment that had ever come within his ken, and it was based on the type of reasoning that had often served him well. He watched it with growing fascination, and in 1936 he was one of the few rich businessmen who strongly favored carrying it through to its logical conclusion. His last important public utterance was a radio broadcast just before the election of 1936 in which he urged the return of President Roosevelt to the White House. He died in Paris in 1937.

IV

Ten years after his death men whose judgment is equally good and whose opportunities of observing Edward A. Filene were equally adequate still disagree flatly about what manner of man he was.

To dispute is not over the facts but over the interpretation to be put upon the facts. The record of Filene's activities is extraordinarily comprehensive. He had the good businessman's respect for documentary evidence developed to a high degree. Apparently he never threw away anything in the nature of a record, not even notebooks in which he jotted down fleeting impressions.

In addition, he was highly articulate. He was able to clothe his ideas in language that made them plain. Not content with that, when he became financially able to do so, he employed literary craftsmen to polish and refine his deliverances, whether speeches, statements to the press, articles, or books.

But these were not ghost writers in the ordinary meaning of the term, that is to say, gentry who supply the ideas as well as the language of a speech to be delivered or a book to be signed by another man. Filene's ghosts had a more exacting task. It was to take his ideas and reduce them to the simplest, clearest, and most succinct terms in which they could be expressed exactly. It was not uncommon for a statement dealing with some trivial matter to be rewritten over and over before he was satisfied that it expressed his thought adequately. When it was a book, or a speech of first-rate importance, there was no limit to his demands for precision.

The result is that the world knows with unusual exactness both what he did and what he thought, and yet there is no agreement as to what he was.

The explanation is that the man had magnitude. To sustain the point it is needful to do no more than consider the most unflattering of all estimates of him, to wit that he was merely an ostentatious trifler. It is an extreme theory. There are countless solid facts that render it untenable, but for the sake of argument accept it. Then it must follow that he was the most tremendous trifler in the history of American business, seeing that the extent of his folly has not been fully measured even ten years after his death.

Under any other theory he becomes important indeed, for he expressed and sometimes embodied in action ideas that are still of great potency in the world. Singularly few of them have been discarded entirely, but many of them have not yet been thoroughly tested, hence the possibility that he may become more important in the future than he has been in the past, because if these untried ideas work they will modify business and politics profoundly. Whether one regards Filene as a great liberal or a dangerous radical does not affect at all the fact that any adequate history of our economy must take account of what he said and did, for it has already had great influence upon our ways of thinking and acting and may have more.

CHAPTER 2

The Merchant

‹‹

I

A SOCIAL HISTORIAN gifted with imagination might deduce a good deal of the commercial history of the United States from observation of the rise, prosperity, and decline of Edward A. Filene's whiskers.

In the eighties they were luxuriant, unrestrained, romantic—and so was American business.

In the nineties, and especially after the collapse of 1893, they were reduced to the decorum of a carefully trimmed Vandyke, somewhat as American business was restricted by the Sherman Antitrust Act.

After the turn of the century they came down, first to burnsides, and then to nothing more than a rather luxuriant handle-bar mustache in the period when Teddy Roosevelt was cracking the whip over "malefactors of great wealth."

But from the First World War on nothing was left except a severe, even austere, close-cropped adornment of the upper lip, such as Pershing wore. By that time it was gray, rapidly turning white, but even after it was snowy it remained a prosaic, no-nonsense sort of mustache, not appropriate to anything as glamorous and mystical as a captain of industry, but well adapted to an economic leader whose faith was in statistics not in romance.

If Edward A. Filene had been an eccentric, this would have

no more meaning than the hirsute vagaries of a sculptor or a landscape painter not quite sure of his own ability and therefore willing to do anything that will make him appear distinctive.

But Filene was anything but an oddity as far as the ordinary social conventions were concerned. In ideas, to be sure, he was individualistic in the extreme, but as far as manners and dress were concerned, the last thing he wished was to seem to be queer. In the matter of hair on the face, as in the matter of clothes, he followed the prevailing fashion whatever it was, because he really didn't care. He took pains always to be presentable, in part because neatness was instinctive with him and in part because he was in a business that calls for neatness. A retail merchant who is sloppy in his personal appearance does not inspire confidence in his good taste.

In the day of President Garfield a magnificent beard was part of the proper accouterment of a gentleman. William Filene had one that bore comparison with that of the President himself, so William's son, as soon as he was able to sprout it, grew a similar one.

But in the day of President Cleveland a certain restraint became evident. The President, being a Democrat and an opponent of the wonderfully bewhiskered Benjamin Harrison, went so far as to shave off everything except a walrus mustache, but business and professional men were content to trim their beards down to pointed Vandykes, and so did Edward A. Filene.

Not until Theodore Roosevelt came to power did the shaven chin really sweep the field. Filene eventually went along with Teddy and Taft—and with J. P. Morgan—in confining his facial adornment to a mustache, but a sweeping and curvilinear one.

Calvinist Wilson went all the way and appeared with a completely naked face, as all his successors have done. So did many businessmen, but some, among them Filene, followed the military style of the close-cropped "toothbrush" mustache.

In all probability Filene never gave it a thought. As a style it was correct in the sense that it was generally accepted and that was enough for him. But sociologists, anthropologists, and ethnologists have confirmed the suspicion of historians that these apparently trifling shifts and changes of fashion frequently reflect changes in social attitudes that are by no means trifling.

Certain it is that Edward A. Filene lived through a period in which the way businessmen in America regarded themselves and the way in which they were regarded by others underwent profound modification.

When Garfield was President and Filene was just beginning his business career, the era of exploitation that followed the Civil War was just climbing to its greatest height. It has been the fashion of late to regard this as a uniquely degraded era, and it is true enough that financial and political probity touched a level perhaps lower than any to which it has descended since. But it is equally true that it was a period of productive energy unparalleled in American history until the period of the Second World War. This had the effect of setting up a double tradition which was followed by American businessmen and politicians in accordance with their various natures. There was the tradition of the robber baron, the exploiter, on the one hand, and there was the tradition of the constructive genius, on the other.

Naturally all men claimed to be following the latter. None, not even Uncle Daniel Drew, admitted that he was solely an exploiter, and in fact many followed both traditions, exploiting with one hand and building with the other. As a result, succeeding generations have been confused when they attempt to trace the history of this period, and there are almost as many interpretations of it as there are historians.

Filene lived his whole business career in the midst of this, but although he dressed his beard in accordance with the

changing fashions, as his photographs show, his ideas remained
remarkably constant in one respect—they were always out of
tune with those of his contemporaries. The ideas themselves
altered incessantly. Some he dropped because, when he applied them practically, he took a terrible beating. Others that
he once advanced confidently he later modified or laid aside,
because further study or the discovery of new information convinced him that they were unsound. Many he never had an
opportunity to test. But some succeeded, and when one did
succeed, its success was likely to be resounding.

A proper gentleman was Mr. Filene in his manners and his
appearance at any stage in his career, but a proper gentleman
he never was at any time in his view of the world, specifically
the business world, which is of course what makes him interesting. He was not even an improper gentleman of the usual
type. Some, in moments of exasperation, denounced him as an
exploiter, a robber baron at heart, but even a superficial view
of his career shows that he does not fit into that classification.
The very existence of the store in Boston is proof that he had
important elements of the constructive type, but his harried
associates eventually became convinced that if left unrestrained he would destroy them all and combined to deprive
him of control. They may have been wrong, but it is impossible
to believe that they were insincere. Their fear was not make
believe.

But if he cannot be neatly labeled as either exploiter or
builder, if he does not fit readily into either of the two existing
categories, it is plainly necessary to find a different sort of place
for him. Perhaps that place is in the category of the pivot men,
the men who are going neither exactly forward, nor exactly
back, but turning in the direction of a new line of march.

This theory has at least the merit of explaining much in his
career that is otherwise incomprehensible. Simple mathematics are capable of handling static measurements, but when the
problem is to discover, not points of the compass nor linear dis-

tance, but the rate of change in relations, one must rely on a calculus that is tricky under any conditions and that is likely to seem utterly nonsensical to the student of geometry and algebra. Filene, the merchant, measured by the rules of logic that make earlier merchants, John Wanamaker, say, or A. T. Stewart, comprehensible, eludes description. Wanamaker and Stewart were merchants and so was Filene, but he certainly wasn't a Wanamaker or a Stewart. It follows that there must be different categories of merchants, and it is possible, although it doesn't necessarily follow, that one of these categories is that of the merchant of the future, and this man belonged to it.

All that is certain is that he was not the kind of merchant that his partner, Louis E. Kirstein, was and not altogether the kind that his own brother, Lincoln Filene, was. And that was where the trouble started.

II

Probably any competent psychologist could demonstrate conclusively that the making of Edward A. Filene into a merchant began far back of Salem and 1860, probably as far back as Filehne, the ribbon dealer of Posen. A boy who from the very cradle heard his elders discussing merchandising problems among themselves and who in childhood knows that the family welfare depends upon a store has gone some way along the road to being a merchant before he is tall enough to see above a counter.

But the development in this case seems to have been quite unforced as far as the parents were concerned. There is little evidence to indicate that William Filene aspired to found a mercantile dynasty. His sons were left to follow their natural bent; and if the second son, by the time he attained years of discretion, had assumed as a matter of course that responsibility for the business would eventually devolve upon him, it was the result of force of circumstances rather than of parental admonitions. His ambition to enter Harvard, for example, was

questioned—if it was questioned at all by his father—solely on
the grounds of practicality, not as being in itself a foolish as-
piration, and when the son demonstrated his ability to pass the
entrance examinations, the father acquiesced readily enough.

William and Clara Filene were on the whole wise parents—
not perfect, for they made obvious mistakes, but at that wiser
than a great many. It is hardly to be doubted that after the accident to their son they tended to protect him too much, and
then, swinging to the opposite extreme, they subjected him to
a discipline so rigorous that it proved disastrous to many a boy
less sensitive and vulnerable than young Edward Filene. When
he was nine years old his mother took all the boys, including
little Lincoln, then seven, back to the old country and entered
the three elder ones in a German military school.

There is no evidence that the Händels Institut in Segnitz was
conspicuously worse than other institutions of its class. On the
contrary in some respects it was distinctly better. It never descended to the barbarous regimen characteristic of some German—and for that matter English and French—boys' schools.
By comparison with the Rugby depicted in *Tom Brown's
School Days*, for instance, the Händels Institut was highly civilized. Nevertheless it was bad enough to make his year and a
half there a searing experience for young Filene. The bitter
unhappiness of his period there undoubtedly drove him back
upon himself, and he was already too much introverted.

Yet it would be patently unfair to blame his parents too
much for this mistake. After all, such institutions were highly
regarded by all their contemporaries, especially in Germany.
This one was what is known as a "select school," and a parent
who chooses the most highly regarded school available for
his offspring may be guilty of unwisdom but certainly cannot
be charged with indifference to their welfare. It was a mistake,
but it was the kind of mistake to which a particularly good
parent is more susceptible than an indifferent one.

The fact remains, however, that the experience certainly did

Edward Filene more harm than good. Perhaps he picked up some small addition to his knowledge of the classics, but he also made the acquaintance of misery much too early in life. After all, he was an American boy being subjected to an intellectual and moral discipline designed for German boys. It didn't fit. One is inclined to suspect—considering the development of educational theory in 1869—that it didn't fit German boys any too well, but as applied to an American, it was almost fabulously wrong.

It was so obviously bad, indeed, that even his German-born parents realized that it wouldn't do and brought the boys back before the end of their second year.

Yet it is possible that this gives too much credit to the senior Filenes. There was another reason for withdrawing the boys from a relatively expensive private school in Europe. It was just at this time that William Filene was running into serious difficulties in New York. In another year he was wiped out financially. Possibly Edward owed his deliverance less to the wisdom of his parents than to their financial catastrophe. In any event, it was a deliverance, and it came none too soon. Already Edward was a brooding, introspective type, and so he remained during the years when he and his brothers were attending the Cobbett School and then the Lynn high school.

He made a sufficiently good record there, and there is no indication that he was regarded as an unfriendly soul, but unquestionably he was somewhat set apart. Earlier, by his own account, he had read Hans Christian Andersen's story of "The Ugly Duckling" and had been powerfully impressed. His sense of realism was already sufficiently developed to make him recognize himself as an ugly duckling in the small world of the school. "I thought I was a swan," he said half a century later, apparently regarding that as the significant part of his childhood attitude. But the significant thing is that he knew he was an ugly duckling; the hope that he was in reality a cygnet followed inevitably. No child realistic enough to perceive his own disability fails to hope that it is only temporary and apparent—none, that is, except a morbid individual already doomed. But not every child is capable of recognizing the truth about himself; it was in this, not in his dreams of possible swanhood, that the boy Filene was unusual.

Probably his childhood was too serious. During the years when he was in high school his father was struggling to reestablish himself in the business world after his catastrophic experience in New York, and Edward, most mature intellectually of the sons, must have had a more complete understanding of the situation than the other boys could attain. It was not a situation designed to induce a gay and frivolous attitude toward life. It was by no means desperate it is true, but it was serious. It was the sort of thing that demanded the utmost realism on the part of those who were to cope with it successfully, and realism, of a sort, young Filene developed.

Unfortunately he never quite understood how restricted a realism it was. He had to learn the business of merchandising, and he learned it swiftly and thoroughly. It was many years later that he began to learn—and he never did learn thoroughly—that there are other realities in life that are quite as solid and refractory as those centering around the operation of making a living. There are no miracles, said Edward A. Filene, which is a doctrine sound enough for practical men, but there are a great many things in the world that to him looked like miracles and that he therefore dismissed as fraudulent whereas they are realities quite as certain as, for example, the law of diminishing returns.

In all that concerns the emotional world he fumbled uncertainly. He prided himself on his own unemotional attitude toward all problems, but he was, of course, intensely emotional. It stands out in everything he did, and nowhere more conspicuously than in what he did wrong. A relatively passionless man

may engage in disputes, but never in such flaming quarrels as
Edward A. Filene constantly entered, to the useless exhaustion
of his own energies and those of his adversaries.

The fact that he had to master business practice early in life
certainly accounts in some measure for his failure to understand the emotional side of life. For business practice, to a degree and in theory at least, is logical, and an adolescent who
concentrates intensely on logic may easily neglect other things
that are quite important. If he neglects them completely
enough and long enough he may diminish, if not lose, his capacity ever to understand them.

Something of the sort seems to have happened to Filene.
Early in life he learned the business approach, the logical
approach, to human problems, and he never learned any other.
He was middle aged or elderly before he began to suspect that
there is any other, and he never understood it perfectly. He was
aware of the existence of the arts, for instance, but rather in the
way that a European of the Middle Ages was aware of the realm
of Prester John. He did not despise the arts. On the contrary, he
always professed the highest respect for them, but they were
on the other side of the earth, and he knew of no road by which
to reach them. Moreover, he maintained a healthy skepticism.
Like the man of the Middle Ages, he had small confidence in
travelers' tales. Medieval Europe knew that most of those who
professed to have visited the court of Prester John were liars
and frauds, but America in the latter half of the nineteenth century had even better cause to be skeptical of those who professed familiarity with the arts, for it is doubtful that any
civilized country ever suffered a worse affliction of artistic char-
latans than this one in the generation after the Civil War when
competent criticism was almost nonexistent.

In the years between his return from Germany and his assumption of a full-time job in the store, that is, between eleven
and nineteen, young Filene developed a mild interest in such
sports as hunting and fishing. A few years later it appeared

that he also knew something about sailing, for there is record of his purchase of a half interest in a boat, and at some time in his younger days he had opportunity to learn at least how to sit on a horse although he never was a real horseman. But at most he took a mild pleasure in these things; none was a real passion.* This is easy to understand, for he had no time to develop a real passion for any kind of sport. What leisure he had out of school hours was devoted to learning the business.

Yet the quality of his mind was such that this devotion to mastery of trade was not deadening. He had intellectual curiosity in abundant measure. Therefore, "we do it this way" was never a sufficient answer to his questions about the operations of the store. He had to know why it was done that way in preference to another way, and that, of course, opened a gate into the whole field of economic theory.

This became his passion, his hobby, his equivalent for the fierce enthusiasm with which other men pursue golf balls, or swordfish, or Utrillos, or first editions of *Tamerlane*. The battle of ideas was his delight, particularly economic ideas, and specifically those economic ideas that have to do with distribution.

Yet here is an apparent contradiction. It has just been stated that Edward A. Filene had no great understanding of the arts and no very strong impulse to acquire that sort of lore. At the same time, the man who finds in the means by which he earns his livelihood also the means by which he comes closest to complete self-expression is essentially an artist. He may be an unconventional artist or a bad artist, but nevertheless, if the work he does for money is work that he would do for nothing except the joy of doing it if he didn't need money, the man is an artist. This unquestionably applies to Filene. When circumstances made it no longer possible for him to develop and apply

---

* The boat, for example, he bought, not out of a passionate love of the sea, but because as a child he had feared the water, and he felt that the best way to get rid of that apprehension was to meet it "a little dangerously." Apparently the method was successful.

his ideas in the store, he nevertheless went on developing and applying his ideas, although now it meant spending money instead of making it.

He would have snorted with disgust at the suggestion that he had any slightest touch of the artistic temperament. It was a point of honor with him to maintain that he was the very model of a practical hard-headed businessman, which he regarded as the very antithesis of an artist. Yet the fact remains that his whole life falls into a comprehensible pattern if one makes the assumption that he was essentially an artist, while it remains largely inexplicable on any other theory.

Naturally, since he insisted on another theory, he remained inexplicable to his associates and therefore annoying. Had he been an opera singer, he would have been much more easily understood, but to conventional minds it is utterly out of character for a businessman to be incessantly searching for a universal harmony, an adjustment of the means of living to truth that is larger than any life, to be profoundly concerned with relations that are not instantly apparent, to be perpetually dissatisfied with the best that exists because it is not consonant with an ideal that exists only in the mind.

But this was Filene. In his early years it was less obvious, because in his early years the steps that he took away from conventional business practice were short ones and not difficult to explain even to people who did not question the existing rules. More than that, in the early days many of these innovations quickly proved to be profitable, some of them immensely profitable. There is no arguing against the sort of success that shows up in large black figures on the company ledger. Competitors who laughed heartily at young Filene's crazy ideas in the beginning sobered when they observed the volume of business he was doing and became deeply respectful when they learned of the profits he was making. Business has its own idea of what constitutes sanity and profit is proof of it; a man whose company never misses a dividend while its surplus swells steadily

is sane, no matter what psychiatrists may say. He may choose
—a tradition says one Bostonian did—to sit on a marble ped-
estal and call himself a bust of Napoleon, but if his company remains consistently in the black and consistently increases its
volume, he is sane in the estimation of his competitors. Indeed he is more than sane; he is foxy.

III

When the executors were going through Edward A. Filene's
papers after his death, they discovered, in a private file to which
he alone had access while he lived, a pathetic souvenir. It was
Certificate Number 276 issued by the acting dean of Harvard
University in June 1879, certifying that Edward A. Filene had
satisfactorily passed examinations in the subjects listed below
and therefore was eligible for entrance into Harvard. The subjects were "Virgil, Latin at sight, Xenophon or Goodwin's
Reader, Greek sentences, German."

It was a memorial to a defeated hope, for it was in midsum-
mer of 1879 that William Filene discovered that he could no
longer carry the burden alone. His son accordingly renounced
his hope of a college career and took his place in the store as a
full-time man. He was nineteen. He made his choice without
hesitation, but it is significant that for fifty-eight years he
treasured the document proving that he was eligible for Harvard, even if he never got there.

The records of his early participation in the business are
fragmentary and inconclusive, but judging by the course of
events, his first important influence upon policy was in the direction of concentration. William Filene was scattering his
fire. He had two stores in Lynn, one in Salem, and one in Bath,
Maine. Apparently it had long been his intention to invade
Boston itself, but for some reason he had never done so. Possibly his multiplicity of small enterprises was developed with
some idea of providing each of his four sons with an independent establishment. Some years later the store at Bath was turned

over to Edward's younger brother, Bertram—incidentally
with results that were none too happy—and it may be that
William Filene's intention was to make similar provision for
the others.

His background lends plausibility to the idea. In Germany a
successful merchant with four sons would surely have dreamed
of setting up each of the younger ones in a business of his own,
preferably in different towns to avoid family competition. The
oldest would naturally have succeeded to the original establishment. But the idea of building up the original store until it
could take care of all was distinctly American rather than European. It was the idea of big business, the idea of an expanding economy in which increasing volume is to be sought more
vigorously than conservation of resources.

In any event, within two years after Edward entered the business on a full-time basis, all the eggs, with the exception of the
one at Bath, were placed in one basket. It was not done with
reckless haste. The Boston store was opened first, and the others
closed out as opportunity offered. But the policy was pursued steadily, and by 1881 it was in full effect.

The store in Boston was a single room on Winter Street. It
was still simply William Filene, Merchant, and it occupied a
space only twenty-four feet square, but already the accent was
on elegance. The establishment boasted of its "genuine marble
floor," and it felt justified in inviting public attention to the
singular attractiveness of its window displays. It is evident
that from its very first days in Boston Filene's had an air; Filene's was not content merely to trail along in the ruck.

But it did not succeed with effortless ease. Competition was
terrific among such small business houses. Survival, not to mention prosperity, depended upon alert and efficient merchandising, and the business mortality was prodigious. William Filene's
health continued to be precarious, so there was a flat necessity
for the young man to learn merchandising, to learn it thoroughly, and to learn it with all possible speed. One of his im-

pelling reasons—not perhaps the dominant one but certainly important—was his determination not to call the other boys into the store until they had had a chance for a better formal education than he had had.

He worked at it so hard that he very nearly killed himself. After four years he collapsed with what is now called a nervous breakdown. Fortunately by that time Lincoln Filene had accumulated age and experience enough to take over, so no disaster to the business resulted, and a long rest including a trip to Europe re-established Edward.

This successful assumption of authority at the age of nineteen is unquestionably the most remarkable feat in Edward A. Filene's career. He did not so regard it. To him it was simply a case of doing what was obviously necessary, and ability to do the obviously necessary he considered among the smallest of the virtues. Yet he was not unaware that shortly before his father's breakdown he himself had undergone a spiritual experience that he found difficult to describe but which affected his personality profoundly. His references to it were always vague, but it had to do with his own physical health, and it probably occurred about the age of seventeen when he suffered an unusually violent and prolonged attack of nervous eczema, which continued for no less than eleven months. Years before, the doctors had told his parents that the eczema certainly, and probably his lameness too, were largely psychological, but only now did he realize what the term meant and that his cure, if cure there were to be, rested with himself, rather than with any medicament that the most skillful apothecary could compound.

A layman would be ill advised indeed were he to try to explain what happened in the boy's mind. A highly skilled psychologist has difficulty enough in explaining it. But to say that it happens constantly is no more than to observe that people do grow up. In this case it happened at about seventeen, which is fairly early, and it happened with spectacular suddenness,

which is fairly uncommon. Young Filene, who had been under-
going treatments of a bewildering variety and some of heroic
austerity, suddenly decided to rely no more on medicated
baths and ointments with which occasionally he had been
smeared from head to foot. He decided quite simply to get
well, and he got well. He had relapses now and then, but they
were of diminishing severity, and within a few years he was
permanently free of both the eczema and the lameness. Not
even six years later, when he really broke under excessive fatigue, did the old malaises recur. He had symptoms in plenty
but not the old ones. They were definitely of the past.

It was, however, a case of straight rationalization. He did
not go over to Christian Science or any other cult that relies
upon invoking the supernatural. It simply dawned upon him
that he had been willing a large part of his own illness, and he
stopped doing so. The small remainder of purely physical
disturbance the doctors took care of easily enough.

The experience, however, unquestionably reinforced his
faith in the efficacy of will power, and it was this will power
that enabled him to meet the necessities that he had to face
when he assumed the main responsibility for the business.
There are a thousand evidences that the man was basically shy.
He knew it, and he regarded it somewhat as he regarded the
physical disabilities that he had overcome because he was determined to overcome them. Shyness had no place in the intensely competitive world that he had now entered, therefore
he renounced it. The result naturally was what the psychologists
call overcompensation. He did not stop with subduing his natural shyness; he became aggressive, especially in business operations. Nearly everyone who worked with him testifies to the
extraordinary difference between Edward A. Filene in his home
and in his office. At home he was rather quiet and could be
charming, but the moment he stepped into the office he began
to bristle.

There is little detail concerning those early years in the existing record. At odd times Filene kept journals that have been preserved, but there is next to nothing about the business in them, and not until later did he develop the habit of keeping records of everything. Apparently he saw no point in recording what he did in the store, for there he was only doing what was obviously necessary. His notes concern lectures he had heard, books he had read, striking observations made by people he met, little about the routine of keeping store.

But from the circumstances it is evident that his first and most intensive training was in merchandising, because that is the great central problem that faces all such establishments. A one-man shop has no administrative problem and a one-family shop not much. Accounting in such a store is simple. Financing the business is frequently, one may say normally, desperate but as a rule not complex. The complicated and harassing problems of personnel that gravely handicap many a huge establishment simply do not exist in a store measuring twenty-four feet square.

But merchandising, that is the operation of acquiring the right goods at the right price and disposing of them swiftly and smoothly, is the dragon with which the small merchant must do battle incessantly, from day's end to day's end and often through sleepless nights. One serious slip in merchandising may sink him forever. One brilliant coup in that field may give him just that slight lead on his competitors that skill and energy can widen indefinitely, even with no further windfalls. If he succeeds in merchandising, his business will grow, and its growth will bring about his ears a hornet swarm of other problems. But he must succeed in merchandising before he can know, except theoretically, that these other problems exist.

The simple fact that Filene's expanded steadily is conclusive proof that the man at its head learned merchandising thoroughly and practiced it successfully. The fact that the business expanded rapidly is proof that he practiced it with brilliance.

By the end of the decade Filene's was no longer a hole-in-the-wall shop but one of the more prominent retail stores of Boston, occupying five floors and a basement in a building around the corner on Washington Street, which was rapidly becoming the center of the shopping district. William Filene now decided that the time had come for him to get out of the way definitely and permanently. Lincoln had made his way through the high schools of Lynn and Boston, had taken his place in the business, and was proving as capable at store management as his brother was at merchandising. Not only was it now safe for the father to retire, it was in his opinion highly desirable; the boys had converted the business into something entirely different from that which he had created, and henceforth his experience, acquired in a different sort of store, would be of relatively little value to them and might indeed turn into a handicap.

The deciding factor no doubt was his health, but it should be remarked in simple justice to him that his illness had not affected his clear-headed logic. The business world is only too well acquainted with that tragic figure, the once able man who is too sick to function efficiently but who will not admit it and who insists upon hanging on after his physical condition has made him more of a hindrance than a help. William Filene deserves credit for avoiding that error. In 1891 he organized William Filene, Sons and Company (shortly to become William Filene's Sons Company) and transferred legal control to Edward A. and Lincoln Filene.

Now the brothers were entirely free to act on their own responsibility, accountable to no one except the stockholders, and the stockholders were themselves and other members of their family. Control was in their own hands, for their father intervened only when he was consulted and then oftener by a letter from some health resort than by a personal appearance. So they were free to show what they could do, and for the next twenty years they showed it, in a way that dazzled first Boston and then the whole fraternity of retail merchants throughout the United States.

IV

Filene's was not and never became a complete department store. To this day it does not handle many kinds of merchandise commonly found in department stores except as those lines may be somehow connected with clothing. It is a clothing store, but it will handle anything and everything that has to do with apparel, and it construes apparel as covering the entire outward appearance of a man or woman. For this reason it is prepared to trim a male customer's hair or furnish a woman with a permanent wave. It has bootblacks and manicurists in attendance, and cosmetics are a strong line. It will supply umbrellas to protect clothing from showers and luggage in which to carry it. A woman may find there jewelry to complete her costume and a man a cane to add the last touch to his.

The result is that nine people out of ten think of it as a department store although it is in reality an organization of specialty shops, all under one roof and one control, yet each to some extent independently pursuing its own objectives in its own way.

It began to take this particular form in the early nineties when Edward A. Filene, greatly daring, put in a line of machine-made dresses. To speak of this as courageous sounds absurd to modern ears, but it was. It must be remembered that by the time the brothers took it over Filene's had built up a very considerable "carriage trade," and there is nothing about which a retail merchant is more nervous than his carriage trade. It is an unpredictable thing to this day, and it was even more so in the nineties when social conventions had a far more powerful grip upon the mind of the average American. To hold the carriage trade a store must have the goods, but it must have more; it must have an atmosphere, an indefinable tone that gives it the cachet of social acceptability. There were a thousand things that might destroy this intangible but very real asset and one that certainly would wipe it out irremediably. That was—and indeed is to this day—the merest suggestion of the cheap-Jack attitude, a hint that low prices were being attained by low quality. The carriage trade wouldn't be caught dead in a store suspected of offering trumpery wares because they were cheap.

Now the machine-made dress, when it was first introduced, unquestionably carried an aura of suspicion. Its cheapness was actually the result of economies in manufacture, but the carriage trade didn't realize that at first, and, in fact, a great many of the first dresses of the sort put on the market were made of rather poor material. Who was going to risk making up a lot of expensive fabric in an untried form? Of course the manufacturers experimented first with the inexpensive.

The problem facing the managing director of better-class retail stores was, would the obvious advantages of large-scale manufacture be great enough to overcome the prejudice against machine-made garments in the minds of women? To guess wrong would be disastrous, for if the new departure failed to take hold, its introduction would have a damaging, perhaps ruinous, effect upon the prestige of the store. A great many merchants nervously refused to guess at all. But Filene risked it, and it was one of the first of his large successes as a merchant.

Examination of how he went about it reveals much about the quality of his mind. In the first place, he examined the theory of the operation rigorously and was unable to discover any flaw in it. He assiduously collected figures on the saving involved and determined that it would be impressive. He considered whether there was anything in the operation that compelled manufacturers to stick either to cheap material or to a monotonous uniformity in their product and could find nothing. He went into conference with manufacturers and found them perfectly willing to manufacture for him the type of dresses that he wished to handle.

His researches led him to the conviction that there was no real objection to the machine-made dress except popular prejudice, and he had confidence enough in the good sense of women to believe that they would not long permit prejudice to deter them from taking advantage of genuine values. Note the successive steps: he determined first that the theory was sound; he determined second that the operation was feasible; he determined third that the necessary technical skill was available. Satisfied of these things, he refused to permit prejudice, convention, precedent, or tradition to stop him.

At the same time he did not proceed recklessly. He would not jeopardize the entire establishment by committing it in its entirety to an untried idea. He set up a separate department for machine-made dresses with its buying system, its accounting, and even its staff personnel so carefully segregated from the rest of the store that in case of failure the whole thing could be swiftly amputated. But it didn't fail. By working constantly, carefully, and skillfully with the manufacturers, Filene obtained dresses that were smart in appearance, excellent in quality, and withal no more expensive than the combined cost of material and the services of a skilled dressmaker. Eventually they came to be less expensive. Above all, the woman who bought at Filene's was saved endless trouble and uncertainty. The department flourished and in time was paralleled by two others.

Incidentally, its relative independence of the rest of the store proved to be no handicap but a positive advantage. The brothers observed this and thereafter as departments were added proceeded to organize them along similar lines, so Filene's grew into a congeries of specialty shops rather than a single organization.

Encouraged by the success of his first venture in backing a well-considered theory against tradition, Filene proceeded to make his most spectacular contribution to the theory and practice of retail merchandising. This was the famous Automatic Bargain Basement.

The truth about this curious institution has never been told for the simple but sufficient reason that no one knows the truth. It was a dazzling success. That much is obvious. It was such a success that at the nadir of the Great Depression, profits from the basement kept Filene's in the black when all eight floors from the street level up were steadily losing money. It succeeded, yes—but why it succeeded is a question that has led to endless bickering and disputation sometimes to resounding battles.

The difficulty is that the Automatic Bargain Basement is in reality three distinct entities. What Edward A. Filene projected is one thing. What was actually put into operation is another and materially different thing, and what the public sees and has always seen in it is a third, fantastically different from the other two. It is certain that each of these three contains some elements of the success of the whole. But what elements, and to what extent are any of them controlling? These points have never been settled and presumably never will be, since the time when it was practicable to test them passed long ago.

Filene's eye, never confined to what was within the four walls of the store, noted that the stream of commerce was clogged at certain points by accumulations of goods that for one reason or another were not flowing freely. He had already begun to regard his store as having a public function, as an instrument of distribution equaling in importance its private function as a source of profit. But here was a field in which it was not functioning in either capacity. It was a challenge to him both as businessman and as theorist.

The goods he had in mind were types not suitable for distribution through the regular Filene organization. In some way they fell short of the standards the store had set or of the standards that any first-class store would set. That was why they failed to move. At the same time these stocks had very considerable values, which were locked up as long as they lay in warehouses. To move them would be a genuine economic service, on the one hand to the manufacturer in that it would release at least part of his investment and on the other to the purchaser, who would receive a genuine bargain. He had in mind such things as goods with slight manufacturing imperfections, goods perfectly made but badly styled, goods slightly damaged by smoke or water in fires, bankrupt stocks, stocks of too-enthusiastic manufacturers who found themselves overextended—all the accumulations resulting from bad guesses and from the unavoidable hazards of doing business.

In the aggregate, Filene believed that they were large enough to constitute an appreciable handicap upon retail trade in two directions. For one thing these masses of slow-moving goods represented so much frozen capital, which reduced the potential activity of the owners of that capital. For another they represented losses that the manufacturer—or jobber, or mortgagee, or whoever was the unfortunate holder of the property— must recoup somehow, presumably by edging up the price on his other goods. That is to say, when the stream of commerce was clogged, the effect always was to make things more expensive, which in turn would slow down trade still more. To move such goods was therefore a contribution to business in general.

The principle of the independent department, already tested in the matter of machine-made dresses, solved part of the problem, but in this case Filene decided upon a physical as well as an administrative separation. He consigned this business to the basement of his building, and he organized it along lines quite different from the organization of the rest of the store. In the basement he wasted no time striving to create an atmosphere except an atmosphere of efficiency. He reduced the number of attendants to the minimum; he refused free delivery service; he refused any kind of fancy wrapping or packing; he made all the service as simple and inexpensive as possible.

Naturally such austerity had to be compensated by the price. Nothing was allowed to go into the basement unless it could be sold at a price that really made it a bargain. It need not necessarily be cheap. Filene's basement has sold fur coats at a thousand dollars each as well as men's socks at four cents a pair. But whatever the price, it had to be conspicuously lower than the usual price for goods of that kind. A fur coat at a thousand dollars is not a cheap article, but if an equivalent garment would cost fifteen hundred dollars anywhere else, the thousand-dollar coat is a bargain. So important is this consideration that Filene would not let his regular buyers supply anything to the basement. His regular buyers were trained to look for quality and price in that order, so he hired a new set to buy for the basement and trained them to look for price and quality in *that* order.

But the spectacular feature, the thing that made the basement the talk of the town within days after its opening, was the "automatic" device. Filene used every possible argument to make his basement buyers realize that the department was there to move the stuff, which meant that it must be priced so that it would move. A buyer must not bring anything into that place except at a price that would move it, and when Filene had exhausted argument, he put a clincher on by establishing an iron-bound rule that he called an automatic price reduction. A buyer bringing an article into the basement could fix on it what price he pleased, but he had to get it out of there, and he had just twelve selling days in which to do it. If it was still there at the end of the twelfth day, he must cut the price 25 per cent; if it still failed to move, at the end of the eighteenth selling day he had to cut it another 25 per cent; if it remained on the shelves at the end of the twenty-fourth day it was to be cut a third 25 per cent; and if it was still sticking at the end of the thirtieth day, it must be given to some local charity that could use it. The inference, too plain for any buyer to miss, was that if much of a man's stuff had to be given away, that buyer would move if the goods didn't.

The plan was rigorously carried out. Occasionally some goods would remain on the thirty-first selling day, and invariably they were offered to charity,* but it soon became abundantly plain that Filene's was losing nothing. The advertising value of the donations was much greater than the cost of the goods. Soon too the public revised its first impression that the basement was a dumping place for goods that couldn't be sold upstairs. Some things did come into it that way but not many; 99 per cent of all the merchandise sold in the basement had never been on the upper floors at all but was bought for the basement.

Nevertheless in Filene's mind it was a clearing ground not for his store specifically but for retail trade in general. He continued to believe that the most important function of the Automatic Bargain Basement was to move goods that were clogging the channels of business. It was necessary to move them at a profit in order to stay in business, but the movement was more important than the profit. The public of course knew nothing of this, and even Filene's associates did not always or fully comprehend it.

Thus there grew up three different impressions of what the Automatic Bargain Basement was and what it should accomplish—Filene's impression, the staff's impression, and the public's impression. This last was one that perhaps neither Filene nor the staff had counted on creating. Filene unquestionably

---

* The word "offered" is used out of respect for precise truth, for E. A. Filene himself is authority for the statement that at least once the goods were not given. Time came when the thirty-first selling day found still on the shelves 2,000 dozen linen collars, the remains of two carloads that a buyer had picked up from a manufacturer going out of business. These collars, mostly sizes 13, 13½, and 18 for which there is little demand, were given to two charitable institutions, but even so the operation showed a profit. So a few months later the buyer was encouraged to take over even more collars from another manufacturer who was also quitting, and this time still more were left on the shelves, but when the charitable institutions were approached, they refused to take them as they still had on hand great numbers of collars from the first donation. In the end the store had to burn them to get rid of them. Filene ironically complimented the buyer on having set a record by buying goods that not only couldn't be sold at any price but couldn't be given away.

regarded the automatic price reductions as the most promising means of keeping his buyers on their toes and therefore making the basement store function as he intended. In the beginning buyers and salespeople doubtless regarded it in the same way. But to the public it added the spicy element of a gambling chance to the dull prosaic business of shopping.

Boston was full of bargain basements. Nearly every big store had one, but none was quite like Filene's, for there you could test your skill and your nerve. Here was, for example, a pair of shoes of the customer's size and of a style that he liked. Bought at a bankrupt sale, they were offered at a price that was a bargain from the first day, yet you knew, since this was Filene's, that if you waited thirteen days you could get them for 25 per cent less. The gambling chance was that someone else would not wait and that on the thirteenth day the shoes would no longer be there. To buy now, or to take a chance and wait? It was a question that added a fillip to shopping in Filene's basement not unlike the pleasurable anxiety of choosing between the bob-tailed nag and the bay at the Camptown Races. It brought the shoppers in swarms, and the basement flourished exceedingly.

This was fine, whether or not it had been foreseen, but the disparity in the attitudes of Filene and the staff led to strain. Harold D. Hodgkinson, now one of the chief executives of the company, was an energetic and ambitious youngster when Filene put him into the basement. Nearly half a century later Mr. Hodgkinson recalled those days with a mixture of wry amusement and nostalgia, but there was nothing amusing in it at the time. Like everyone who worked closely with Filene, the young enthusiast spent his days being dragged in opposite directions by intense admiration and equally intense fury. He regarded Filene as unquestionably the greatest merchant he had ever encountered and at the same time the hardest taskmaster.

"He was partly right," said Mr. Hodgkinson, smiling thinly, "but so was I."

He looked around. It was 1947, when Edward A. Filene had
been dead for ten years. The place was the enormous restaurant on the top floor of Filene's, one of the most popular
luncheon places in Boston. Hundreds of customers were being
served, yet there was a long line behind the barrier at the door.
The menu featured an unknown item—you paid so much and
you ate what the waitress brought—again the sporting touch
that was to be found below, eight stories plus, in the Automatic
Bargain Basement. Yet you were pretty safe, for whatever you
got would be good; as there was nothing in the basement that
wasn't a bargain, so there was nothing in the restaurant that
wasn't eatable.

"He created it, make no mistake about that," said Mr. Hodgkinson, and you knew he was not referring specifically to the
restaurant, but to the whole vast establishment, now occupying
the entire square bounded by Winter, Washington, Hawley,
and Franklin streets.

"But with all his genius, he never could make himself understood. He tried. He wanted to be understood, to be liked. He
was not a misanthrope, but he lacked the gift of getting in
touch with other minds. I think in part it was because his own
was so swift; he would explain half an idea, then his mind
would leap ahead to the conclusion, and he couldn't believe
that he hadn't explained it all."

He told Hodgkinson that the fundamental idea of the basement was to move goods that had been sticking, and the young
man understood, but he also told him that he must make a
profit, and the young man understood that much better. He
proceeded to make a profit, and then Filene denounced him
for not moving more goods.

Looking back over the years the man who later became basement manager illustrated with an incident, quoting fictitious
figures (the true ones would have been larger) that nevertheless revealed his position.

"I would discover a bargain," he explained, "but one decidedly too big for the store to handle, let us say three thousand blue serge suits. The unit price was attractive, but circumstances were such that it was a case of taking all or none, and I knew that six hundred suits were about my limit for one season. At the same time it was a standard item not much affected by sudden changes of fashion, and the price was one that I could not hope to match again. So I would buy the whole lot and throw six hundred suits on the counters. Sure enough, at the end of thirty days we had sold five hundred and ninety-eight, giving two to charity. The operation netted a profit, and it could be repeated at appropriate intervals until all the suits were gone.

"I would be inclined to pat myself on the back, but Mr. Filene wouldn't. He would give me the devil. He would say that it was unethical to hold back anything, that the purpose of the basement was to move goods, and by holding back I was defeating its purpose.

"As I said, I see now that he was partly right, but so was I. To call the transaction unethical was nonsense, but when he said that putting those suits in a warehouse tended to defeat the purpose of the basement, he had a point. But that didn't soothe the feelings of a youngster who felt that he had done well but found himself upbraided."

Yet Filene hated injustice, really hated it. The trouble was that he couldn't see any injustice in such incidents. That very power of concentration that enabled him to get through an incredible amount of work every day made it difficult if not impossible to adjust his mind to another's point of view. So intensely did he concentrate on his main objective that minor objectives faded into relative insignificance in his mind, and it irritated him to find others concentrating on them. He couldn't understand why. Most certainly he could not understand why they should expect praise for good work, even brilliant work, if it were done on secondary matters to the neglect of the primary.

Yet men who had done good work did expect praise, and

when they did not get it, they accused Filene of being crochety, unreasonable, and unjust. Like Hodgkinson they were partly right. Merely because Filene's intelligence was powerful and his ideas magnificent in their scope, one cannot acquit him of all blame for the incessant misunderstandings that harassed and handicapped him. He was aware that certain subjects that he needed to know—statistics for example—were crabbed, thorny, bewildering, and he accepted that condition. The patience he brought to the mastery of such a subject was inexhaustible; any amount of time, any amount of labor that might be necessary he would devote to it without a murmur until he had grasped it with an unbreakable grip. But he never realized that the study of human nature is quite as abstruse and difficult and deserves quite as much intensive labor as any branch of mathematics ever invented. He didn't see why it should be so, and he didn't believe it was so. Man, the authorities had told him, is a reasoning being. Then let him reason, and if he appears not to be reasoning, denounce him. If he had had to live with a wife and a house full of children, he might have learned that the authorities are not altogether to be relied on and that man is a reasoning being only by fits and starts. But living alone he never learned it, and that ignorance was the heel of Achilles.

V

Twenty years after Edward A. and Lincoln Filene assumed legal control of the business, it became plain that a crisis was approaching. Four times the premises had had to be enlarged by expedients that were by no means always satisfactory. For a while the store was cut in two. It was housed in two separate structures with another building intervening so that customers who wished to pass from one department to another had to go out into the street. Unfortunately the intervening building— it was Oliver Ditson's music store—was a relatively new and expensive one, but in the end Filene's bought it at some financial strain.

Even so, the place was unsatisfactory. None of the buildings had been erected to serve the purpose to which they were now put, and alterations, no matter how clever, were never exactly what was wanted. By 1911 it was clear that the time had come to attack the problem, not piecemeal but by an all-out frontal assault. The store must have its own home, designed for it from the beginning and big enough to allow for future expansion. They set about assembling the real estate and, greatly daring, determined to break into the new subway with a station in the store's basement.

The corner of Washington and Winter streets was obviously the proper location, so they negotiated for property there and then set architects to work on building plans.

Here was a problem that would absorb the best brains in the organization for a considerable time, but in addition to it there was an equally serious problem of internal administration. Filene's had long since grown to the point at which the work of the two brothers consisted entirely of organization. True, both of them, and especially Edward, believed strongly in keeping an eye on things, and made it a point to walk through the store frequently noting details, but their real job no longer had anything to do directly with customers or goods. Their work was to keep the organization adjusted and running smoothly.

Even that was rapidly assuming proportions beyond the capacity of any two men. They had able assistants, but they needed something more than assistants; they needed competent advisers who had at stake something over and above merely a good job. That sort of thing is seldom to be obtained from a salaried employee, no matter how able.

In addition both Filenes were convinced that a first-rate man who throws all his energies into developing a business over a long period of years is entitled to more than a salary. A man who is absolutely first rate works for something besides money. He wants recognition, and while money is its first form, it is not the only form. There are subtler but no less satisfying forms of recognition—power, dignity, deference from associates, honorable status in the business world—to which long and exceptionally able service entitles a man.

Again, the brothers were now in middle age, at the top of their mental and physical powers; in the course of nature time must take its toll, and they could expect to become less not more efficient. They had seen too much of the world not to know how common it is for aging men to grow increasingly arrogant, and they had no desire to see Filene's develop into an iron-bound tyranny, for they were sure that any such development would mean the decline of the business. Edward in particular was convinced that more or less democratic control is the best assurance of permanence in business as it is in politics.

But a word of warning should be inserted here. Not for a moment did he accept the modern heresy of regarding democracy as a synonym for equality. He knew that men are not equal, and he was strongly, even violently, opposed to placing authority in the hands of inferior men. But he knew that there is no automatic sifter that may be relied on to separate superior from inferior types of humanity. Blood will not do it nor money nor formal education. He had seen with his own eyes that a man may have a distinguished ancestry or money or both, and a Ph.D. to boot, and still be a fool. Yet he had seen that under the existing system a fool in possession of these things can frequently maintain a great position by means of them, holding good men down.

Democracy he regarded as simply the best system yet devised for permitting brains to rise to the top unhindered by artificial blocks. For that reason he supported it passionately, and he regarded its operation as no less salutary in business than it is in politics.

Toward the end of 1911 therefore the Filenes determined not only to erect a great building but also to reorganize the business in such a way as to decentralize authority and, as they hoped, to assure the permanence of able control. Long before

Paul Mazur formulated it in words they had recognized the fact that the operation of a large retail store falls naturally into the four great divisions of merchandising, management, publicity, and control. Accordingly, they proposed to appoint a chief for each of these divisions—"pyramids of authority" was Edward A. Filene's somewhat fanciful name for them—and to allow each of the four to acquire first a considerable interest in the business at once and second the hope of becoming eventually one of a group that would have entire control.

It is highly important to note here that it was the intention of the brothers in time to pass control to a larger group. To Edward A. Filene, in particular, this was of the essence. He regarded two-man control, even at the stage of the business in 1911 and 1912, as less than ideal from the standpoint of the business, and he was quite sure that if it expanded largely, as he expected it to do and as it did, two-man control would be progressively less efficient. He wished to see not less than four men at the top, and the brothers actually provided for six, themselves and the four division chiefs.

As regards three of the four managers, there was no problem. In E. J. Frost, for example, long the chief accountant of the business, they had the man who should obviously head the division of control, responsible for all financial and statistical matters; J. R. Simpson, also an employee of long standing, was as obviously the man for publicity, which includes display as well as advertising; and T. K. Cory had developed under Lincoln Filene into an able specialist in store management.

The hitch came in the matter of selecting a merchandising man. They had no one in the organization available, for Filene's was contemplating a radical departure in that line. Hitherto it had been strictly a women's shop and its merchandising personnel were all trained to that business. But the brothers had decided to go into men's clothing, as well, as soon as their new building should be completed, and the head of the division of merchandising must know something about men's as well as women's clothing. For this post it would be necessary to bring in a man from outside.

In an evil hour, as far as Edward A. Filene was concerned, their choice fell upon Louis E. Kirstein.

VI

At the time though it seemed a logical enough selection. Kirstein, son of a dealer in optical goods in Rochester, New York, had come up the hard way, entering business when still a boy and by sheer ability making good in a highly competitive field. He did not stay long in his father's business, soon turning to the industry that dominated Rochester, men's clothing. In 1911 at the age of forty-four he was already an important figure in the Stein-Bloch Company, a tailoring concern with a national reputation. He had accumulated a respectable amount of money and a more than respectable reputation as an expert in men's clothing. Both Filenes were pleased with him, and apparently they were equally eager to bring him into their organization.

But it required some finesse to accomplish it. Kirstein was a man of means, and he wished to invest his money as well as his energies. He was not disposed to enter the firm on the same footing as men who were brought up from the ranks. On the other hand, the Filenes were in no great need of his money and not at all disposed to sell their business, but they did need his services as a merchandising man and especially as a specialist in men's clothing.

In the end a compromise was worked out. Kirstein was permitted to invest a quarter of a million of his own money, but he had to take nonvoting preferred stock. The common stock, that is to say power of control of the business, was divided into one hundred parts, of which Edward A. and Lincoln Filene each retained twenty-six, while Frost, Cory, Simpson, and Kirstein each acquired twelve. This left the brothers with 52 per cent of the common stock so that together their control was absolute, while the remainder was divided equally among the four others,

who were designated managers. The six men, together with five
salaried executives, would compose the board of directors. Kirstein, by reason of his holding of preferred stock, would receive
a larger share of the profits than Frost, Cory, or Simpson but
would have no more say in the management of the business
than they had.

But all this was more or less routine. The matter of first importance to all the managers, above all to Kirstein, was the Filenes' pledge eventually to turn over control to the men who
helped them build the business. To effect this an elaborate
agreement was drawn up and, after protracted negotiations,
became effective in 1913.

It must be borne in mind that the Filenes at this time were
still vigorous, but they were under no illusions. They gave themselves at most fifteen years of efficiency at a high level after
which their value to the business would certainly decline. To
provide against all contingencies that could be foreseen, they
first went into an agreement between themselves by which, in
the event of the death or disability of either, the other would
have the right to purchase his stock at a price to be determined
by means written into the agreement.

They then proceeded to enter jointly into an agreement with
the four managers in which they promised, on January 1, 1928
—that is approximately fifteen years later—to sell to "the owners of 48 per cent of the stock" an additional 4 per cent out of
their own holdings. This would reverse the position, giving the
four managers 52 per cent with control of the business, while
the Filenes would be left with 48 per cent between them.

However, in order to prevent unwelcome intrusions all four
managers, in their turn, agreed that in the event of the withdrawal of any, whether by death, disability, or other cause, his
stock should not be offered for sale publicly but could be
bought at a price to be determined by means set forth in the
agreement either by the company or by a person designated by
the surviving parties to the agreement.

To Edward A. Filene this meant assurance after 1928 of four-man control even if he and his brother dropped out altogether. In his mind this was the whole point of the arrangement, because it was to assure broader control that the four managers had been brought in. The matter of justice to the men might have been arranged in far simpler ways; it was the assurance of broader control that required such elaborate precautions.

Characteristically he ignored the possibility that what was quite plain to him might not be plain to all the others. Perhaps ignored is hardly the word since to many people it implies that he put the thought away from him. That is probably not true. The thought simply did not occur to him, so he did not have to put it away. He knew what he knew, and that was that. If other people didn't know it, then they must be evading or avoiding the truth, which is a long step removed from honesty.

However, for the moment the question did not arise. Edward A. Filene turned his attention to the erection of the new building and for many months practically abandoned the store, which was a matter of no great moment since the new organization under Lincoln's general supervision was functioning smoothly. As for Edward, he performed a minor miracle or the contractors and builders did under his vigorous urging. Between February and September a veritable temple of commerce rose on the corner of Washington and Summer streets, a building rising eight stories above the surface and sinking the equivalent of three stories below it—basement, subbasement, and cellar, the last-named containing the heating plant, dynamos, and other machinery necessary to operate the building. The selling floor of the basement opened directly into a subway station so that on the stormiest day a customer could come from many miles away into Filene's without being touched by a drop of rain.

It is a tribute to Filene's vision that after thirty-five years the main store is still an excellent one. Many changes have been made in store building since 1912, and even this building has

had to be redecorated and in large part re-equipped because
the original installations wore out. Technological improvements
in lighting also have been adopted as they came along, and such
things as air conditioning have been installed, but nothing radical has ever been done to the building itself nor apparently ever
will become necessary until the fabric disintegrates under the
tooth of time, for it was built right in the first place.

True it soon proved to be inadequate in size, although it covered about a fourth of a city square. The firm has bought or
leased one building after another until it eventually came to
control everything bounded by the four streets; but the original
building, in spite of the speed with which it went up, remains a
first-rate store.

The construction of the new building was Edward A. Filene's last great achievement as a merchant. He was to do a
great deal more work in the world and still to achieve the larger
part of his fame, but strictly as a merchant he did little more
that the world remembers now. When the building program
was over in 1913, and he was able to turn his attention once
more to the ordinary work of the store, he found that he had
caught a tartar. Kirstein had then been in the organization for
something over two years, which was ample time for so vigorous
a personality to take over and to a large extent he had taken
over.

Louis E. Kirstein was physically and psychically the very antithesis of Edward A. Filene. He was a large man, bull-necked
with broad hunched shoulders and a shambling gait. He had
the retail merchant's appreciation of the value of a good appearance and spent plenty of money and time on his clothes.
His extensive wardrobe, in fact, became a standing joke among
the salespeople. But the tailor never lived who could make such
a man look dapper; it simply wasn't in nature, and while to
many people he suggested a dressed-up fullback, he reminded
no one of a fop.

Edward A. Filene by contrast was small, alert, quick yet

precise in his movements, and in appearance almost an exquisite. He had that rather rare gift, the ability to wear clothes. As a matter of good business practice he was always well dressed in the store, but he could wear anything and still look like a bit of a dandy. His pictures taken on hunting and fishing trips frequently show him in old and rough garments, but even in that garb there clung to him some faint suggestion of the Brummel.

But it was not their differences, it was their similarities that produced the trouble. They were exactly alike in that each was endowed wih ambition, driving energy, and an iron will. To add fuel to the flames each was a merchandising man. Filene was far too intelligent not to defer to superior knowledge when he knew it was superior. When Frost, for example, who had spent his life juggling with figures, insisted that such and such an accounting policy was more efficient than any other, Filene would sometimes admit that he was arguing with a specialist and yield the point. Simpson could occasionally put over an advertising idea by persuading Filene that he really knew more about it than others who had not made his special study of the problem. But it was vastly more difficult for Kirstein to have his way in anything connected with merchandising, for was not Filene a merchandising man himself? On that particular phase of the business he deferred to nobody, for he did not concede that anyone had superior knowledge.

This did not contribute to Kirstein's happiness, but it had no effect in lessening his determination. Kirstein was not in business for happiness; he was there for profit, and he meant to have it. Anyone who stood between him and his objective he would crush if he could, and the fact that his opponent might be one of the bosses made not the slightest difference. There was no more timidity in Kirstein than there is in a steam roller.

This is not to say, however, that he was a mere moneygrubber. On the contrary, he was a notably generous man with a keen sense of the social responsibility that economic success imposes. He was on the boards of half a dozen hospitals; for some time he headed the Boston Jewish charities; he served as president of the board of trustees of the public library; he gave much money and more time to the Harvard School of Business Administration; he was interested in the Boy Scout movement and assisted it with both money and advice; he freely spent his money and his labor on many other public enterprises. To look upon him as a modern Ebenezer Scrooge would be a fantastic misconception. Filene's fixed opinion to the contrary notwithstanding, he was a valuable citizen full of civic virtues and, according to his lights, as honest as Filene himself.

More than that, he was an extremely able merchant. Even this Filene eventually came to deny, but the facts are against him. It seems to be true that the men's clothing department got off to a slow start and did not measure up to the rest of the store for some years, but it would have been remarkable indeed had the firm's invasion of a new and fiercely competitive field been attended by instant success. Kirstein's energy and ability were valuable to the whole organization, however, and before the fight became bitter, Filene knew it. Unquestionably that is why he did not try to eject the man in the early days when his ejection would have been practicable, perhaps easy.

But Louis Kirstein was a merchant of the old style—a very good one indeed yet definitely of the old style and flatly determined not to change. He was up to date in the sense that he was willing enough not to follow but to keep just a step ahead of the vagaries of fashion, for that was and always had been an essential part of successful merchandising. But as for viewing the store as an integral part of the social order with a duty to perform in keeping the national economy functioning, he would have none of it. He believed that all such theorizing was arrant nonsense, and for the theorists he had nothing but disdain.

To Kirstein the agreement of 1913 meant a promise by the Filene brothers to transfer control of the store to their associates in fifteen years. The fact that there were four associates was to him merely a fortuitous circumstance, having no bearing on the validity of the agreement. Arguments in favor of democratizing control by broadening the base of authority could hardly be expected to appeal to a man who regarded the store as a source of profit and a social institution only to the extent that every profit-making enterprise is a social institution. Control was to be transferred. That was the point, and he saw nothing illegitimate in taking measures to be in position to gather that control into his own hands when it was transferred.

Therefore, as time passed and he realized the wide range of Edward A. Filene's ideas, he became alarmed and there is no reason to doubt the genuineness of his alarm. That he set himself to undermine Filene's influence and eventually to remove him from the organization is true beyond a doubt. More than that, he did it. But that his motives were as low as Filene supposed is very much open to doubt. Simple greed was Filene's contemptuous explanation, avidity for money and power. But this is by no means certain. Kirstein liked both money and power of course, but it is easily conceivable that he sincerely believed that the removal of Filene was essential for the preservation of the business and for the safety of his associates, as well as himself. Inconceivable as it was to Filene, Kirstein may have regarded himself as performing a public service in striving to gag and bind what seemed to him a dangerous radical.

The first link in the chain of events was the retirement of Simpson in 1915 on account of ill health. In accordance with the agreement he offered his 12 per cent of the common stock to his associates at the price provided, and the tender was accepted. Edward A. Filene wished to designate at once another man to buy the stock and take Simpson's place among the managers, but Kirstein objected and managed to delay the designation. But Simpson needed his money, and if his stock were not taken up within a specified time, he had the right under the agreement to sell it to the firstcomer. To avert this, the company itself purchased the stock and made it over to a trustee to be held until an individual purchaser should be designated. None was ever named.

Six years later Cory died, and this time Frost and Kirstein stepped in and bought the stock from the estate without reference to the Filenes. Edward protested and brought legal proceedings to enjoin the purchase, but Frost and Kirstein already had the stock and divided it equally. Edward A. Filene's challenge of its legality made their right of possession doubtful, but they held on grimly so that each now laid claim to 18 per cent of the total.

This purchase, if held valid, would effectively block Edward A. Filene's idea of four-man control. Even if two other men were brought in to succeed Simpson and Cory, there would be only 12 per cent of the stock to divide between them. The new men with 6 per cent each would be on no real level of equality with Frost and Kirstein holding 18 per cent each. Filene therefore redoubled his efforts in the courts as the critical moment approached, and litigation multiplied prodigiously. Naturally tension within the organization grew constantly worse. The five employee directors, Edward A. Filene found, or thought he found, were in fact dummies under the control of Frost and Kirstein, but they had power to isolate him whenever the board took a vote.

He was not slow to express his dissatisfaction in scathing terms, but he got it right back in terms just as scathing. If he accused Kirstein of double-dealing, Kirstein accused him of imbecility, and each believed his accusation. Kirstein was just as much a fighting man as Filene and just as much inclined to take any opposition as a personal affront probably based on worse than doubtful motives. What had begun as a difference over policy developed into bitter animosity that poisoned the atmosphere of the whole organization.

The chief victim of the feud was Lincoln Filene, caught in the crossfire. Lincoln admired his brother, but he did not altogether understand him. He also admired Kirstein and did understand him. Above all, he understood very clearly indeed that a feud of this kind among the owners was likely to prove highly detrimental and possibly disastrous to the business, so he struggled for years to adjust matters, but his efforts succeeded only in making both antagonists suspicious of him. As 1928 approached he had to act, and in the end he did with a bold resolution that must command respect whatever one thinks of the wisdom of his decision. He threw his brother overboard.

But that harsh statement requires some modification in justice to the younger Filene. He agreed to vote his stock with Frost and Kirstein but only on certain conditions. He would tolerate no public humiliation of Edward A. Filene nor would he have him penalized financially. In the end an arrangement was worked out whereby Edward A. Filene was to remain president of the company for life; he was to occupy the president's office with all the appurtenances thereof, including the office staff; he was to retain 30 per cent of the total capital stock of the company; he was to draw the same salary as Kirstein, Frost, and Lincoln Filene, to wit, one hundred thousand dollars a year; he was to devote such time as he saw fit to any outside activity that pleased him except a mercantile business in competition with Filene's; but he was in no way to interfere with the conduct of the store, although he might make recommendations to the board of managers.

In other words he was reduced to impotence, but Lincoln saw to it that it should be a very grand impotence. Yet Edward never forgave him.

Such was the end of the career of Edward A. Filene as a merchant. He died regarding himself as the victim of a disgraceful betrayal, and betrayed he certainly was, but that it was disgraceful is a debatable question. Perhaps it was inevitable. Conditions being as they were and human nature being what it is, it is easily conceivable that the others could not have acted otherwise.

Edward A. Filene's real misfortune was not that he cherished

vipers in his bosom, but that he could never understand how
far he was ahead of his time and how necessary it was to explain over and over to his associates what he was doing and
why. Kirstein was not a bad man; he was simply an old-fash-
ioned man, extremely practical, content to adhere to ideas that
had been tested and proved good. He was constitutionally suspicious of criticism of such ideas. He always doubted the motive
of really searching criticism. He was inclined to believe that
anyone who wished to abandon time-tested methods was more
anxious to create trouble than to create a better order. In short,
he was a conservative "of the most straitest sect" in business,
although not necessarily so in his political and social views.
That Filene could ever have converted him is doubtful, and
if he couldn't be converted, he certainly couldn't be dominated. It was the more important that all the others should
comprehend the progressive ideas—frequently progressive to
the point of radicalism—that Filene was generating, but he
was too impatient to be a good teacher.

In this he resembled Woodrow Wilson, another man ahead
of his time who also ran into trouble. Wilson always believed
that to explain a thing once to an intelligent man was sufficient;
if the matter were put before him clearly and he still professed
to be confused, there must be some insincerity in his attitude,
and insincere opposition is not open to argument. It must be
beaten down.

Filene harbored the same delusion. The speed of his own
mental processes was not apparent to him, and when others
failed to keep up, he was pretty sure to think it was because
they would not follow when sometimes they could not. As for
Kirstein, he seems to have been temperamentally scornful of
Filene's basic philosophy, which was regrettable but not a
crime. Kirstein was ambitious, ruthless, and not too fastidious
in his choice of methods, but if it comes to that, so was Filene.
The evidence of actual bad faith on either side is not convincing to an outsider; it is more likely that each man was

convinced that he was working primarily for the good of the whole group and therefore operated with a clear conscience, even when he was doing his utmost to sink the knife into the other.

Nevertheless the outcome was to bring to an abrupt halt the development of Filene's ideas in the field of distribution. This unquestionably represented a social loss, not a net loss since it was at least partially compensated by his work in other fields but nevertheless a loss. Twenty years later it is clear enough that the field of distribution presents some of our most perplexing economic problems; if this man had been permitted to proceed we might have the answers to some of them today. It is true that he might have found the answers by smashing his own concern, which would have been a disaster to Filene but not necessarily to the rest of the world, for proof that a given hypothesis is untenable is a contribution to knowledge and may represent a distinct step in advance, as every scientist admits.

The elimination of Edward A. Filene as a merchant certainly did not destroy William Filene's Sons Company, so one cannot flatly deny the possibility that the elimination may have saved it. In that case Kirstein was a hero to the company. But he is no hero to the rest of the world, for if he saved the company, he saved it by stopping an experiment of great educational and possibly of great financial value to the nation. It was a triumph of the spirit of conservatism over that of bold experimentation. Such triumphs sometimes have a negative value in preventing losses, but they contribute nothing to progress.

CHAPTER 3

The Citizen

<<<<<<<<<<<<<<<<<<<<<<<<<<<<<<<<<<<<<<<<<<<<<<<<<<<<<<

I

"My first ambition as a boy was the usual one—I wanted to keep a candy store," Edward A. Filene wrote when he was an elderly man. That desire faded as the passing years brought him his first contact with the tragedy of human existence, the somber realization that there is a stomach-ache in too much candy.

But it was succeeded by others of a similar order. "I changed my ambition, and an engineer operating a railroad engine seemed a god worthy of imitation. Next I wanted to be a conqueror—to ride on a big black horse with nodding plumes and go out into battle with a sharp flashing sword, cut off four heads at one time and come back riding through streets with the assembled multitudes waving flags and acclaiming me as a hero and strewing roses in my path.

"But there came a day when I realized that to ride back from battle on a big black horse along a rose-strewn road, having killed men and left their families to suffer from want and starvation, also had an ache in it."

So he compromised on a determination to become a savant. "I remember my disappointment and how ill used I felt myself to be when I could not go to Harvard. I thought I should never now be a learned man, never be a very useful one, without this Harvard education." But he did what he could. "I began to

78

study subjects with which my work brought me into contact in a practical way—that is, subjects that would correct or amplify the theories I was applying to the problems of my business. . . . I gradually came to understand that the intelligent running of a store was a very good substitute for a college. After a while I became reconciled to my lot."

In this summary of the education of a practical man it is highly probable that Filene spoke not for himself alone but for any number of Harvard graduates as well. The college training, lack of which he regretted so sharply, at most would have speeded the process of his real education, and even that is not certain. Realization of his lack may have made Filene work harder than he would have worked otherwise and so may have brought him to a knowledge of himself and his world as soon as he would have reached it by aid of formal instruction for four years.

"I think shopkeeping is like sin," he continued; "first you endure and then you embrace it." But although one might not become learned in a shop as the schools understand learning, it is possible that there "one may become wiser than some of the men who go through Harvard, if wisdom means having the things you know or have learned permeated with love and sympathy and understanding for your fellow men. . . .

"I have gotten into a work . . . which gives me hope that even if I do not become learned before I die, I shall at least from year to year be likely to know more and perhaps be more useful. And that, I think, is an ambition which it is worth while to try to satisfy. I would not change this, even if I could, for the engine cab or the big black horse."

The question unanswered, or not answered explicitly, in this is "useful to whom?" Perhaps it is a silly question. Filene would have thought it so. It never occurred to him that any man, or certainly any intelligent man, could wish to be useful to anything except to society, to the commonweal.

Yet it is of course a highly unusual ambition. Oh, it is common enough for men to profess it. Every candidate for every office from township constable to President makes the welkin ring with proclamations of his desire to be useful to the state. Every clergyman, including the most self-seeking, proclaims his desire to be useful to morality and righteousness; every lawyer, the shyster most loudly of all, by his own account is devoted to justice; every doctor, the quack leading, would advance health and longevity; every businessman, and most blatantly the one with the conscience of Uriah Heep and the ethical code of a pirate, asserts his devotion to service in general.

So common indeed have false professions of a desire to be useful to society become that a cynical world receives them all with sneers. One among many may be telling the truth, but he is not to be believed on his own assertion, not to be believed at all unless the evidence is clear, cogent, and convincing. Edward A. Filene's statement of his concept of citizenship—year by year to know more and to be more useful—is admirable, but any hypocrite can make an admirable statement. The question is, what steps did he take to make the statement good?

One may as well begin with the admission that his record is a long way from consistent. Wisdom he described as "having the things you know or have learned permeated with love and sympathy and understanding for your fellow men." Merely as a definition that is good, very good; it is not easy to produce a better—merely as a definition. But as a description of an attitude coming from Filene, it is justification for much lifting of the eyebrows among those who knew him. Love and sympathy and understanding some persons did receive from him, but it was not the common experience of individuals who approached him. On the surface indeed it was rather the reverse, and not many of us penetrate beneath the surface of personal contacts.

Sometimes he could be genuinely sympathetic and understanding in very rough ways, ways so rough that they gave him
a reputation for being anything but sympathetic and understanding. For one thing, although he was tolerant of labor's
aspirations to a degree that exasperated his business associates,
he drove his office assistants mercilessly. Naturally this generated in exhausted assistants, secretaries, and stenographers
dark suspicions that his tolerant attitude was only a pose, and
one after another quit his service in fury.

Yet the record shows that it was a rare occurrence for one of
Filene's ex-secretaries to sink into obscurity after leaving him.
Nearly all were successful, and some rose to high places in business and the arts and sciences. Obviously then Filene did not
break them, yet there is no manner of doubt that he pounded
them heavily. It is a matter of common knowledge that when
a man takes a real battering in his youth—and Filene custom-
arily picked them relatively young—if the metal of his character
doesn't break, it is forged and comes out of the experience
vastly stronger than it was before. Filene was not an infallible
judge of men, but he had a sharp eye for innate ability in a
young man, and he was not often deceived. But he had also a
keen realization of the fact that natural ability is not always
accompanied by a resolute will to develop it.

If then he perceived high ability in a young man and also
perceived that the young man was not developing his powers
to anything like their capacity, it cannot be said that he lacked
understanding. Then to compel that youth to extend himself, to compel him even by force and violence to do his best, to
do better than what he had considered his best, was not in the
long run detrimental; on the contrary it might be highly bene-
ficial. The strikingly good record in later life of this man's former employees is consistent with the theory that he spurred
them into developing powers that might otherwise have lain
unused.

Nor is it possible to maintain that such treatment was basically unsympathetic or unloving. All that one can say of it confidently is that it was unsentimental and that Filene himself
was ready enough to admit. He would have done more—he
would have boasted of it—for he prided himself on being devoid of sentimentality. To give a man increased confidence in
his own powers is certainly a magnificent gift, and if Filene
gave that to his men* he would have worried little over the
methods by which he conferred it.

He would have worried too little. Sentimental treatment is
poisonous to an adult, but there is a wide area between sentimentality and stark ruthlessness. This Filene never quite
realized. Had he done so, he would have been a happier man
and probably a more successful man, for even an honest cru-
sader needs the good will of his fellows.

At the same time there is no reasonable doubt that when he
described wisdom as knowledge permeated with sympathy,
love, and understanding, he was writing with complete sincerity. He did love his fellow men. He did sympathize with
them. He did understand a great deal about them even if he
was utterly ignorant of some of the most important things.

Filene was one of those not uncommon characters who love
people and despise persons. This sounds like a paradox, but it
is in fact a well-known quirk of human nature, and it is quite
consistent with greatness. Woodrow Wilson was a conspicuous example of the type. John Adams and his son, John Quincy
Adams, were examples. George Washington had more than a
touch of it. John Randolph of Roanoke is an extraordinary

* As this book was being written one of these men was editor of one of the
world's greatest newspapers, two had been famous college presidents, two were
directors of great foundations, and others were on their boards, while several
were genuine tycoons in business and the professions. One or two had died,
but not one was in either a penitentiary or an almshouse. With all the hatred
he inspired, Filene apparently never broke a man's spirit, or the people who
worked for him would have been no good afterward.

instance, because he recognized it in himself and by flaunting it actually turned it into a political asset.*

In any event, Filene's success as a citizen is certainly not to be measured by his success in making himself universally beloved, for the net balance there is on the wrong side of the ledger. He was respected, yes. He was admired, albeit in a somewhat guarded way. But he never was in any danger of becoming a popular idol.

Yet this, like most positive assertions about anything as complex as a personality, is subject to one reservation, for there was an element of the population with which his success was spectacular. Children adored him. The reason was that he exacted nothing of them and expected nothing of them except to be happy. To see a child's face light up gave him unalloyed pleasure, which is the one facet of his character which may safely be described as altogether charming.

One of his joys in life was to roam about the store watching the children accompanying their mothers on what was to them a boring expedition. Filene would choose one looking particularly bored and engage in a conversation which invariably culminated in a visit to a toy counter where he would present the child with a gift; or still more thrilling, to his office, where he kept a big drawer in a filing cabinet filled with marvels for little women. Boys sometimes came away with a large silver dollar.

Cynics, of course, were not at a loss for a deprecatory comment, even on this. "Good business," they said, pointing out

* On the other hand, Alexander Hamilton seems to have liked persons and detested people. So did such disparate characters as Henry Adams, W. G. Sumner and Ambrose Bierce.
"I wish I liked the human race,
I wish I liked its silly face,"
wailed that most charming of Oxford dons who was almost obliterated by being named Sir Walter Raleigh; perhaps he was sighing for the quintessence of supreme greatness.

that the mother was invariably pleased and flattered while the child would go away with an impression of Filene's as a place where delightful things could happen in the most unexpected fashion. That was true enough, and if the child were a girl, she might grow into a woman with a subconscious attachment to Filene's as strong as it was illogical. As a matter of fact, there are gray-haired women in Boston today who admit that in their minds the name of the store is linked with childhood memories of a sort of a fairy godfather who popped up from nowhere and transformed an ordinary day into a golden one.

Doubtless it was good business, but doubtless he liked it, anyhow. Nor does the suggestion of business apply to one feature that attended the Christmas party he gave to a group of children every year. This feature was the dumping on the floor of the living room of a tremendous pile, a peck or so, of bright new pennies. The host would then get down on his hands and knees, inviting the guests to imitate him, and offer a prize to the child who could sort out exactly one hundred pennies faster than he could. Competition was strenuous, and Filene worked at it as earnestly as he ever did at solving a business problem. There is no rational explanation of his repeating the stunt year after year except that he liked it, and his liking it gives the world a glimpse of a man who must have been far removed from a misanthrope.

II

Filene, the merchant, may have been more important to the city of Boston than Filene, the citizen, but the rest of the world takes a different view. The fact that he was a champion among sellers of pins contributed handsomely to the prosperity of his native city, which is reason enough for Boston to esteem him but is of no great interest to anyone else. It is the fact that he was full of novel, interesting, and sometimes challenging no-

tions about citizenship that makes him worth the attention of
people far removed from the scene of his activities.

Yet he was decidedly Bostonian, especially in his earlier
years. No doubt every man is shaped by his environment to
some extent, but Boston seems to be exceptionally potent in
stamping a characteristic mark upon her progeny. This is
not to say that they are uniform; on the contrary Bostonians
from the beginning have been extraordinarily diverse, and in
her two extremes she is matchless. No other city has produced
philosophers as stately or rogues as fantastic as those that come
from Boston. One of her savants exhorted the city to plain
living and high thinking, but Boston has put her own interpretation upon the exhortation by becoming the country's most
remarkable exponent of high thinking and low living. True, it
was after Filene's death that she accomplished the unprecedented feat of having for her mayor a character then living at
the taxpayers' expense in a prison cell, but even in the nineties,
when the young Filene was first beginning to look about him
with a judicious eye, Boston was a curious and startling city.

There was the usual hookup between crooked politics and
sanctimonious business. A highly respectable merchant who
wished to park his trucks in a no-parking zone, a landlord who
wished the building inspectors to overlook inadequate fire es-
capes, a manufacturer who would have been put to great expense had he complied exactly with the sanitary laws, all knew
whom to see and about how much of a contribution to the "campaign fund" would be required to adjust matters. None would
admit even to himself that in making such arrangements he was
corrupting public officials, undermining the law, and poisoning
the government—in short, that he was a crook and a dangerous
one.

In the last days of the nineteenth century and the early ones
of the twentieth, communism was still largely a dictionary
word, familiar to sociologists and historians, but rarely to be

found in the newspapers. However the idea that half a century later is conveyed to most American minds by the word communism was well known to Boston right after the Spanish-American War and was feared and hated. They called it anarchism. The average Bostonian's definition of anarchism had no more relation to the theories of Prince Kropotkin* than his modern definition of communism has to do with those of Nicholas Lenin; in fact, anarchist was then exactly what communist became later, not a label but an epithet. Anyone who was thoroughly horrible was an anarchist, and the most horrible of all people were those who were willing, or were thought to be willing, to subvert law and order to further their own ends. The denunciation of anarchists was as much the duty of respectable Bostonians as contributing to charity and in the statelier clubs of the city the name was a hissing and a byword.

The fact that these clubs were hotbeds of anarchy escaped all but a few minds. The slums where immigrants swarmed produced not nearly as large a proportion of men willing to subvert law and order to further their own ends, for there was hardly a businessman among them and not many property holders who had not quietly arranged to have the law set aside in some particular to serve his profit or convenience. The difference was that some of the professed anarchists were theorists who held to anarchism on principle, while no businessman was an anarchist for anything except his private advantage.

The facts did not escape Filene, but what to make of them he had no idea. Yet as time passed and increasing prosperity lessened the pressure of business upon his time and energy, he became more and more convinced that he ought to make something of them. This too was a typically Bostonian reaction, al-

---

* Incidentally, although he had no sympathy with Kropotkin's views, Edward A. Filene was one of those who at least knew what they were. In later years he was an acquaintance of Princess Kropotkin, the philosopher's widow, who called at Filene's office at least once.

though there is hardly a doubt that it was inspired in part by old William Filene's stern sense of duty.

For this contradictory city has ever been prolific of two diametrically opposite types of intellectual, one the battling reformer, the other the intellectual anchorite, best represented perhaps by Charles Sumner and Ralph Waldo Emerson. From the beginning the cultivation of one's own personality has been an ideal esteemed in Boston, which in no wise reduces its esteem for the other ideal of the cultivation of the personality of everyone else, whether he likes it or not. The lily-fingered inhabitant of the ivory tower, who disdains the sordid vulgarity of political strife, is as familiar to Boston as he was to intellectual circles in Europe before the rise of Hitler proved that the intellectual life is encompassed by the political life and that a malignant growth in one will, if left unchecked, inevitably destroy the other.

At the same time, the Boston Brahmin rarely goes as far as Simeon Stylites, who would descend from his pillar for no purpose whatsoever. There are some things that will fetch all Beacon Hill swarming down to the plain in fighting array, and one of them occurred at about the time Filene began to consider his civic duty rather more than his mercantile interest. The local transit company proposed to run a streetcar line right across Boston Common.

This attempted sacrilege was defeated but not without a long and arduous contest that revealed a deplorable state of affairs. The city was in the grip of a transportation monopoly grown arrogant in the strength of its position, which threatened to become all powerful. To prevent the violation of the Common all sorts of people had banded together, and after that was accomplished some of them, including some of the Beacon Hill aristocrats, refused to lay down their weapons. They remained combined in what they called the Public Franchise League to defend the interests of the public during the great expansion of transportation facilities that was plainly inevitable.

From 1897 on the league made war against the efforts of the traction company to acquire a monopoly and control the use of the public streets without providing adequate transportation facilities. The fight raged for years through the courts, the legislature, and political campaigns, spreading to involve the gas companies and other utilities. The question of the ownership of the new subway system was the storm center, and eventually the city won, if not a complete victory, still a reasonable degree of security.

One of the most difficult phases of the combat was that of public education, for without public support based on accurate information nothing could be done in the legislature, and no victory in the courts would last long if the legislature chose to rewrite the law. At this Bloody Angle the Public Franchise League posted Filene as chairman of the publicity committee, and the mere fact that victory was won is evidence enough that he acquitted himself well.

It was essential, of course, for the chairman of the publicity committee to keep in close touch with all that was done in the courts and the legislature. The legal phase of the battle was in the charge of a man whom Filene had long known as one of the smartest corporation lawyers in Boston, but with whom he had had no particularly close association until the franchise fight; long before that fight was over, however, the merchant was tremendously impressed by the league's chief counsel. The mild-mannered ethereal-looking figure resembled some medieval ascetic rather than a man-at-arms, but in court, or before a legislative committee, he was prodigious.

On one day in particular Filene was amazed when counsel for the traction company at a legislative hearing suddenly shifted his whole attack and undertook to prove that certain operations apparently showing a profit had really been conducted at a loss. For two hours he reeled off statistics taken from a huge mass of documents piled on the table before him. The Public Franchise League had had no idea that anything like this was coming, and Filene, at least, was utterly confused. But not the league's counsel. When the company lawyer finished, he rose armed only with notes scribbled during the speech and took up the argument point by point. "This is a misstatement," he said; "the true figures are these . . . ," and "this is a misinterpretation; the true meaning of the clause, as the courts have held in such-and-such cases, is this . . . ," and "this is bad bookkeeping; the item should not be deducted from this total, but added to that, as any accountant will tell you." In thirty minutes the whole long argument was wrecked, and Filene knew he was dealing not merely with a first-rate lawyer but with an extraordinary intelligence in this man, whose name was Louis D. Brandeis.

The impression was deepened when at the end of the long exhausting battle Brandeis refused to accept a fee for his services. Filene was inclined to be a little fussy about it; he pointed out that the lawyer had been regularly retained, and he, for one, would feel embarrassed if the committee failed to compensate him; in fact, he wanted to write his own check for at least part of the fee.

"If you have a right to give your money to the public service, Mr. Filene," said Brandeis, "I claim an equal right to give my time."

Filene subsided, but from that time on Brandeis' firm was retained by the store to represent it in any negotiation that promised to be difficult, and Brandeis himself was consulted on any matter of public interest in which Filene was involved.

His advice was not always followed for on at least one point their philosophies were directly opposed, and neither changed. Brandeis was afraid of sheer size, Filene not in the least. Brandeis believed that man's capacity to organize efficiently is strictly limited, and therefore that any organization spreading beyond that limit is bound to be inefficient and is likely to work against the interest it was originally designed to serve. Filene could perceive no convincing evidence that this is true, and even if such a limit exists he was quite certain that it has, been approached in very few, if any, lines of human endeavor. Accordingly he went ahead blithely, organizing whatever he could lay his hands on, sometimes to Brandeis' perturbation.

III

The franchise fight had persuaded him that one thing very much in need of organization was the city of Boston itself. People had been drawn into the Public Franchise League by all sorts of motives—the Brahmins originally to protect the Common, the Washington Street merchants originally to prevent their street from becoming so hopelessly choked that it would no longer function as a thoroughfare, suburban dwellers and real-estate interests to secure faster and more adequate service to the business center. But before it was over, all were fighting to save the city from losing control of its own destiny and becoming a satrapy ruled by irresponsible private interests.

As they assembled, Filene had been amazed to discover how ignorant they were of each other's very existence, to say nothing of each other's enthusiasms, prejudices, and points of view. United they had triumphed over an entrenched and powerful financial interest. It was plain that united they were very nearly invincible.

Nor was there any apparent reason why they should not be united, at least on all the major interests confronting the citizenry. They all lived in the same city, and any improvement in the safety, convenience, and attractiveness of that city was to the advantage of them all—the private as well as the public advantage. Union therefore seemed to be dictated by enlightened selfishness as well as by other considerations. Filene proceeded to promote it by every device that occurred to him.

What struck him most forcibly was the fragmentation of the city's business interests. The merchants had an association, the manufacturers had another, the real-estate men had half a dozen, the hotels had their organization, the saloonkeepers theirs, while the neighborhood groups associated for local improvement were numberless, but there was no general organization representing all the business interests of the city of Boston. This anomalous situation Filene set out to correct.

It was an undertaking of large proportions but of no complexity whatever. The situation was familiar to the whole business community, and practically everyone agreed that it should be corrected; all that was required was a leader with time, energy, and persistence. Vast numbers of letters had to be written, innumerable conferences arranged, many minor disagreements had to be ironed out, but nobody had to be convinced of the desirability of the project. Once Filene went into action, he found a great many helpers, some of them highly efficient. The Boston Chamber of Commerce, as it eventually came into existence, was by no means exclusively his work. Toward the end indeed he became little more than the liaison officer, the point of contact, between groups and individuals all working toward the same end.

Nevertheless, one is justified in saying that he founded the Boston Chamber of Commerce, if it is understood that the word means that he furnished the initial impulse not that he did all the work. He had time, he had energy, he had persistence, the three elements needed for the work, and he put them all into the job without stint. With that done, the situation crystallized rapidly, and he brought the organization into being with relative ease—that is to say it involved a great deal of routine labor but not much hard thinking.

Encouraged by his success, he went on to organize the State Chamber of Commerce on a similar plan and eventually played a large part in organizing the United States Chamber of Commerce.

These activities were not regarded with unbounded enthusiasm by all his associates. In the store Kirstein in particular was critical. Filene, he thought, was squandering on public affairs time and energy that belonged to William Filene's Sons Company. If there had been any temperamental sympathy between the two men, he might have reserved judgment at least, but instead of sympathy there was the basic antagonism that inevitably exists between conservative and progressive. He didn't like Filene, and all this public activity, far from commanding his admiration, increased his dislike. The fact that it was highly successful, at least on the surface, only made matters worse. Kirstein smoldered.

On the other side Brandeis also regarded it somewhat doubtfully. With his chronic distrust of bigness he perceived that increasing the power of the business organization increased its potency for evil as well as for good. As Filene proceeded from city to state and from state to nation, he thought with increasing uneasiness of what might happen to such efficient machinery in the hands of reactionary forces.

"Filene," he remarked to Lincoln Steffens, "is always making weapons for the enemy."*

A full generation later candor compels the admission that both Kirstein and Brandeis were partly right. If one assumes that Filene's principal reason for being was to make money for the store as rapidly as possible, then he would have accomplished that purpose more readily by spending all his time and energy upon the store. To this extent Kirstein was correct.

But there is another point of view regarding the store, a perfectly valid point of view, although it is more generally accepted in Europe than in this country. A store or any other business enterprise may be regarded solely as a source of immediate income, which is the point of view more widely accepted in a country in which, as a French observer has put it, "a man changes his occupation as readily as he changes his shirt"; or it may be regarded as a European family regards its

* *The Autobiography of Lincoln Steffens*, p. 601. Harcourt, Brace, New York, 1931.

landed estate, as a sort of trust that the contemporary generation may enjoy but which it should pass along to the next generation improved, not impaired.

Even Americans once accepted this point of view as applied
to land, and the Boston Brahmins accept it as applied to urban
real property, but only occasionally does one find an industrialist or merchant taking that view of his business, because such
men are rarely true proprietors. They are usually agents for
an amorphous group of stockholders in whom ownership is
vested and who are only too willing to get rid of their holdings
the moment income from the business is seriously threatened.

Both the Filenes, however, were genuine proprietors. They
had built their business from an insignificant side-street shop
into the greatest of its kind. To them it was a source of pride
as well as profit, and they were both much more interested in
its permanence than stockholders usually are. Lincoln understood as well as Edward that the prosperity of Filene's as an
institution was closely linked with the prosperity of Boston as a
city. Lincoln could therefore appreciate the value of work for
the general benefit of the city, even long-term work whose full
benefit might not appear for a decade or even a generation. He
was in the early days by no means unsympathetic with his
brother's public activities even though they absorbed more and
more of his time. Lincoln certainly did not yet regard them
as inconsistent with the long-term advantage of the store.

But not even his brother understood the full scope of
Edward A. Filene's thinking about the relation of the businessman to his community. This is not astonishing, for it is
doubtful if Filene himself had as yet perceived clearly what
it was that he wished to do.

Evidence of this is the fact that in 1909 he brought in a man
to help him think, and his selection was an extraordinary choice
for a capitalist, an employer, and a millionaire. Lincoln Steffens, indeed, was extraordinary from any standpoint. Little,
lean, and goat bearded, he bore a striking physical resemblance

to the Russian leader, Leon Trotsky, and he had something of Trotsky's shrewdness and energy with a great deal more intellectual integrity.

Steffens was one of a group of writers, largely newspapermen, who are almost forgotten today but who in 1909 were shaking the country. They were "exponents of the neglected truth" in that they were describing the more unpleasant facts of American life, particularly in the overlapping fields of politics and economics. The alliance between big business and dirty politics was their theme, and in the beginning they were hailed by liberals as champions of their cause. But they ranged far and wide, and eventually their investigations began to drag in so many of the once respectable that they became embarrassing; so that champion phrasemaker, Theodore Roosevelt, then President, in an attempt to discredit them compared them to the man in Bunyan's *Pilgrim's Progress* who did not perceive an angel standing above him and offering him a crown because his eyes were fixed on the muck he was raking together in the street. Bunyan's allegory of course was directed against avarice, but Roosevelt turned it to his own uses so neatly that muckraker became a generic name for a writer who attacked any phase of the existing order.

One of the ablest—if you admired them, or one of the most notorious if you didn't—of the muckrakers was Lincoln Steffens, newspaper and magazine writer, whose specialty was the corruption of municipal government. He had investigated, one after another, half a dozen American cities and in each had discovered the same pattern—an alliance between "respectable" businessmen and disreputable gang politicians to rob the taxpayers, always of their money and frequently of their rights. Over and over Steffens had shown how for every dollar spent on public improvements another had to go to some thief and how slums, firetraps, and brothels menacing the health, lives, and morals of the public continued to exist because inspectors and other officials had been bribed, sometimes directly, more often indirectly, by landlords who were frequently pious church-men and pillars of the community.

Naturally Steffens was loathed and feared by all those ele-ments that prefer not to be informed of nastiness in their own communities, for once informed, their pretensions to righteous-ness compel them to do something toward cleaning it up. But his activities had resulted in an immense amount of sweeping and swabbing in the cities he had visited, so reformers held him in high esteem.

Filene made up his mind that an exposure by Lincoln Steffens would be good for Boston, so he sought the man out and, when other persuasion failed, actually hired him to come and see what he could find. Naturally this did not increase Filene's popularity among conservative Bostonians, and even his brother began to wonder what effect enterprises of this sort might have upon the store.

But the outcome was not exactly what anyone had expected. Steffens, unlike some of the muckrakers, was honest intellec-tually as well as financially. He had not written his exposures of the cities solely because magazine editors were willing to pay high prices for them but because he wanted to know the truth and to understand the nature and origin of social evils. When he found that wherever he went the pattern was the same except for minor variations easily explained by local conditions, he began to suspect that the real trouble lies too deep to be reached by conventional reform, and since reform is based on conventional morality, he began to suspect that too. By the time he came to Boston, he was pretty thoroughly sick of the sort of thing he had been doing in Philadelphia, in Cleveland, and elsewhere. He had developed from an investigator and re-porter into a social philosopher.

In Boston he had no difficulty in discovering the old fa-miliar pattern and, in fulfillment of his agreement with Filene, he wrote a book about it. Boston differed from other American cities only in that the dirty work was done somewhat more circuitously than elsewhere, but it was quite as effective, and with slightly more labor it could be traced.

Steffens put in about a year on the job and in due season delivered the manuscript to Filene's committee. But it was never published. Steffens says in his autobiography that he knew rumors spread abroad that the book was suppressed by the influence of powerful financial and social interests that were able to terrorize the committee into withholding it, but he asserts that that was not the case. According to him, the truth was that the book simply lacked the punch he had put into his earlier work because he no longer believed in the efficacy of the remedies he had once advocated.

In support of this he asserts that when Upton Sinclair was writing his book on Boston he asked Steffens to be shown the manuscript, and Steffens sent it to him. But Sinclair made no use of it whatever, and a book that Upton Sinclair could not use obviously was not particularly damaging to vested interests.

But although no sensational exposure eventuated from Lincoln Steffens' presence in Boston, it had a marked effect on Filene's thinking and, at least temporarily, on his action. The two men's minds moved in parallel lines. Filene had always been skeptical of panaceas. "There are no miracles," was a favorite saying of his. Steffens began by believing in every panacea, but he was too honest to reject the evidence of his own eyes, and long observation had at last convinced him that none of them worked.

The easy recourse of men who have reached this state of mind is to fall into cynicism and apathy. If there is no answer to the questions one has been asking, it is obviously a waste of energy to keep on asking. Some of the muckrakers who had been Steffens' colleagues in the early days fell into this attitude and were converted into bitter reactionaries, but Steffens took the line that a physicist or a biologist takes when one of his hypotheses is proved untenable—if there is no answer to his question, then it is the question not the universe that is idiotic.

Filene readily admitted that his thinking was influenced by Steffens, but we are left to surmise to what extent Steffens' thinking was influenced by Filene. Starting with the firm conviction that there are no miracles, the merchant had never felt the writer's temptation to pin his faith to formulas, except, perhaps, in his early youth. He said once that if he had a son who was not a Socialist before he was twenty, he would disinherit the boy, but if he remained a Socialist after he was twenty, he would be disinherited just as ruthlessly.

Steffens was incapable of taking this severely pragmatic view, but there is no doubt that in Boston he realized that the philosophy of the muckrakers was too simple and easy to account for the things he saw. It is not unreasonable to assume that his association with Filene contributed to this realization, for he had no doubt of Filene's sincerity nor any doubt that the merchant was doomed to defeat. Steffens asserts that it was about this time that he discovered the futility of conventional morality, and it is hard to think of anything more likely to precipitate such a discovery than the spectacle of a man completely honest, highly intelligent, and a hard worker who was getting nowhere.

That this was Steffens' view of Filene is made plain in the former's autobiography. That Filene held toward Steffens the same attitude of admiration mingled with exasperation is nowhere directly stated, but it is implicit in his whole course. He was convinced of Steffens' honesty, he respected his intelligence, and he admired his diligence, but no disillusionment, no series of disillusionments could ever quite cure the writer of the obsession that somewhere there are miracles. To Filene this was simply a flaw in the writer's mental equipment, but he overlooked it since there was obviously nothing to be done about it.

What fascinates the student of personality is that these two attained the same point of view although they approached it from opposite sides. They were both liberals in the sense that

they were hospitable to new ideas, but they were hospitable
for opposite reasons. Ten years after this Boston association
they were both to be fascinated by the new idea represented
by the Russian revolution, but Steffens welcomed it because
he hoped the Russians might show us the right road to the
good society, Filene because he was certain that it showed us
where we were in some respects on the wrong road. Steffens
was filled with enthusiasm, Filene with curiosity, but they
agreed that the experiment should be given a fair trial and
watched with close attention. Steffens in his enthusiasm became temporarily a fellow traveler if not a Communist; Filene
in his curiosity was not for a moment tempted to join the movement, but he did wish to see what the Russians could make of
it. They agreed that Communism ought not to be suppressed
by force but should be given a fair chance to show what it
could do, so in the estimation of the more fanatical conservatives they were lumped together, and there was a time when
both were suspected of being disciples of Lenin.

IV

But the Bolshevik Revolution was still ten years in the future
when Lincoln Steffens came to Boston and joined Edward A.
Filene in one of the most curious campaigns for civic betterment ever undertaken in an American city. Indeed, curious
is a mild word. In some ways it merits the adjective, fantastic,
that not a few Bostonians applied to it. The project was badly
designed and fumblingly executed; it accomplished little and
was generally regarded in Boston as a complete failure. Yet its
basic principles were never disproved, and the subsequent development of municipal government in American cities affords
more than a suggestion that these men were on the right track
and that their failure was due to technical incompetence rather than to basic error.

Filene had not forgotten his astonishment when he learned
during the franchise fight how little Bostonians knew about

Boston. The city was divided into watertight compartments, and men of force and character on Beacon Hill were hardly aware of the existence of men of equal force and character in sections into which one could almost throw a stone from the top of the hill. Intellectuals had not even a passing acquaintance with industrialists, and popular leaders knew neither.

Steffens had found in other cities, and he found again in Boston, that a political boss, an industrial boss, and a financial boss are much more like each other than any of the three is like one of his own followers. He had acquired a clearer understanding of the leadership principle than Hitler ever had, but he found that he was almost alone in his possession of the information. Most Bostonians cherished the illusion that the cleavage of the classes is vertical instead of horizontal and that leaders of the "nice" people are altogether different from leaders of the unnice. Steffens knew that a leader is a leader, whether in the slums or in Louisburg Square, and is divided from all followers by a gap much wider than the one that separates him from other leaders.

Both men were aware that all these people lived in the same city and that all had a selfish interest in making that city safe, convenient, and attractive. Both held the more questionable belief that if all these men knew each other they might work together more effectively for their common advantage. They agreed therefore that the logical first step was to bring them all together.

Steffens asserts that the idea of organizing the Boston City Club was his, but he concedes that Filene did much of the work. The basis of the project was the selection of genuine leaders, which could not be done out of the city directory, nor from rosters of membership in various organizations, nor even from a directory of directors. It took careful and skillful investigation.

Yet it was after all merely a matter of care and skill. It was not impossible, it was not even difficult if the right people were consulted, to discover who really ran the various organizations in the city, whether they were social clubs, business groups, or political wards. What was more difficult was to convince these leaders that they were not being drawn into some sort of trap. To effect this the first inviolable rule adopted was that the Boston City Club should do nothing whatever in its official capacity. It was to be a place for discussion and investigation not for action. The expression of any and every sort of opinion was to be welcomed, and controversy was never to be suppressed, but the club was to have no power to commit anyone to anything.

One highly practical aspect of the project Filene attended to alone. He was aware that the very foundation of a successful club is the provision of good food at reasonable prices. A club with the dullest and most unimaginative of presidents can survive and flourish as long as it possesses a first-rate steward, but with a genius for president it will soon be in trouble if its steward is incompetent. Filene went into this with his customary thoroughness, and a refractory job it was, but eventually, in New York, he found the right man and promptly dragged him to Boston.

Finally enough members were rounded up to make a start. Nobody was really against the project; the general reluctance was based on people's inability to see anything in it. But once it got under way, the rest was easy. Men discovered that there was, in fact, much to be said for meeting on common ground; for the first few years the City Club furnished that ground, and leaders of all types used it. The result was a lively interest that for some time made it the most vital place in Boston, a true Areopagus, not in the sense of a court but in that of the place where men went, in the scriptural phrase, "to hear some new thing."

But although it was debarred from action, behind the City Club there was an ulterior motive in the minds of its projectors. It was a place for talk, but they did not expect it to be idle talk; they intended to use it to give the spark to a much larger concept, which eventually acquired a somewhat amorphous identity under the name of "Boston 1915."

Nearly forty years later it is easy to perceive that from the start this scheme was ill conceived and mismanaged. Steffens formulated it, and he was not the man to work out detailed plans for a project of the kind. Filene managed it in large part, and he was not the man for that job. The formulator should have had a sharp, definitive, severely practical mind, which is as far as possible from Steffens' mind. The manager should have been a suave, diplomatic, infinitely patient man, which is as far as possible from the sort of man that Filene was. But it is certain that there were not two other men in Boston, and probably not two in America, who combined the vision to conceive the project and the boldness to attempt it.

Just what "Boston 1915" was the city hasn't found out to this day, and therein was the assurance of its failure. It may be labeled—although a label is no definition—as a classical example, a textbook case, of impractical idealism. But Filene might have objected that this is a contradiction in terms, for the very basis of his philosophy was that idealism is never impractical. The methods by which men seek to realize it may be—with depressing frequency are—impractical, but the thing itself is the only real practicality.

All that the city discovered, and this only little by little, was what "Boston 1915" was not, and it was not so many things that a large proportion of the population eventually acquired the conviction that it was not anything. It was not a scheme to bring more factories to Boston. It was not a scheme to bring more people to Boston. It was not primarily even a scheme to bring more wealth to Boston although Filene believed that increased weath would have been one of its incidental results. In 1909 it was the general assumption in Boston, and in every other American city for that matter, that improvement of the city necessarily meant increasing its business activity, its population, and its wealth. If "Boston 1915" was not aimed directly at any of these, it could have no aim or none that could interest a reasonable man.

The flat truth is that this was correct. The movement did not have an aim that interested the population in general, and that was the failure of its projectors. They had an aim, but they did not make it interesting by defining it sharply and clearly enough to bring it within the comprehension of the masses, and hence they could not control the energy of the masses sufficiently to channel it into the right direction. Nevertheless this failure throws more light upon Filene as a citizen than is shed by many of his successes.

He and Steffens started with two perfectly sound premises from which they drew the wrong conclusion, but it was a failure in logic which the temperaments of the two men rendered almost inevitable.

Their first premise was that there existed conditions in the city of Boston that added to the inconvenience, danger, and general discomfort of living in the city. Over this there was no debate. Everyone knew that there were slums that were a menace to public health, criminals who were a menace to property, firetraps that were a menace to both life and property, faults in the school system that were a menace to the intelligence of the next generation, political corruption that was a menace to democratic government. Everyone could see the traffic congestion that was exhausting the time and the patience of citizens. Everyone knew that not only the rich but people of moderate incomes were escaping to suburbs that became more and more remote as the automobile came into more general use, with the result that residential property in the city itself was steadily declining in value, thereby forcing up the tax rate on business property. Everyone knew that the public health service was neither as efficient nor as extensive as it should be. Everyone knew that more open spaces, especially playgrounds, were needed in the crowded sections. The better informed knew that Boston was meeting increasingly severe competition from other Atlantic ports and that the harbor and wharf facilities needed attention. In short everyone knew that plenty of bad conditions existed.

All informed persons were aware too that the existence of these conditions barred a great many people from any real par‑ ticipation in the civilization of the city. Boston had developed a culture in which it took justifiable pride, but it was a culture that left some people out. There were plenty of Boston citizens who worked hard, stayed sober, and never gambled, but at that had great difficulty in feeding and clothing their families, with no surplus either of money or of time to devote to enjoyment of the facilities that existed for their recreation and development.

To Filene's mind this meant that the existing facilities were largely wasted, and civic waste meant money out of every man's pocket. A huge public library with a wonderful collection used to only half its capacity, magnificent art galleries with only a handful of spectators, splendid parks so located that masses of the population could never reach them—such things to him represented money gone down the drain. But to berate the pop‑ ulace for its neglect of such advantages was futile as long as the lives of many people were cast in such molds as to make their enjoyment of cultural facilities impossible.

The second premise was that nobody liked this situation. As to this there was debate. Down in the poorer sections there were men—not among the mentally handicapped either but shrewd intelligent men, some of them powerful leaders—who firmly believed that the rich were perfectly satisfied with exist‑ ing conditions. Why not? As far as the poor could see, the rich were doing very well for themselves with things as they were; it was not to be supposed that they desired any real change. Among the rich and particularly among the socially elect, who were farther removed than businessmen from contact with the populace, there was a general assumption that the ward bosses were equally content; with things as they were, they could ex‑ ploit the taxpayers, so it was not to be supposed that they de‑ sired any real change.

The point of view of each rested upon an assumption of moral superiority on his own part. This allowed one to believe that the class to which he did not belong, being morally inferior, actually enjoyed and approved the existence of squalor, vice, and corruption. The two great divisions of the rich and the poor were the main ones, but there were innumerable subdivisions, each cherishing its own brood of suspicions. Even within the world of business, for example, the industrialists suspected the merchants and both suspected the bankers of moral delinquency permitting the approval of evil from which they might extract a personal profit.

To Steffens it was a familiar picture. He had seen it in every city he had studied, and Boston was not materially different from the rest. To Filene it was an illogical picture. He saw it plainly enough, but he could see no reason for its existence except lack of information, and that could be remedied.

So they set out to remedy it. The Boston City Club was one means to this end, but that was a discussion group or at most a fact-finding agency. Something more dynamic was needed, and "Boston 1915" was contrived to supply it.

In his autobiography Steffens has a fascinating account of his endeavor to convince one group of Brahmins that the worst political bosses in the city really disliked both corruption and strong-arm tactics although they were given to routine employment of both. The group hooted, so Steffens challenged them to name the most objectionable boss in the city and promised to visit him and argue with him.

They promptly named one Martin Lomasny, whom Steffens proceeded to visit. He was received with suspicion and heard with frank incredulity, but he had been prepared for both. He refused to take any high moral tone with the boss. He merely argued that corruption in municipal offices and fraud in elections profited nobody in the long run. This the boss not only admitted but enlarged upon with great bitterness. No Brahmin in the group Steffens had just left regarded the existing system with more distaste than the boss who was manipulating it. Indeed his intimate acquaintance with it enabled him to cite many of its evils which they had overlooked.

One thing led to another. After several interviews Lomasny called in his lieutenants, and there was more suspicion and more incredulity. In the end however they agreed that Steffens, at least, was straight. They told him they would deliver their ward for any public improvement project he might designate, and they did. They said frankly that they were taking a chance, but they had sporting blood, and Steffens found them far more reliable than his aristocratic associates.

It is an interesting commentary on American municipal government that Steffens explains the disruption of the arrangement some two years later as due to the fact that the upper classes, for political advantage, double-crossed the boss. He saved an election bill for them, although he was a Democrat and most of them were Republicans, whereupon some of them telegraphed Theodore Roosevelt that his powerful influence exerted through his local followers had whipped the bosses. Naturally Lomasny resented being sold out, so he was through.

Thus, knowing that evil conditions existed and believing that nobody liked them, that is to say, from two premises both perfectly sound Filene and Steffens drew the conclusion that men, once informed of the true situation, would work together to remove those things that were hurtful to everyone. This was a blatant *non sequitur*.

A few years later Walter Lippmann, who had also worked with Steffens, pointed out that men in general really are not much interested in their interests, not nearly as much as they are in their prejudices and emotions. If the morning paper, for instance, contains an account of Congressional action on a tariff bill that directly affects the pocketbook of every man and woman in the country, the average reader will skip over it to read of a sexy murder case in which he has nothing whatever at stake and the outcome of which cannot possibly affect his interests in any way.

This is illogical, and Edward A. Filene's heaviest handicap was his inability to make room for the illogical in his thinking about public affairs. He did not allow for it in planning "Boston 1915," and it tripped him.

The scheme was to make a survey of the city as a whole, to spot those conditions which everybody agreed were bad, and to employ the energies of all classes against them. To tighten up the effort it was agreed to set a time limit, and the year 1915 was chosen because it was approximately five years ahead by the time the program was fully organized. It was hoped that the Boston of 1915 could look back upon the Boston of 1910 and perceive a vast improvement.

But it was clearly, definitely, and emphatically not a moralistic endeavor. On May 13, 1909, the Committee on Municipal Resources, which was the powerhouse of the movement up to that point, issued a public statement in which it strove to present the idea clearly. That statement read:

> The Boston-1915 movement is based upon the fact that it should be possible for a willing worker earning an average amount to live, himself and his family, healthfully and comfortably; to bring up his children in good surroundings; to educate them so that they may be truly useful, good citizens; and to lay aside enough to provide for himself and wife in their old age. A city which provides less than that directly must make up for the deficiency in a more costly indirect way; there is no escaping this alternative. Therefore the committee should determine how much Boston is paying indirectly because it does not provide for old age, proper education for the children, etc. This should be stated in dollards and cents as nearly as can be, and should be the basis for the Boston-1915 work for saving of waste.

The very mudsill of Edward A. Filene's social philosophy is embedded in the words *there is no escaping this alternative*. All the rest might have been written by some evangelist inspired by religious fervor and summoning men to bring forth works acceptable to God to further their souls' salvation. But if one really believes that a city is going to pay somehow and that, if it doesn't pay out of its pocket, it will pay through the nose much more painfully, then one requires no religious inspiration to favor paying out of the pocket. It is a matter of common sense.

Yet there are few things harder to believe than that a wise social policy is financially profitable to a city even though at first it may involve a material increase in the tax rate. Of course everyone says he believes it, and some think they are telling the truth in saying so, but what they really mean is that they do not deny it.

The sort of belief that is mere acceptance spurs nobody into action. Men do not deny that the sun is ninety-three million miles distant, and if asked they will say that they believe it, but it occurs to nobody to act on the belief. But if a man has reason not, indeed, to believe but merely to suspect that his house is afire, he acts with all the rapidity and energy of which he is capable. The evidence that discloses the distance of the sun is no more convincing than the evidence that discloses the wastefulness of a feeble and inadequate social policy. No informed person denies either, but very few people seem disposed to act on either.

To Edward A. Filene however this sort of loss seemed as deplorable as loss incurred by fire or flood or any other catastrophe. He was able to convince a few others, but not enough* to

* The original board of directors of "Boston 1915" included, besides Filene, Louis D. Brandeis, John H. Fahey, Bernard J. Rothwell, George S. Smith, James L. Richards, and James J. Storrow, to whom were added later Richard C. Cabot, Michael H. Sullivan, James P. Munroe, Thomas I. Gasson, Henry

assure full success. Indeed, the fullest success could have been assured only by enlisting every man and woman residing not merely within the legal boundaries of the city but in the larger community of which the city was the center. A few of the ablest men in Boston supported the movement wholeheartedly. Many supported it halfheartedly. Nobody of importance actually fought it. Yet at the end of two and a half years it was evident that the main object was not going to be achieved by this method, and it was abandoned.

Yet the failure was far from complete. The material achievements of "Boston 1915" were considerable, especially in the schools, in harbor improvement, in the beautification of the city, and in public health. Where it failed was in the larger field, in the establishment of the habit of working together, in the creation of a sense of solidarity among all groups interested in the improvement of the city.

That this failure was attributable, at least in part, to Filene's weaknesses as a leader is hardly to be denied. He was not conspicuous for his patience, and this project called for a man of infinite patience. He was not conspicuous for tact, and this job called for a supremely tactful man. His knowledge of human nature was restricted, and this job called for a man of the widest familiarity with every type of human being. "Boston 1915" was no more than under way before its troubles began to multiply. Some of the committees into which it was subdivided could not be spurred into activity of any sort. Some, on the other hand, were altogether too active, rushing into projects that in Filene's estimation contributed not at all to the main objective or even militated against it. When Filene expressed his opinions with characteristic vigor, he aroused resentment that hobbled, if it did not paralyze, further effort. Some of those originally most

Abrahams, Arthur M. Huddell, Frank A. Day, Joseph C. Peletier, Robert A. Woods, Dr. Arcturus Z. Conrad, and the Rev. John H. Denison. The multitudinous committees included members as various as A. Lawrence Lowell, president of Harvard, and John F. Fitzgerald ("Honey Fitz"), mayor of Boston.

interested gradually came to believe that he aspired to domi-
nate rather than improve the city and quit, filled with bitterness and disillusionment.

The biographer with any respect for truth cannot deny that
there was some justification for this attitude. Filene after all was
a businessman, a successful executive of a large and complex
organization. None but a dominant character ever succeeds in
such a position. Business, especially big business, is by its very
nature something of a dictatorship. If it operates in a highly
competitive field such as retail merchandising, the necessity for
prompt and final decision becomes imperative. The first-rate
executive is never an impulsive man, but he is always a decisive
one. If he is highly competent, he will make no decision until
all the facts have been presented, weighed, and considered, but
once he has made up his mind, he hates wasting more time in
explanations. He knows what he is doing, and it is not necessary
to the success of the enterprise that others should know everything about it. If they will merely carry out their orders
promptly and efficiently, things will go well enough.

But public affairs are conducted on a different basis, and this
Filene, like most successful businessmen, found it extremely
difficult to understand or to remember. In public affairs one
must persuade because he cannot command, and persuasion
involves endless reiteration. Filene too often tried to command
and thereby won a reputation for arrogance that damaged his
influence and contributed to skepticism of his motives. This was
the case, and it would be futile to attempt to deny it or to gloss
it over.

But what evoked the real bitterness was not his bearing itself
but the assumption that it must be based on a towering contempt for the capacity and opinions of others. In nine cases out
of ten that is the real basis of arrogance, so the assumption was
natural enough, but it is not sustained by the facts. The facts
all go to show that Filene was distinctly an impressionable man,
indeed a hero worshiper. He constantly sought advice, and if

he deemed it good service, the source meant nothing whatever. It is probable that he made more mistakes by giving undue weight to advice than he did by rejecting it altogether. A manner so forceful that many people regarded it as overbearing was a necessary part of his equipment in business; to apply that equipment where it was not appropriate was an error but an error that had no basis in contempt for his fellow men.

The fact is that "Boston 1915" was an attempt to set up in the city a genuine representative democracy, which is a very different thing from the democracy constantly sung by the yearners who think it possible to work out a government policy without reference to the past. Representative democracy, as it was understood by some very great Americans, notably Jefferson, is not egalitarian nor moralistic. It is simple recognition of a fact demonstrated by experience. It is the fact that the sum total of intelligence linked with integrity in any community, be it a family, a village, a city, or a large nation, is never more than sufficient for the proper conduct of its affairs. There never was a surplus of brains and character in this or any other country, in Boston or any other city. On the contrary there is, there always has been, and presumably there always will be, a shortage.

It follows that a community should use its best endeavor to employ such resources as it does possess to the limit of their capacity. Emphatically it should permit no artificial barrier to keep from participation in public affairs any honest and intelligent man, not so much in justice to the man as in justice to the community, which never has enough such people in its service.

Filene and Steffens found that Boston was employing in its civic affairs—not merely in municipal politics, but in all its multitudinous operations as a city—only a small proportion of the men of ability and integrity who inhabited the place. Furthermore they found, or thought they found, that this waste of talent was in many instances due to artificial barriers erected by law only infrequently but by custom, by caste, and especially by sheer ignorance. Steffens's experience with Martin Lomasny was a case in point. The proper gentlemen in aristocratic circles had not the faintest idea what the political boss was like. They may have believed vaguely that he could, but none thought that he would, be of tremendous assistance to them in perfectly legitimate enterprises. The two enthusiasts assumed that, if such misinformation and misapprehensions were swept away, the really superior men, that is men superior by reason of talent not by some fortuitous advantage such as money or social position, would easily be enlisted in the service of the community.

But it did not work out that way or at least not for long. "Boston 1915" started with a tremendous rush, but bit by bit the original enthusiasm petered out. After a year and a half in Boston Steffens went on his way, and soon thereafter Filene himself began to perceive that the movement was failing to achieve some of the things he thought most important and was achieving some others that he thought not worth the effort. The even advance all along the civic front that he had envisaged was not being achieved. The thing was growing lopsided, not because it was an utter failure but because it was only a partial success. By 1912 he could see no further merit in it and, with the advice and consent of his surviving associates, called it off.

Here was a failure certainly, and it is hardly to be attributed to extraneous ciecumstances. To begin with there was enough money. Filene himself put up considerable sums, and others contributed. As a matter of fact no very large sums were needed for an enterprise of this sort, and quite enough for the purpose was available. But additional money failed to come in. It was not for lack of energy. Filene worked very hard for a long time, and while some of his associates soon exhibited a tendency to lie down on the job, others put forth vigorous efforts. But energy tended to be exhausted and was not renewed. It was not due to an intransigent organized opposition, for there was no opposition of that sort.

Plainly then the collapse was due to some inherent weakness

in the scheme itself. This has led cynics to aver that the thing
was a farce from start to finish, a woozy romantic notion based
upon an astuteness and unselfishness that mankind doesn't possess. They suspected Filene of having concealed somewhere in
his psychological make-up a broad streak of the Jean Jacques
Rousseau temperament, and they laughed him to scorn.

Unfortunately for the cynics their basic assumption is not in
accord with the facts. The very first principle of "Boston 1915"
was that it was not altruistic. Far from being asked to ignore
their own interests, the men who participated in it were urged
to take a shrewder and more comprehensive view of what constitutes their real profit and to work to enhance that profit. "Boston 1915" was designed to stop a thousand little leaks that were
draining values, financial values, out of the city.

After nearly forty years it is fairly plain that it must have
failed largely because it was not completely understood. The
men who participated in it no doubt were men of average intelligence and of average selfishness, but they had no need to be
geniuses or saints. What they really needed was to be thoroughly convinced.

We have come a long way since this movement was launched.
It is not hard now to convince businessmen in any large city
that traffic congestion costs money. With their own eyes they
have seen property values decline in hopelessly congested districts. They have traced the falling off in patronage of their own
concerns when customers found it too difficult to get there. In
1947 New York merchants and industrialists were told that the
congestion of the downtown streets was costing them a million
dollars a day, and they accepted the figure without question. If
anything, they thought it too low.

No one today has to argue with businessmen that a menace to
public health is a menace to profits. The influenza epidemic of
1918 was argument enough to establish that for all time. Every
large employer of labor knows that absenteeism due to the common cold runs up his costs, and in no negligible sum, every win-

ter. American business contributes enormous sums annually to accident-prevention work and regards them as insurance premiums not charity.

The size of the toll that criminality and vice exact from business is far better understood today than it was forty years ago. A businessman need not be particularly moral himself to be strongly in favor of an honest and efficient police force that will hold down not only footpads and burglars, but also panders, narcotics dispensers, and illicit liquor sellers.

To stand for and work for a more convenient, more comfortable, and more attractive city is not now regarded as the mark of a conspicuously virtuous man. It is rather the mark of an alert citizen with a shrewd appreciation of his own interest.

The quality of Edward A. Filene as a citizen is revealed, not by the fact that he understood this, but by the fact that he grasped the truth twenty years ahead of most of us. He never asserted any moral superiority, but to be farsighted is certainly a virtue of citizenship however it may rank in morals and ethics.

But if his quality is revealed by his launching "Boston 1915" when he did, his disqualification is revealed by his managing it the way he did. He missed one of the fundamentals, to wit, the necessity of explaining and explaining and explaining again if his followers were to be thoroughly convinced before he took an additional step.

Successful exposition is not a science; it is an art closely akin to the art of dramaturgy. Filene was fascinated by the scientific method almost to the point of idolatry, and he fell into the delusion that the successful management of men is to be achieved through application of the scientific method. Any ward heeler in Boston knew better. Steffens knew better. Certainly Lincoln Filene, managing a thousand employees every day in the store, knew better. But they couldn't tell Edward. Nobody could tell him. Perhaps, indeed, nobody can tell any man. Perhaps it is one of those things that each must learn for himself through intimate physical and emotional contact with people. Edward A.

Filene was physically in contact with any number of people, but emotionally he was not tightly bound. With neither wife nor child, he was a little aloof, just enough withdrawn never quite to understand the lesson that human beings, in the large, are not directed, they are persuaded.

Perhaps if he had had a bit more of the actor in him, he might have overcome this handicap even without family ties. Within limits he was an actor. He was well aware that there are times when putting on a good show is highly important, and at such times the act he could stage was remarkably effective. He liked applause too and liked it more and more as he grew older. But this was superficial. The histrionic was not bred in his bone as it is in that of the great actor, or a great politician, or a great cleric, or a great trial lawyer.

Basically he was sure that to show a man where his interest lies is to convince him. Over and over he stated his conviction that the fundamental motivation of mankind is self-interest, but he overlooked, if he ever comprehended at all, the fact that fundamental motivation is frequently modified out of all recognition by more superficial factors. It seemed to him therefore that to show citizens of Boston in which direction their true interest lay would be to send them in that direction. Logically it should. But human nature is incorrigibly illogical, and that is why the scientific method never fits it exactly. If one had stated formally the proposition, "Human nature is illogical," no doubt Filene would have accepted it—formally. But he never accepted it deeply. He could see no reason for its being so, therefore he could never really feel that it was so.

To launch such a project as "Boston 1915" on a sound basis required scientific thinking—straight, logical, yet imaginative. Filene had that. But to carry it through to success after it was launched called for a different sort of equipment. This task needed the ability to dramatize, to simplify without falsifying, to perceive and illuminate relations, and to resolve discords, functions that belong to the field of art, rather than to that of science. In short, it required a skillful popular leader, which Filene was not.

The popularizer is doubtless a second-rate genius, but he has his uses. "Boston 1915" had everything else, correct principles, logical conclusions, clearly perceptive vision. But lacking the expositor, the unpredictable artist who may degenerate into a demagogue on the one hand or rise into the prophet on the other, it failed.

Yet like all the conspicuous failures of the "unsuccessful millionaire," this one was not altogether convincing. A nagging doubt persists that it really failed because it was basically wrong. It is too easy to account for the defeat by errors of timing, of method, and of other circumstances that were temporary or local. "Boston 1915" is dead, but will it stay dead? Many cities have already taken over some of its main ideas, and more are being adopted every year. Filene is dead, but a great deal that he said makes better sense today than it seemed to when he said it. This possibility that the world eventually will follow him, after all, is what gives him significance for the rising generation.

V

There is one aspect of his quality as a citizen however that belonged strictly to his own time and place. This was his languid interest in conventional eleemosynary institutions.

It infuriated some people, notably Filene's partner, Kirstein, who saw in it an unaccountable inconsistency. Kirstein was a man full of good works. For years he headed the Jewish charities, but his time and his purse were available for any worthy benevolence regardless of sectarianism. He was on the boards of half a dozen hospitals, he participated in countless fund-raising campaigns for building orphanages, for disaster relief, and for combatting the effects of poverty, disease, and vice, and to any plan for social amelioration he never refused either counsel or cash.

To the warm-hearted Kirstein his partner's attitude toward

But social disease was another matter. Specific social maladies of course Boston had always recognized. "Thou shalt not suffer a witch to live," was an injunction it had always taken with great seriousness from the days of the Salem affair to the days of Sacco and Vanzetti. It was famous for its vast production of abolitionists, prohibitionists, transcendentalists and pickers-up of fallen women. But in the early days of the century the broader problem of social health, the creation of a disease-resistant population, was only beginning to dawn upon its consciousness. Some of its more alert and perceptive citizens had seen the point, and among them was Filene. These people, living in a city so generous in conventional ways, were justified in confining their own efforts to a neglected field, but of course they were misunderstood.

In justice to the many Bostonians who had no idea what this farsighted group was seeking and who were therefore inclined to deride them or even to denounce them, it must be confessed that frequently and for long periods they did not themselves understand clearly what they were seeking. They were men of vision, but they were a long way from omniscience. They misjudged men and measures; they took wrong turnings; they confused their directions; they made all sorts of blunders that enabled the scornful to jeer. In short, they made the usual mistakes of pathfinders seeking to break open new avenues to progress. The skeptics could find any numbers of instances of error and failure at which to laugh. They did. Laughing at Filene and his associates was one of Boston's most popular sports for thirty years.

But they got results. They did not remake the city of Boston, but they learned much, and some of them developed remarkable powers. It was in these years and in this setting that Louis D. Brandeis, for one, was developing his juristic philosophy that later was to have a profound effect upon the whole country. John H. Fahey was another who was learning things about citizenship that were to affect events far beyond Boston. John J.

Mahoney was a third who was learning things about teaching
that he found in no textbook of pedagogy. There were others
blundering along with Filene but out of their blunders distilling
wisdom that was not to be wasted.

Furthermore it is fairly evident to the distant observer that
they had a good time. They did not think so. Both as individuals and as a group they were filled with frustration, exasperation, and indignation. They were incessantly suffering defeats,
betrayals, bafflements, and harassments, and they probably
considered themselves ill used, not without reason. But in reality they had a good time, as any strong man struggling with a
job a little too big for him has a good time even though he may
be convinced that the business is driving him crazy. The proof
of it is the simple fact that they never quit. They abandoned
one project after another, and not a few of them eventually
abandoned Boston, but not one ever abandoned the attempt to
bring more reason and order into the organization of society.
Most of them have died, but the few survivors are still at it although they are old men now, and no man ever came up to and
passed the Psalmist's span of years still working at a job from
which he derived no joy at all.

One of Filene's notions, acquired partly in the franchise fight,
partly in "Boston 1915," and largely no doubt from Steffens, was
the desirability not to say the absolute necessity of somehow
enlisting political ability among the forces of civic betterment.
He was more or less dimly aware that a first-class politician, like
a poet of genius, is born and not made, so he began to cast about
for some young man who had demonstrated conspicuous ability in swinging votes and who might be persuaded to become
the standard-bearer of the effort to make Boston a better city.

His first choice was none too fortunate. He found the man, all
right—young, vigorous, a marvelously effective campaigner,
yet gifted with a quick penetrating intelligence. He cultivated
this man's acquaintance, and the more he talked with him the
more he was impressed by his capacity to master intricate prob-

lems with speed and to bring to their solution clear logical thinking. The young man was interested in Filene's ideas and seemed to comprehend them; Filene and his associates were charmed and threw their influence to him; he progressed rapidly from the State Legislature, to the Board of Aldermen, to Congress, to the mayoralty. His name was James Michael Curley.

Of course the alliance did not last long. Within a very few years Curley, one of the cleverest and most cynical masters of machine politics the country has ever produced, showed his true colors and Filene's critics had the laugh on him again. It was a bad blunder, and Filene was deeply chagrined, but there is this to be noted—he was deceived as to the man's character but not as to his ability. Any man who can retain political control of a large city even while serving a term in jail, as Jim Curley did, is certainly no blockhead. Filene could pick them. He who, selecting relatively unknown young men to act as secretaries or literary assistants, chose successively Glenn Frank, later president of the University of Wisconsin, Ernest M. Hopkins, later president of Dartmouth College, and Charles Merz, now editor of the *New York Times*, certainly knew a bright young man when he saw one.

Nor was the startling alliance between the idealist and the excessively "practical" politician wholly unproductive. The well-meaning gentlemen who were going to advise the rising young politician to the benefit of everyone did not get far with that project, but out of their association grew the Fact-Finding Committee that was Filene's last important contribution to the city of Boston—Filene's in that he was the moving spirit in its organization not in the sense that he did it all.

Later he was to establish and endow foundations from which Boston would benefit, but these were not primarily municipal enterprises. To the end of his life he remained interested in civic affairs and participated in a vast number of projects, many of them highly successful, but these were all limited in scope, so

it is substantially true to say that the Fact-Finding Committee
was his last large-scale strictly Bostonian project, just as the
erection of the new building was his last great contribution to
the store although he remained associated with it while he
lived.

Filene dropped Curley long before the high-flying mayor—
later to be governor and then mayor again—came into collision
with the law. Filene quit when Curley, in defiance of the warning, urging, and pleading of the advisory group, made an ap-
pointment that threw the educational system into the grip of
machine politicians. Curley's lurid subsequent career gave Filene cause to congratulate himself that he had cut loose when
he did, but it seems also to have convinced him that he would
be well advised not to intervene directly in local politics again.
If direct intervention meant building up such a character as
Jim Curley, then it certainly should not be tried.

The Fact-Finding Committee accordingly was organized
like the original Boston City Club not to act but merely to in-
form. It set itself the task of digging out and explaining the real
meaning of official documents, statistical tables, reports, statements to the press, and proposed legislation. Because it did no
more than make information public, its influence is hard to
measure, but it is significant to note that every progressive city
in the country today has an analogous organization, usually
with much firmer official standing than the Boston Committee
had. The work of an organization that undertakes to correct
mistakes is easy to measure because the records are plain, but
one that seeks to prevent mistakes before they are made works
in an anonymity that is hard to penetrate. Yet as Filene grew
older, he was more and more strongly convinced that this is
the sort of work that is most worth doing. Probably the experience with Curley also strengthened his conviction that it
was also the sort of work to which he had better confine himself, seeing that he was obviously not the man to handle a political genius.

But long before the Fact-Finding Committee had come into existence, before the new store was built, even before 1909 when "Boston 1915" was projected, the man's thinking had spread beyond the problems of the city of Boston and the state of Massachusetts. The larger field absorbed more and more of his energies as time went on, and after the outbreak of the First World War it almost monopolized them. The man who started as predominantly a merchant had become predominantly a civic leader and now was to become predominantly a national figure, "not without dust and heat," as Milton says of freedom's victories, but nevertheless effectively.

Henry Ford had been pursuing his meteoric career, and that amazing spectacle fascinated Edward A. Filene. Characteristically he thought far ahead of most of his contemporaries. He recognized Ford as a wizard while the rest of the world still thought of him as a joke, and by the time the rest of the world had come around to recognizing the wizard, Filene had already discovered the fallacy in the philosophy of mass production and was seeking to eliminate it. Naturally this brought him more misunderstanding than credit. In the early days, when he took Ford seriously, people laughed at him, and later, when he ceased to take Ford seriously, they laughed at him again. But he was right both times, and because his thinking was accurate, it reached out naturally and inevitably toward horizons that forever retreated and covered fields that as steadily expanded.

CHAPTER 4

The Patriot

<<<<<<<<<<<<<<<<<<<<<<<<<<<<<<<<<<<<<<<<<<<<<<<<<<<<<<<<

I

THIS CHAPTER heading and the previous one are admittedly arbitrary. A good citizen is of necessity a patriot, and an unpatriotic man cannot be a good citizen. The words are employed here simply to designate the local and the general application of the same qualities of mind and character.

The distinction might have been clearer if instead of citizen and patriot the words Bostonian and American had been used, but that would have been to make one point clear at the cost of obscuring another. Edward A. Filene lived in Boston, but he would have been interested in the same things and probably would have pursued the same general course of action had he lived in Atlanta, or Peoria, or San Diego; he was an American, and he could not have acted precisely as he did had he been anything else, but he would have thought the same way had he been an Englishman, or a Frenchman, or a German.

It seems worth while to consider separately his course as a member of the community and as a member of the nation because, while his course of action undoubtedly was somewhat modified by the accident of his residence in Boston, his course in national affairs was much more strongly modified by his nationality. Any other country might have produced his type of mind—indeed from time to time every other country does so. But it is doubtful in the extreme that any other country could have produced Filene's career, and it is certain that none has done so. That is to say, his Americanism was much more strongly marked than his Bostonianism, which makes it convenient to consider them separately although in reality there was no separation.

There is little reason to doubt that the making of Filene into a strong American began when he was nine years old or that it began with him, as with many another, in a journey abroad. The miserably unhappy year and a half he spent in the German boys' school certainly did nothing to weaken his devotion to America, and attitudes developed at that age are persistent.

However it must have been no more than an attitude, for it would be absurd to claim that a child so young worked out a reasoned philosophy. It was to be a long time before any outward manifestation appeared of which one can say with conviction, this is American.

In fact it was twenty years or more unless one characterizes as typically American his belief at seventeen that he must have a college education if he hoped to amount to anything important. The explanation is simple enough. For those twenty years his energies were so completely absorbed in getting his business established upon a solid foundation that it was impossible for him to give much attention to anything else. Not until he was approaching thirty was he in position to devote any considerable amount of time and thought to those things he preferred to do rather than to those he had to do, so not until then did the character of his thinking with regard to affairs beyond the parochial begin to become clearly apparent.

It was not that he was at any time indifferent to what was going on beyond the municipal limits of Boston. On the contrary he was interested from early youth, but he was uninformed and knew it. Even in his busiest years he contrived to find time for a certain amount of study and discussion.

"There are two ways of becoming good," he said when he

had only three years yet to live. "One is to become interested in goodness. The other is to become interested in the facts of life."

This was not hearsay evidence. He had tried both, and while he never denied validity to the first way, he found that it was not for him and had turned to the second way before he became perceptible as anything more than a successful retail merchant.

It may be argued with some plausibility that this was a characteristically Bostonian procedure. Certainly that city has been prolific of people who were interested in goodness as such; indeed the transcendentalists remain to this day the country's most impressive exponents of that mode of life, and transcendentalism was substantially a Boston idea. When Ralph Waldo Emerson died, Filene was twenty-two years old; it would have been strange indeed if a young man endowed with intellectual curiosity had not felt the impact of such a force.

He did feel it. At the Liberal Club, for instance, the ideas discussed were far from exclusively political. Thorny problems of ethics and morals were constantly being posed and discussed by speakers with at least the reputation of great profundity, and young Filene listened attentively. He did more than hear. He pondered also. His notebooks of the period are studded with references to the dark questions raised by something he had heard or read in the endless debate over monism and pluralism and similar recondite matters—references often placed in odd juxtaposition with comments on the price of lace per yard or reminders to speak to a department chief about a display of gloves.

As his economic position became more and more assured, his interest in broader questions increased. For some years he attended—and made financial contributions to—a summer conference at Greenacres, in New Hampshire, where speakers did not hesitate to plunge into the darkest mysteries of human

existence. Occasionally practical reformers of the type of Anna
Howard Shaw appeared on its lecture platform, but on the
whole its main interest lay in the development of the individual personality, or, as the more top-lofty enthusiasts preferred to express it, the cultivation of one's own soul.

It is possible that Filene's interest in this sort of thing may
have owed something in the beginning to fashion. The intellectual atmosphere of Boston at the time was tremendously
solemn. Everyone was peering busily into the mysteries of the
psyche and few paid much heed to the mysteries of physics.
Too much interest in the world of phenomena, in what was
actually happening to men and women, was in fact regarded
as a bit low. It was supposed to reveal a tendency toward
gross materialism. The superior person strove rather to develop
his own inner resources.

It would be remarkable if young Filene had not gone along
with the crowd, at least for a while, and it is evident that he did.
He was a young man, he had never been to college, and the
greater part of his time was spent in the market place. Why
should he not have been impressed by the eminently respectable men of letters, philosophers, and theologians who were
proclaiming the doctrines of ethical culture as the road to
salvation? He was impressed, at least enough to sit at their feet
summer after summer for half a dozen years and to give them
substantial assistance in maintaining their forum.

But he did not remain in that camp. He never challenged
it. He was always willing to admit that for certain types the
ivory tower may be a satisfactory place of residence where they
may become good by becoming interested in goodness. But in
the end he determined that it was not for him. By 1890 he
seemed to be definitely an adherent of the Socratic doctrine
that virtue is knowledge, a doctrine on which he acted for
many years.

There is an ironic touch in the fact that on the same page—

the one for January 25, 1890—on which he recorded this sentiment he also confessed a certain uneasiness because his brother, Lincoln Filene, was then at sea on the French liner, *La Bourgoyne.* "But," added Edward, "he is on a good ship and I will not worry." Eight years later this same ship went down in a collision with a loss of five hundred and sixty lives, at the time attributed in part to bad conduct on the part of the crew. In that instance lack of knowledge was, if not a virtue, at least a comfort to the man who made the notation, for if he had known that Lincoln was on an almost fabulously bad ship he would have done plenty of worrying.

At about this time he also entered in his notebooks a long analysis of the argument in Edward Payson's *The Law of Equivalents,* which he had just read and by which he was much impressed. It is not difficult in fact to trace certain ideas he cited from Payson in Filene's thinking for the rest of his life. There is not much doubt that this book influenced him profoundly.

Yet Edward Payson has been so completely forgotten that in 1947 none of the common reference books mentioned him at all. This was not Edward Payson, the theologian, who remains fairly well known, appearing even in the *Encyclopaedia Britannica,* nor was it Edward Payson Payson, the sociologist, likewise fairly well known. Edward Payson, the nonreverend son of the theologian, was a man from Maine who seems to have been interested, as were most of the intellectuals of his time, in the correlation of physical laws and the principles of ethics and morals. His *The Law of Equivalents* apparently was based on the notion that the conservation of energy has its analogue in the nonmaterial realm. Payson was certainly not a modern psychologist, and it is inconceivable that he had ever heard of Sigmund Freud, who was then little more than a brilliant pupil of Charcot, but Filene picked up from him ideas strikingly similar to Freud's later teachings regarding repressions.

It would seem that almost nobody else saw much in this man.

Neither Vernon Parrington nor Merle Curti* mentions him, nor
is his name to be found in the *Dictionary of American Biography* or the *Encyclopaedia of the Social Sciences,* not to
mention less hospitable reference works. Yet if Payson did in
fact determine the direction that Edward A. Filene's thought
was to take, it cannot be said that the man from Maine was
without influence. It is rather another bit of evidence to prove
that an author needs only one reader in order to make an impression upon his time—if he can get the right reader.

But by the early nineties Filene was pretty well through with
cultists of all sorts. This is not to say that he was through with
enthusiasms. On the contrary he was just beginning to develop
a long series of enthusiasms, which sometimes carried him into
ill-considered courses of action, so that he was frequently accused of developing a cult of his own. But by 1896 he was satisfied that whatever doctor, scholiast, rabbi, or swami might
say, there is no touchstone that may be relied on to identify
truth. "There are no miracles," was the fixed conviction of this
man, who nevertheless spent the rest of his days trying to work
what most of his fellows regarded as nothing short of miracles.

II

Filene's initial adventures in the realm of general ideas were
made naturally in his own field, that of retail merchandising.
His intellectual progress was strictly logical—from passing pins
across a counter to retail merchandising in general, from retail
merchandising to distribution in general, from distribution to
economic theory, and from economics to all the problems of
the great society. Or, as one might say, from clerk, to merchant,
to business consultant, to theorist, and at last to something that
it is still too early to define with assurance, but that we may

---

* Yet unlearned laymen had cherished the illusion that Parrington's *Main
Currents in American Thought* and Curti's *Growth of American Thought* between them mention every serious book that this country has produced. Evidently, universal learning doesn't exist.

call hypothesist if we always bear in mind that the maker of accurate hypotheses is a prophet.

Because he was a successful retail merchant, other retail merchants were interested in his ideas and his first public appearances were at meetings of merchants' associations and similar groups, while his first writings were concerned with the problems of a retail store. He became a more and more frequent contributor to trade journals, and as the ideas that he had proved by the test of experiment in his own establishment accumulated, he gathered them into books. Most of them were eventually assembled in two volumes, *More Profits from Merchandising* and *The Model Stock Plan,* whose titles indicate their nature. They are of no great interest today, even to merchants, because a good many of the ideas in them failed to stand the test of practical application. A third book, *Next Steps Forward in Retailing,* written in collaboration with Werner Gabler and Percy S. Brown, had better success and is still used as a college text.

The reason for mentioning them here is simply to emphasize the point that Filene accepted the world as he found it. He was not content with it—who is?—but he did not regard it with revulsion even as a base of operations. That is to say he was an evolutionist never a revolutionist. His more conservative associates doubted this, for to them a man who seeks to effect any change whatever is a subversive character, but true revolutionists were in no doubt whatever.

"Do you think then, Mr. Filene," demanded Nicholas Lenin, furiously, "that the workers are fools?"

No, he didn't think it. Having been one himself, having worked with them, talked with them, and observed them through a long life, he knew beyond peradventure that they are fools. But he knew also that bankers, merchants, industrialists, and statesmen are constantly perpetrating follies as egregious as any of which the workers are guilty. He knew that all men are foolish at times and that among them a conspicuous perpetrator of follies was one named Karl Marx. Edward A. Filene found himself born into a world of a particular kind, not in his opinion the best of all possible worlds but the only one he had, so he was content to start from there and see what he could do in the way of improvement.

But he agreed with Lenin that improvement is not to be achieved until the men who desire it have first achieved power; the basic difference was that Lenin construed this to mean political power exclusively, whereas Filene believed that many kinds of power, indeed any kind of power, might be used to attain desirable ends. For a man of his talents in his environment, what was most readily attainable was financial power, so he went after it and counseled his followers to imitate him. "Put money in thy purse" may have been the advice of Iago, but it may be followed by an honest man to the advantage of all.

If he seemed revolutionary even in the limited field of merchandising to some of his more conservative competitors it was because of his basic idea, which he never was able to establish as accepted practice. This was the idea that inordinate costs of distribution are the retail merchant's great foe.

Here is another of those notions that everyone says he accepts and that many think they accept but that few really believe. It has had only one really brilliant demonstration, and that came when Filene was already a man of middle age. This was Henry Ford's career in the automobile industry. Ford proved beyond any reasonable doubt that in special circumstances the theory is true, but to this day many businessmen doubt that it has anything like universal application.

When Filene first went into business the overwhelming majority of merchants accepted it as an absolute truth that it is better to sell an article at a profit of one dollar than to sell it at a profit of one cent. Filene was one of the handful who realized that this is not an absolute but only a conditional truth. If by selling at a profit of one cent you can multiply the num-

ber of your sales by one hundred and one, then the profit of a
cent on each sale brings in more money. The central problem
of merchandising therefore is the problem of multiplication of
sales. A profit margin must exist, but its size is irrelevant; any
margin at all down to a one-cent margin will do, provided the
multiplication of sales proceeds satisfactorily.

Today, thanks largely to the success of Ford in industry and
of Filene and the chain stores in merchandising, merchants
in general admit that that largest attainable income is derived
from a small unit profit on a large volume of business. But to
this day not many accept in full Filene's notion of how best to
acquire the necessary large volume. In fact he never worked
out a procedure that fully satisfied his own mind; he was still
experimenting when death overtook him.

The fundamental idea, though, he grasped firmly relatively
early in his career, and it was upon this idea—fully shared by
his brother—that the lasting success of Filene's was based.
It was expressed in a bewildering succession of innovations that
competitors called stunts, tricks, and follies or sometimes, in
moments of forced admiration, strokes of genius. Most competitors attributed the success to the innovations and credited
the Filene brothers with nothing more than extraordinary ingenuity, although they, Edward in particular, were constantly
telling the world exactly what it was that underlay all their
ideas.

This fundamental principle was the theory that the merchant's function is to satisfy a genuine want adequately. They
held that to concentrate all his attention on merely selling the
goods on his shelves is for the merchant to lose sight of his true
function and to drift into a course that will end in a smaller
profit and a shakier business position than he might have
had.

A genuine want is one felt by the customer without the stim-
ulation of high-pressure salesmanship, and it can be satisfied
adequately only by an article of good quality sold at a price

that the customer can afford to pay. Acting on this theory Filene
gave his salespeople advice that to many of them seemed sheer
heresy. For one thing he forbade them to make special efforts
to sell slow-moving goods. That, he maintained, would be to
conceal one mistake by making another. In the first place how
would the store's buyer know that he had bought a sticker unless it stuck? If high-pressure salesmanship, not their quality
and price, moved the goods, then the buyer would buy more of
the same type. His mistake would be covered, even perhaps
from his own eyes. In the second place to sell a customer an
article he really does not want is to sacrifice good will for an
immediate profit, which is a mistake in itself. Thus the store
would be guilty of two mistakes and might continue a bad business practice indefinitely.

Another injunction even more startling to the conventional
mind was that if an article happens to be out of stock and the
clerk knows where it is to be procured he should send the customer there, even if it is into the store of the chief competitor,
but he must never fail to report the incident. This, said Filene,
would serve the double purpose of placating the customer and
revealing inadequacies in the line. If it happened repeatedly,
he assured the salespeople, there would be an explosion all
right but not among the clerks; it would blow up the higher
officials who had failed to keep the shelves supplied with
wanted goods.

These ideas may have been directly opposed to accepted
theories of selling, but they were strictly in line with the theory
that the merchant's true function is satisfying genuine wants
adequately. To simplify them for the staff he reduced them to
the injunction, never sell a woman customer an article that you
would hesitate to sell to your mother, assuming that she had
the customer's money and the customer's desire. He knew that
no sales girl would attempt to foist off on her mother a shoddy
article or one absurdly overpriced, and he wanted no such
goods sold to his customers.

To understand Filene's mind, though, it must never be forgotten that he did not urge this course because it was ethical. It was ethical to be sure, but he believed from the bottom of his heart that it was also the more profitable course for a man who intended to remain in business. The modern notion that the profit motive is essentially and inherently evil he scouted. The trouble is that men do not understand where the greater profit lies. No doubt he was a profoundly moral man, but he always maintained that his utter contempt for sharp practices and crooked practices was based not on their immorality but on their stupidity. He loathed stupidity, and crooked business he regarded as the very acme of the stupid.

It was many years before Filene formulated this philosophy in a Weinstock Lecture at the University of California, and he never generalized it, but it is clear that in the early years of the century, certainly before the outbreak of war in 1914, he had become convinced not from the study of books but through business experience that what is called conventional morality is of very doubtful validity. He made the discovery—and made it for himself—that genuine morality consists in acting not in conformity to any code but in harmony with the truth. But he had discovered—again by experience not by indoctrination— that a business policy in harmony with the truth is profitable, highly and steadily profitable. Hence he inferred that a profit honorably gained is profoundly moral.

But the evidence of his own eyes taught him that the world is full of businessmen whose very adherence to a code drives them into bad business practice. These were to Filene a far greater menace than the relatively small number of out-and-out crooks infesting the business world. Crooks can be caught and jailed, but what can be done with a completely honest man who is inflicting social and economic damage upon the country every day through adherence to a code that is outmoded? Filene didn't know. Certainly the law is impotent, and conventional morality is satisfied. Yet the damage goes on.

The good man in a bad fix [said Filene, but not until the lecture referred to, delivered in 1934] doesn't see any way out of his difficulties except high-pressure salesmanship—forcing on his customers those goods he happens to have in stock. But the fact-finder [note that Filene had not yet gone so far as to call this fact-finder the really moral man] will not do this. He will not do it because he does not want to drive his customers away—which may seem like a base motive but see how it works out.

He too talks to his sales force, and he says things which startle them. He doesn't suggest any new tricks of salesmanship. He suggests, rather, that they make no particular effort to get rid of certain goods, lest in doing so they get rid of certain customers.

"The safe plan," he explains, "is to treat every customer as you would treat your own parents if they were at your counter. Find out what they want. Remember how little money they have to spend, and how much it means to them to pay more than it is necessary to pay for anything. Then, if you have what they really want, at a price which they can afford to pay, let them have it. If you cannot fill their orders in this way, however, and you know of some place where they can get better value for the money, *send them there.*"

This sounds so amazingly unselfish that the salespeople may wonder if the boss is in his right mind.

"You don't mean to send them to some other store?" they may ask.

Surely. Why not? If they buy something they do not want at his store they will go to some other store eventually. The way to keep them coming to his store, he has discovered, is to make sure that they always get their money's worth whenever they do trade with him.*

This, be it observed, was no innovation, no trick, no clever advertising dodge contrived to draw customers into Filene's.

---

* Edward Albert Filene, *Morals in Business*. University of California, Berkeley.

It was a general principle of merchandising, applicable to any kind of store in any kind of place. The Filene brothers, and especially the astute men they employed to handle details, were full of tricks and dodges to be sure. They kept competition on the jump year after year with ingenious surprises, and right heartily were they detested for it. But the basic idea was nothing peculiar to Filene's and certainly no trade secret. It was as old as the Greeks at least, and it had been known to wise men of all nations.

Its vigorous propagation was Edward A. Filene's first notable contribution to citizenship in the larger field outside the doors of his store and beyond the boundaries of the city of Boston. If it be objected that it is wrong to call his a contribution that is as old as philosophy itself, the answer is that no really valuable contribution to society is ever new. Every concept of permanent value is simply the rediscovery of some phase of truth and its restatement in terms that catch the attention of contemporaries. A redefinition of the true function of the merchant was needed when Filene made it, and because he made it loudly and with unusual sharpness, it attracted attention and undoubtedly influenced the thinking of men far away from Boston. It is therefore definitely a stage in the development of his thinking and perhaps a stage in the development of merchandising in America.

III

Along with it came another perception that was to carry Filene even further away from the store and into the realm of general ideas. It too was derived from his study of what had happened to him in his business career and to other businessmen, with some of whom he had worked while others he had merely observed. It was his acceptance of the inevitability of change, which was the basis of his liberalism.

Every man of experience knows that change is inevitable, but not all accept the knowledge cheerfully. The desire for stabil-

ity and permanence is so deeply embedded in all of us that it
can never be eradicated, and it usually grows stronger with the
passage of time. That Filene felt the strength of this impulse
to seek the eternal is implicit in everything he wrote, but what
engaged his attention was not the search itself but the fact that
it is so often and so blatantly misdirected.

Early in life he had discovered that a good man in business
is not necessarily a good businessman. He observed moreover
that a man who is good and who devotes himself largely to remaining good frequently is driven into bad business practices
by forces that he does not comprehend, much less control. To
Filene a bad business practice is not merely one that loses
money for the practitioner, but one that deprives society of any
kind of value, financial or other. No man was better aware
that there are many profits and losses that never show up on the
ledger of the most skillful accountant, but that nevertheless in
the course of time affect the business beneficially or detrimen-
tally. It is not impossible to make money for a time in a business
that is essentially unprofitable. He saw men doing it, and he
sought the reason diligently.

Still thinking in terms of his own experience, he found that
good men become bad merchants because in the majority of
cases they fall into the logical error of attributing eternal verity
to something that is transitory, or into the equally common error
of attributing effects to causes that are really irrelevant.

Filene put it into simpler words. Good men become bad
merchants, he said, because they will not find the facts about
their own business. Therein he fell into an error of his own.
The word to express what he had in mind was not facts. The
men he criticised had found the facts, all right. What they were
ignoring was the truth behind the facts, specifically the truth
that facts are subject to change.

A team of horses, for example, is a fact, visible, tangible,
audible, and certainly smellable, capable of being perceived
through at least four senses. But the truth about this fact al-

tered materially within Filene's own lifetime. When he was a boy, a team was the principal means of short-haul transportation both of goods and of persons, but by the time he had reached middle age that particular fact had lost that particular part of its truth. The internal combustion engine was then the principal means of short-haul and an increasingly important means of long-haul transportation. Today with fast passenger and express traffic largely committed either to airplanes or to Diesel locomotives, the internal combustion engine is an even larger factor in transportation.

A businessman who took no account of this shift would be out of his mind, unless he were some such rarity as certain big-city specialty shops that still make their deliveries in horse-drawn vehicles as a publicity stunt. But there were in Filene's time and still are certain ideas just as antiquated to which business men cling stubbornly, because they are facts that once embodied the truth.

It is a fact that before the industrial revolution and for more than a century after it began the production of goods was never, except spasmodically in certain lines and in limited areas, equal to the existent demand, and therefore the market was normally a seller's market. That is to say the principal economic problem was that of production, and the problem of distribution was subsidiary. It was a fact and businessmen found that it was a fact. Historically it is still a fact, but prior to the war of 1914-18 the truth behind that fact had shifted. The world market had become increasingly a buyer's market because production had overtaken and overburdened the existing means of distribution, therefore the problem of distribution had become primary while the problem of production took the subsidiary place. Yet the vast majority of businessmen, having found a fact that embodied the truth prior to 1750, assumed that it still embodied the truth in 1912.

This was what Filene had in mind when he clamored for

fact finding in the business world. What he meant was find the truth, for the facts are obvious.

> Morals always begin with facts [said Filene], mainly with the facts of human relations. Those practices which have worked well are codified, and those who obey the code are considered good people, while those who disobey are considered bad.
>
> This is all right for awhile. This is all right until the facts begin to change; for there is little deviation at first between the letter of the code and the facts of human experience. . . .
>
> Those who are most passionately interested in goodness are likely to be least interested in improving the code. It worked, therefore it was good. It was good, therefore it became sacred. It is sacred, therefore it is not to be altered. The bulk of the moral passion of the community is often directed, not toward finding a better way of living, but toward the preservation of a code under which, because of changed conditions, it has become possible to do no end of harm.*

This protest reveals the sum and substance of Filene's liberalism. The only emotional element in it, that is to say the sole element not supported by strictly rational argument, is the assumption that change may be controlled at least to the extent of directing it toward socially desirable ends. Granted that, the rest falls into place readily. The cheerfulness with which Filene accepted the thesis that change is the condition of mundane existence comes from that assumption added to confidence in the suppleness of his own mind. He had no doubt that he could adapt himself to any change that might come about except one effected by sudden violence. He was not in the least afraid of changes brought about by natural laws, no matter how radical they might be.

* Edward Albert Filene, *Speaking of Change; a Selection of Speeches and Articles,* p. 179. National Home Library, Washington, D. C.

This perhaps made him inclined to be somewhat less than fair to men not gifted with his high adaptability. Men who can retain their mental agility beyond the age of fifty are not common. They remember how long and painful was the process by which they learned their business and a suggestion that they may have to learn it all over again usually means to them that they will have to repeat the whole agonizing process. Naturally they repel such a suggestion with the utmost energy, sometimes with an energy that blinds them to the obvious and ruins them or certainly ejects them from the ranks of first-rate businessmen.

Somehow Edward A. Filene discovered the error in this attitude. How he did so is not immediately apparent, for there is nothing in the record to show that extraneous circumstances thrust it upon him, as they have thrust it upon some men, notably those who work in the physical and biological sciences. An eminent physicist once told the writer that he had spent thirty years of study and had reached the age of fifty before he felt that he was a master of his science, and at that moment the discoveries of mathematicians shattered the accepted principles of physics so completely that he was faced with the necessity of learning it all over again. He was appalled, but he had no choice, and he discovered that he had learned how to learn so that in five years he covered as much ground as he had before in thirty. Ten years later, Einstein and his accomplices arrived, and physics was blown up again, but at this third effort our man covered the necessary ground in two years.

Somewhere Filene learned how to learn and was aware of his ability. Therefore he could afford to be a liberal, always looking on change with a tolerant eye and usually welcoming it. He had no fear that his intellectual muscles and tendons would be unequal to the task of adapting themselves to unfamiliar uses, so perhaps he was a little toplofty in his attitude toward men stiffer in the mental joints. Certainly not a few of them thought so and were the readier to denounce him as a *poseur,* an exhibitionist, a traitor to his class, and probably at heart a flaming revolutionist. It was silly, but there is much reason to doubt that it was the malicious slander that Filene thought it.

However it is not to be inferred from this that he was omniscient. At this very time he was himself pursuing courses that in later years he came to regard as very dubious indeed. For instance, he was swept along with the crowd into the cult of "service," which was then burgeoning mightily. Not a store in Boston was ahead of Filene's in devising little attentions— and a good many not by any means little as measured by the expense they involved—to please its customers.

But as early as the middle twenties, when the cult of service was still raging like wildfire through American business, Filene was already beginning to suspect that he had been helping create a Frankenstein's monster in promoting it. To Paul M. Mazur, an investment banker forced by the exigencies of his business to become in some sort a merchant, he wrote: *

> I have lived through the years in which the modern system of service was built up. That system was an established thing when your career began and it is natural that the relation óf cause and effect is not as definitely impressed upon you as it is upon my memory. . . . The public of fifty years ago knew very little of free delivery, charge accounts, luxurious fittings, personal service, C.O.D., etc. The customer of today knows them because the merchant has taught him to want these things.
>
> If these extravagant and costly services, then, add to the cost of distribution, why do customers patronize the department stores, instead of the individual small shops which cannot give such service? The reason is clear. The proprietor of the small shop has not the bulk purchasing power of the large store, must buy from the middleman and often

---

* Excerpts from a letter to P. M. Mazur, under date of October 30, 1925, in the Filene papers.

cannot discount his bills. The result is that the small shop
is forced to get as much money for its merchandise, even
though it dispenses with the extravagant service. . . .

Notwithstanding the foregoing, I still am in favor of a
high grade of service and improved service as time goes on,
but only such services as will pay for themselves by the
additional amount of business which they will attract to
the store are justifiable. . . . It follows, therefore, that the
quality of service given is not a justification for an increase
in the cost of distribution.

If there is any doubt as to whether the general public
really imperatively demands a high grade of service, one
need only look to the cash-and-carry chain stores and see
what effect their policy of dispensing with unnecessary
services and consequent lowering prices has had on the
grocery stores, for example, which had charge accounts,
free delivery, telephone order department, etc.

This was written, be it remembered, in the gaudy twenties,
in the new era when poverty was abolished and the country was
being assured of permanent prosperity "on a high plateau."
Filene no doubt enjoyed the prosperity of those roaring days
as much as anyone, but even then he knew that the problem of
distribution was not being solved and that it was paramount.
Four years later the failure to solve that problem exacted its
toll and turned the gay parade into a funeral procession.

But long before he wrote that letter, more than a dozen years
earlier, Filene had perceived and had begun to proclaim the
necessity of the merchant's recognizing changed conditions and
adapting his course to them. The merchant's function—he still
talked about merchants, specifically retail merchants, bringing
in other businessmen whose problems he knew less intimately
only by inference—was to satisfy his customers' genuine wants.
But one of these wants, and a very genuine one indeed, was
nothing that lay upon the merchant's shelves. It was a reduction
in the spread between the cost of production of merchandise

and its cost to the customer in a retail store. If that spread narrowed, the customer's money would buy more. If the customer bought more, the merchant would do a larger business, would hire more people, and by increasing his orders compel the manufacturer, in turn, to hire more.

But it wasn't narrowing. Even from 1890 to 1914 it had widened considerably. When Filene began to cry out against this, even before the First World War, he made his second notable contribution to the thought of the country beyond the confines of the city of Boston.

IV

The shock of the first blood bath of this gory century disheartened him, as indeed it did every man whose outlook on life was more than parochial.

He was in Paris when the storm broke. Like many other Americans he had developed a partiality for the cure at Carlsbad and tried to arrange to spend some weeks there whenever he went to Europe. He and John H. Fahey had gone to Carlsbad after a meeting of the International Chamber of Commerce in June of 1914. Nearly thirty-five years later Mr. Fahey remembered with wry amusement how the Americans had been taken on a tour of inspection of the great Schneider locomotive works—a polite euphemism for arsenal—at Creusot, how the French showed with frank pride their latest models of artillery and machine guns, and how the Americans nevertheless made speeches congratulating all concerned on the way modern civilization had beaten its swords into plowshares and its spears into pruning hooks.

But at Carlsbad in early July—the heir to the Austrian throne had been assassinated at Sarajevo on June 28—the attitude of everyone, French, German, or British, was one of fatalistic resignation to a war regarded as inevitable. It was incomprehensible to the Americans, but they felt it. Things grew so tense that within a few days Fahey got out, but Filene had started

on a three weeks' cure and refused to cut it short.* He barely
made it to Paris before the outbreak of hostilities closed the
frontier. But even then he refused to rush for home. He remained in Paris during the terrific six weeks leading up to the
first battle of the Marne, and when he came away, he
had learned a great deal about war through the evidence of
his own eyes.

To Filene it brought keen personal distress because much
that he knew and loved was imperiled. He was a first-genera-
tion American, and German anti-Semitism had not yet become
so virulent as to extinguish the sentimental attachment of German Jews to the land of their fathers. He was not pro-German.
He was too well informed and had too much respect for the
logic of events to cherish any sympathy for aggressive German industrialism or for the Prussian military caste, which had
combined to precipitate the war upon the world.

But inevitably he was filled with regret for the destruction of
so much that was valuable not to Germany alone but to all the
world. The worst of it was that he did not believe for a moment
that war was inevitable.

Like most highly civilized Americans, he misinterpreted the
significance of the catastrophe, to some extent. He perceived
the collision of economic imperialisms clearly enough, and he
perceived that the very economic forces that had brought on
the war might just as readily if properly directed have strengthened and solidified the peace of the world.

But he grossly underestimated the importance of that slip-
pery Proteus then appearing as Pan-Germanism, later to be
transformed into Nazism, and nearly a dozen years after Filene's death threatening to materialize again under new names
and in new forms, but still the mortal foe of civilization.

Not many of his fellow citizens are in position to criticize
Filene for this error since we all fell into it. Obscurantism,
chauvinism, xenophobia are words that a civilized man finds in

* John H. Fahey in an interview with the author, 1947.

his dictionary and with whose definitions he may be familiar, but he really knows little about them. They are forms of fanaticism that are removed from his experience by the very fact of his being civilized. He may read endless ingenious analyses of the primitive mind, but he cannot actually feel and so finds it hard to measure the forces that set the whirling dervishes to spinning in Arabia, the voodoo drums to pounding in Haiti, or the Ku Klux mob to howling in Mississippi. Usually—or so it was to 1914 and with many civilized people up to 1939—he hugs the comforting delusion that the enlightenment of mankind exorcised these evil spirits or reduced them to impotence long ago.

Doubtless they still infested certain dark crannies in our social structure. So much was made startlingly plain when some old woman was murdered in Pennsylvania because she had hexed her neighbor, or when wild celebrants handled rattlesnakes in the southern Appalachians, or when social workers uncovered incredible blood relationships and mass imbecility in the pine barrens of New Jersey. But that the primitive mind could obtain dominance over great, highly developed nations was regarded as an absurdity even after a troglodyte, crawling out of the cellars of Munich, had begun to threaten the world.

In 1914 the world was even blinder. Men of large affairs, men whose sanity was beyond question, actually asserted in the summer of 1914 that the war could not last more than ninety days because by that time all the participants would be bankrupt; they really believed that such a theoretical condition as bankruptcy would stop a frenetic nation and were dazed when it failed to do so.

Filene was somewhat better informed, but at that he knew very little about what had actually happened. Like all his generation he attributed much more solidity than it had to the long cessation of general hostilities between Waterloo and Sarajevo, and when the thing collapsed, he sought reasons for its collapse in its structural weaknesses, especially in its economic strains, for he could not admit that the very foundations of civilization were insecure. Most civilized men felt the same reluctance, nor did they admit it until the rise of Nazism forced upon them the knowledge that we remain much closer to barbarism than we had thought.

In Filene's case confusion was not resolved by his intimate acquaintance with Europe. On the contrary it was probably made worse, for he knew so much to say on all sides.

As early as 1886 he had begun making periodic trips to Europe, increased in frequency until they became annual jaunts, unless some emergency at home prevented his traveling. The first trip was made in the interest of his health; in the early years, after his father's collapse and partial withdrawal from business, Edward A. Filene overworked and by 1886 broke down completely. A long rest was not a matter of choice but a grim necessity, so he appeared in Europe, for the first time since his childhood, not even as an ordinary tourist but as a convalescent thinking first of regaining his strength.

In 1888 he returned and thereafter visited Europe with increasing frequency. On all these journeys he made voluminous notes, but there is not much in them that is worth repeating. He saw the usual things, experienced the usual sensations, and made the usual comments that American tourists see, feel, and make. He visited Venice and was impressed by the Grand Canal, he visited Paris and was impressed by the Louvre, London and was impressed by the Abbey. Who isn't? In these records there is hardly anything that differentiates Filene sharply from thousands of other well-to-do Americans surveying the continent from which their forefathers came. There is a certain interest in noting one negative factor—from the records of these trips it is evident that aesthetic sensibility was not Filene's strong point. He dutifully visited all the famous art galleries, cathedrals, and palaces and dutifully admired them, but there is no convincing evidence that he was ever really enraptured by a masterpiece of art, for nowhere does he make a strikingly original comment.

But if his acquaintance with the Europe of the great past remained on a somewhat formal basis, his acquaintance with contemporary Europe became intimate. Never after 1886 did he go to Europe strictly in the character of a tourist. His business was expanding rapidly, and after 1891 his was the chief responsibility for supplying the succession of new ideas necessary to keep it in the front rank. Europe he found was a fertile source of such ideas, and after the first trip or two his main interest was not in what he could see and admire but in what he could bring away for use in Boston.

At first he bought goods, but in the course of time he turned over most of that work to professional buyers while he sought for ideas, particularly ideas having to do with the whole theory of merchandising rather than with the clever handling of a specific article. He spent more and more time seeking the company of conspicuously able merchants and discussing with them the larger problems that affect all big stores, whether in Boston, or in Vienna, or Paris, or Berlin. He had known Harry Gordon Selfridge in Chicago when Selfridge was on the staff of Marshall Field and Company, and after the American moved to London in 1904, Filene never failed to seek him out. Partly through Selfridge but largely on his own initiative, he became acquainted with the chief retail merchants in every capital in Europe and through them with manufacturers and other businessmen.

There is little indication that Filene as yet bothered much about political affairs. It is probable that he shared the common delusion that in the modern world politics is bound to the chariot wheels of economics and that he didn't discover that the reverse is the truth until the catastrophe of 1914 battered it into his mind. But his contacts in Europe did spread far beyond the field of retail merchandising. His study of retailing inevitably led to study of trade in general, and his investigation of trade as inevitably raised problems of economic theory. By the time war broke, Filene had at least a passing acquaintance with practically every important economist in Europe and with numbers of government officials, such as ministers of finance and commerce, and with an occasional opposition leader if his opposition was based on governmental fiscal and commercial policies.

But he knew more than the mighty princes of commerce and the great officers of state. The German language he had learned as a child, and later he had acquired sufficient command of French to be able to converse easily with all sorts of people. Whenever he visited an important city he made it a point to take some time off to spend in talking to unimportant people—cab drivers, policemen, street sweepers, concierges, anybody and everybody who could give him information on how the mass of the people lived.

This was neither idle curiosity nor an outbreak of the missionary spirit; it was a necessary part of his inquiries. To understand trade in Europe or anywhere else it is not enough to know the merchants; one must also have some understanding of the customers. The more Filene investigated conditions in such countries as France and Germany the stronger became his conviction that the first duty of merchandising in the modern world is to bring the prices of goods within the range of the customers' purchasing power. Naturally the greater that power, the easier is the merchant's task, but the increase of purchasing power calls for the joint efforts of every member of the economic system. It extends far beyond the utmost bounds of retail trade.

Thus when war broke out, he was not only much better able to appreciate its economic significance than was the average American, but he also knew a great many of the personalities involved on the higher levels and much about the types of humanity on the lower levels. He knew through his own con-

tact with them that these men were not the bloodthirsty crea-
tures of the cartoonists' imagination, but victims caught and
whirled along by forces beyond their comprehension, to say
nothing of their control. It followed therefore that assiduous
and careful study of these forces, to the end of discovering means of bringing them under control was a matter of such
vast importance that it transcended any other labor in which a
man might engage.

To be sure, in war the laws, even economic laws, are silent.
For four years there was nothing Filene could do except attend to his own business and prepare to act when the artillery
fell silent. This was the process by which the merchant become a citizen and then a patriot reached another boundary
and stepped into the international field.

V

But more than a decade before 1914 another event had occurred that affected Filene, the American, as profoundly as the
war itself. In 1903 the Ford Motor Company had been organized by the most amazing business genius of our times, and
Filene had watched its progress with an interest that swiftly
mounted into fascination and eventually into stupefaction. In
this he differed little from other businessmen and the public at
large except that it happened to him about ten years earlier
than to most people.

Henry Ford, it seemed to Filene, was making the first
shrewdly planned and competently executed attack on the
problem of distribution. Most of the world regarded it as an
attack on the problem of production, but Filene was not deceived. All the mechanical wonders of the Ford establishment,
from the assembly line up and down, were in reality old stuff,
familiar to industrialists for a generation, some of them for centuries. The only novelty in Ford's employment of them was the
colossal scale on which he operated. Filene brushed them aside.

What was new was Ford's determination to make a car that

the largest possible number of customers could afford to buy. His success in doing this resulted in the production of masses of cars, but this interested Filene, the merchant, but little. What fascinated the merchant was not the production but the selling end of the job—not the way Ford made millions of cars but the way he got rid of them. Perhaps because he was a merchant, very early Filene perceived that the miracle of Ford's mass production was his mass production of customers not of cars.

From this he evolved the thesis that he was to proclaim over and over to the end of his life—true mass production is not production *of* masses of goods but production *for* masses of people. As Ford's profits soared to fantastic heights, one conviction struck deeper and deeper roots into Filene's mind. It was the conviction that the price at which an article should sell to yield the largest attainable income is not to be figured on a cost-plus basis but solely on the average customer's power to purchase.

Twenty years later this became fairly plain to everyone, but when Filene first began to preach it, he had great difficulty in making himself understood. Businessmen persistently held that he was demanding consideration for the customer, which they admitted was very praiseworthy but which they regarded as hardly a sound basis for a business policy. That it was an argument for increased profits was not clearly apparent to men still imbued with the ideas appropriate to an economy of scarcity. Not until Ford's success had attained astounding proportions and General Motors had imitated him with comparable success, did any considerable section of the business world begin to realize that perhaps Filene's head was somewhat harder than they had believed.

The criticism to which he was subjected must have made Filene examine his own premises with care, and as he did so, a curious fact became clear. In the most literal sense the critics were right. He was in fact arguing for ethics as the foundation of business policy. To set as one's first objective the goal of giving the customer full value for his money unquestionably is ethical regardless of one's motive. Where the critics erred was in plotting Filene's line of approach. They assumed that he perceived that his policy was ethical and then tried to prove that it was profitable. The truth was that he perceived that it was profitable and then found, perhaps somewhat to his surprise, that it was ethical.

The critics were at no loss for facts with which to attack the Filene theories. They could point to any number of cases in which those theories did not work and never would work. They could point to successes, some of them impressively large successes, in the business world that had been built on diametrically opposite reasoning. What they failed to perceive was that these facts for the most part were not relevant. When Filene spoke of a businessman he did not mean every man engaged in trading for profit. There is a type of trader to whom none of his ideas apply. This is the buccaneer type whose method of doing business is to see an opportunity, rush in, make a killing, and get out with all possible speed. The perfect representative of this type is the stock-market gambler, but men of that sort are to be found in all lines of business including retail merchandising.

In this type Filene had no interest whatever. He regarded them not as businessmen at all, but as parasites upon business. What he meant by a businessman is one who sets up an establishment in a particular field with the hope and expectation of spending the rest of his life prosperously in that establishment, finally to hand it over to his sons or grandsons in better shape than it was when he began. Such a man is less interested in immediate profit than in the maintenance of steady healthy growth, and to such men he directed his argument.

But the discovery that by the road of profit seeking he had arrived at a position that compelled him to support principles that had all the appearance of altruism had a profound effect upon his thinking. In the end, as will be seen in a later chapter, it led him to the conviction that there is no distinction between the principles of good business and the principles of good morals and that the immorality characterizing much business activity is simply evidence that relatively few businessmen understand their own interests.

Needless to say he did not work through this maze by one swift, sure, and errorless drive. He made many mistakes, some due to faulty logic but more to the very error that he condemned most eloquently, the error of failing to take into account all the facts. For one thing, in later years he came to see that he had greatly oversimplified the case of Henry Ford. He failed in the beginning to give anything like sufficient weight to Ford's position as a proprietor, a position almost unique in the American business world.

Ford owned his company outright, which gave him an independence in policy making forever impossible to a manager responsible to directors who are, in turn, responsible to hundreds or thousands of stockholders who are in no sense proprietors. A manager must show an annual profit or run a grave risk of losing his job. Ford was responsible to nobody. He could and once did operate at a loss for eleven consecutive years before his policy justified itself. True the profits when they did begin to come in were prodigious, but the point is that Ford could do what most men cannot, therefore his example had less immediate significance than Filene was inclined to give it.

Before this became plain to him, he concentrated on Ford's methods of reducing costs and saw quickly that it was essentially economy of man power, especially brain power. Ford was one of the world's greatest adepts at using managerial ability to its utmost capacity. Any competent gang boss can drive manual labor to the limit, but the best use of muscle power is simplicity itself in comparison with the intricate business of applying brain power where it will accomplish most.

Filene thought this over in relation to retail merchandising and saw at once that it was applicable. Indeed it was already being applied in certain lines and with conspicuous success.

Filene himself was employing certain persons of exceptional native ability developed by experience into skill of a very high type, notably buyers. A first-rate buyer commanded a large salary because he was worth it, but his value rested not upon the amount of labor he performed but on the excellence of his judgment. His decision to purchase article A rather than article B, if it were accurate, meant large profits to Filene's, profits large enough to justify his salary, but that decision might be applied to twenty stores as easily as to one.

Furthermore, as between two buyers of equal ability, the one who bought in enormous quantities could usually command a better price than the one who bought in small quantities. The highest ability therefore was partially wasted if it were employed in small transactions, and the price of high ability applied to small transactions necessarily meant a material increase in the unit cost of goods, whereas if it were spread over a large volume, it would affect the unit price hardly at all.

So for a time he became obsessed with the idea that chain-store organization was the answer to the problem of reducing the cost of distribution and became one of the most vigorous and persuasive advocates of that idea, to the exasperation of Brandeis and others of his friends, who feared the development of the monopolistic element in the chain-store system more than they valued its elimination of waste. Applying the compartment idea that had worked well in his own store, Filene talked of the development of a chain of chains, that is a chain of department stores in which each department should itself be part of a chain. If the main chain consisted of twenty department stores, each selling shoes, then each shoe department would be a link in a chain of shoe stores, sheltered under the roofs of the twenty department stores, but with little organic connection.

The idea was to economize managerial ability not only in merchandising but in accounting, publicity, and store management as well. However the thing never was clearly worked out and probably should be listed among Filene's failures. Theoretically it would effect certain savings, but it would inevitably involve certain wastes as well, and these might offset the gains. Adequate means of avoiding the wastes in such a scheme have not yet been devised.

The vigor of Filene's advocacy of the chain-store idea disconcerted some of his friends and gave ammunition to such critics as were willing to attack his sincerity. It seemed to line him up with those who would tolerate, even if they would not advocate, monopoly. But an apparent inconsistency of this sort could not stop him. He was no worshiper of words, and competition for its own sake interested him not at all. If the social value of competition is its effect in reducing the price of goods and services, when it ceases to have that effect, it ceases to have value. He did not believe that a system of trading devoted primarily to reducing the cost of distribution would lead to monopoly, but if it did, yet at the same time eliminated extortion, wherein would the public be worse off?

Eventually, though, his own thinking brought about a modification of his enthusiasm for the chain-store idea. For one thing he began to appreciate more fully the importance of Henry Ford's independence of financiers, whether bankers or stockholders. More and more clearly he perceived the immense difficulty of applying invested capital to the reduction of the costs of distribution. This brought him face to face with the immensely thorny problem of re-establishing the investor as a true proprietor.

His approach to that problem was by the two avenues of credit unions and consumer co-operatives, but he was given time to make only some short steps toward it. He was still engaged in opening up the avenues when he died.

VI

If no man is to be regarded as a great American unless he has taught us the solution of some of the problems that beset us, then Edward A. Filene may be dismissed at once, for it is hard to think of any question of importance to which he furnished a conclusive, complete, and final answer. His role was to ask questions, not to answer them.

This was conspicuously true in his management of his own business. A subordinate who was not prepared to withstand a barrage of questions was foolish to submit an idea to him at all. Some questions he asked so often that he grew tired of expending breath upon them and so had them molded into rubber stamps. When a proposition was submitted in writing, if it were not crystal clear, he would reach for a rubber stamp and give the document a bang, whereupon it would bear in ominously large letters the question, "How can we make or save a dollar on this?" This was not at all the equivalent of absolute disapproval. The proponent had a right to answer the question, and if he could do so adequately, his scheme would be adopted, but it was an effective reminder that he had not made things clear in the first instance, therefore it did not encourage self-esteem.

Every good executive of course is a formidable critic. One of his most important functions is to detect and expose the fallacies in his subordinates' reasoning, and there is no more efficient means of doing this than the Socratic method of the searching question. But Edward A. Filene carried it far beyond the office practice of the ordinary executive. He questioned everything, and there was nothing that he questioned more sharply than success. One of his most maddening inquiries, and one that lost him the services of man after man, was to say when a particularly good job was reported, "Why didn't you do it better?"

He questioned profits, but that is perhaps no more than evidence that he rated somewhere above the rank of a merely good executive. Really top-flight businessmen always question profits, because they know all too well how illusory a bookkeeper's profit may be and are never satisfied until they know be-

yond peradventure that what is being saved at the spigot isn't
being wasted at the bung.

He questioned ethics and morals as they were currently
accepted in the business world, but this again is far from
unique. Most men of long experience in the ways of the world
know that conventional morality is pretty dubious and are little
impressed by long prayers and broad phylacteries.

But Filene went a length to which few have followed him in
questioning vice. He was far from certain that the total eradi-
cation of greed from human nature, even if it could be done,
would be desirable. Greed is a fine spur. It activates brawn
and brain and makes industrious men who without it would
be incorrigibly lazy and inert. In Filene's opinion greed becomes vicious only when it is stupidly misdirected; as long as
it is held in the channels through which it may attain its own
ends most efficiently it is what he termed "enlightened selfishness" and by no means an antisocial force.

Whatever the philosophical validity of this attitude, it had
the effect of putting barbs on his questions. He came preaching the gospel of lower prices not for the altruistic reason that
the poor might profit but for the selfish reason that the rich
might profit the more. Therefore he could not be dismissed as
an ordinary evangelist.

Americans are certainly among the most preached-at people in human history. In 1940 we had no less than 140,000 regularly recognized clergymen, 76,000 college professors, and
75,000 social and welfare workers, all of whom spend a large
part of their time asking us if we are doing our duty. From
the present state of the nation it is fairly plain that we have become relatively immune to preachments, and a question as to
whether we are doing our duty arouses but a languid response.

But here was a doctrinaire who said nothing about our duty
but asked us if we were missing a bet. That was profoundly
disturbing. That was a question that struck and stuck. At the
turn of the century American businessmen readily admitted

that American business might have its faults and even its vices, but they believed, not without apparent reason, that none could question its efficiency. Here was a man who did. He did not denounce businessmen for acquiring riches, as the conventional moralists did. He derided them for cheating themselves out of still larger profits, and that struck home.

It is evident that Filene, like every man who has been perceptibly ahead of his time, never altogether comprehended his own position. He was always convinced either that he had the answer to the current problem or that he was on the verge of discovering it, and he incessantly made proclamation to that effect. He thought of himself as constantly endeavoring to soothe men's minds, whereas his achievement was to upset them.

He accomplished this the more effectively because he was gifted with great clarity of expression. It is true enough that the extreme lucidity of his public utterances was not due entirely to his own literary skill. Part of it he bought in the market place. From Glenn Frank to Charles Wood, he had in his employment a long succession of highly skillful writers who gave his phrases a polish that he could have achieved only after long effort if at all. But they were not ghost writers* in the ordinary sense. They were rather lapidaries who cut and polished the stone but did not provide it.

As a matter of fact the inquisitive Mr. Filene did not vanish from the world of American business even when the Boston merchant of that name died. He had made provision for the

---

* I have this from Mr. Wood, who asserted it in the strongest terms and who knows whereof he speaks, for he has done plenty of real ghostwriting in his time. He remained with Filene for ten years, a record by long odds, made possible, he thinks, because his contract covered one week only. Any Saturday night Filene was at liberty to fire him, or he was free to walk out; they quarreled incessantly, but when he did quit, it was on account of illness and to Filene's frankly expressed regret. Mr. Wood declared positively that in those ten years during which he handled an immense number of speeches and articles, he never inserted an idea that had not been given him by Filene.

questioning to go on indefinitely. He had established and endowed the Twentieth Century Fund, which he described as a fact-finding organization but which has developed into more of a question raiser. The Twentieth Century Fund does, in fact, turn up a tremendous lot of information that had been buried out of sight until it began to burrow, but it is true that for every fact it has found it has flushed a whole covey of further questions. It could hardly be otherwise, since "to study and advance the next step forward" is the way Filene described its function, which necessarily means asking questions.

The Twentieth Century Fund has a history of its own that is not at all the story of Edward A. Filene. In 1928 he made over to this foundation the income from his holdings in the William Filene's Sons Company,* which is to say, the bulk of his fortune, and he served as its president, but he did not control it at any time. He had no wish to do so. The men who constituted its board had been chosen for the reason that they knew more, or were supposed to know more, about the sort of thing the fund was intended to accomplish than Filene did. Therefore, while he was prolific with suggestions—he wouldn't have been Filene had he not had an idea on every conceivable subject—he submitted gracefully when his suggestions were voted down, as they frequently were.**

Hence the significance of the Twentieth Century Fund in the story of Filene is not to be found in the details of its operations but in the character of the work. It raised questions consistently and persistently. To that extent it reflected the mind and temperament of its founder. Its first significant work was with the credit-union movement, which was essentially raising a question as to the efficiency of the American banking system in supplying credit at the point where it would be most bene-

* At Filene's death ownership of this stock passed to the fund and proceeds from it constitute substantially all its endowment.

** John H. Fahey, a member of the board, insists that Filene's scrupulous care not to try to impose his opinions upon the membership should acquit him of the charges of arrogant stubbornness that his enemies bandied about.

ficial to the national economy. In all its important operations since, the facts that it has presented have necessarily implied a question as to whether we are acting in accordance with the facts, which is as searching a question as can be put to a self-governing people.

The other public trust set up by this man and to which he gave the remainder of his fortune, the Good Will Fund (substantially replaced after his death by the Edward A. Filene Good Will Fund) was a questioner too. Specifically it questioned Filene's own business, retail merchandising, through its work with consumer co-operatives. But the Good Will Fund belongs to a later stage in his thinking when the internationalist had become as important as the patriot and the sometime dispenser of pins had become a penetrating analyst of the basic principles of trade.

As an American—in contradistinction from the internationalist on the one hand and the Bostonian on the other—Filene's role was that of the questioner but not that of the skeptic. The genuine skeptic believes nothing; Filene, far from rejecting everything, had a tremendous faith in practically everything if only things were well ordered. It was the vast disorder of the world that troubled him, not the futility of "the scheme of things entire." To the very end he believed that the American way of life is well designed as far as its structural elements are concerned. The trouble, as he saw it, is not with the basic design but with the fripperies and oddments, many of them foolish and not a few pernicious, that have been permitted to obstruct and burden the fundamental design. Were these removed and corrected, he had no doubt an admirable social order could be established and maintained.

This attitude made him the despair of extremists on both wings. Extremists always hate a man who cannot be readily classified. Lenin's scornful inquiry as to whether Mr. Filene considered the workers fools masked a real dread of a man who could defend capitalism without for a moment defending capitalism's errors, for the errors of capitalism are the communists' arsenal. Nothing fills a communist with a more bitter sense of injury than a demand that he disregard his feelings and begin to think.

On the other hand reactionaries had no love for a man who would not dignify them by classifying them as villains but who held them up to scorn as idiots working against their own interests. They could denounce him as a communist at heart, but they couldn't convince many people that a man who had made millions by his own shrewd trading was a communist. The capitalistic system had worked too well for Filene; people simply couldn't believe that he hated it. Yet the only alternative was to believe that he did see faults and flaws in it that called for correction, and this idea is always hateful to reactionaries.

The fact is that he, like every man whose thoughts run somewhat ahead of his time, was a troublesome fellow. The world dislikes thinking and proceeds to it only under pressure of necessity, and the necessity is always resented. Filene stated his ideas so loudly, so clearly, and so incessantly that he forced a certain amount of thinking. This was salubrious, no doubt, but it did not add to his popularity.

The merchant whose energy and ingenuity kept competitors guessing and swearing evolved into a citizen who kept Boston in a turmoil for decades. The citizen evolved into a patriot who filled the country with questions about things that hadn't been questioned for years, perhaps generations—a man who doubted that American business was efficient, that American banking was sound, that American morality was always moral, and that even the vice of greed was always vicious. An interesting man he was, no doubt, but a bother, at that. It is not a cause for wonder that he founded no school, no party, not even a faction. The wonder is rather that he escaped with relatively little annoyance from the upholders of things as they were.

But his evolution was not complete when he emerged on the national scene. He still had far to go.

CHAPTER 5

The Internationalist

<<<<<<<<<<<<<<<<<<<<<<<<<<<<<<<<<<<<<<<<<<<<<<<<<<<<<<<<<

I

NEAR THE FOOT of the western slope of Beacon Hill is a quiet court called Otis Place, and here at number twelve Edward A. Filene lived during his last twenty years. Otis Place is attractive but not impressive in any way. Besides one apartment building it contains little more than a dozen red brick houses, tidy, correct, perhaps a little prim but by no means ostentatious. Number twelve, located on the western, that is to say the downhill side, is not conspicuously different from the rest; like all of Otis Place, it is compact, dignified, neat, eloquent of a correct and orderly life, narrow perhaps but swept and garnished, monotonous possibly but in irreproachable taste and highly sanitary.

But number twelve has its distinction. In front it is merely a town house, but at the back a small garden extends to the grass border of the riverside park called the Esplanade. A great, wide window in the rear wall looks out, not into another neat and narrow Boston street, but to the Esplanade and beyond that up a long reach of the Charles River, which is no river but an estuary a mile or so across. On the other side, away to the right as one stands at the library window, a glimpse of domes and white columns marks the Massachusetts Institute of Technology, and in the far background a mighty bridge sweeps across to Cambridge and Harvard University.

159

The view is made the more impressive by contrast—at the front of the house, Otis Place, scrubbed, proper, mannerly, but small and smug; at the back, immensity. One can easily imagine that it corresponded to something basic in Filene's nature to live thus between the correct and narrow and vast stretches of sea and sky. He went in and out through Otis Place, doubtless with great satisfaction for he had a sincere love of Boston, but he cherished the view.

Immediately below his window, but at a sufficient distance to give perspective, was the Charles River Basin, harbor for small boats ranging down to toys. There on summer days came boys, adults, and occasionally old men to sail their model yachts. In his younger days Filene had been something of a sailor himself and part owner of a pleasure boat. He understood, perhaps he shared, the impulse that brought the people to the spot, for when his own end was near, he expressed the curious wish that his ashes might be scattered in the Charles River Basin.

He made no explanation and perhaps he never stopped to analyze his own impulse, but it may be that the model yachtsmen are the key. For they are dreamers who recognize the limitations of their powers yet are not content to lay their dreams aside. It is not given to them to cruise among tropic islands, or breast the long seas of mid-Atlantic, or contend with the furious winds that howl around the Horn, but in imagination they will convert Charles River Basin into a limitless ocean and the toy they hold in their hands into a tall ship or into a millionaire's palatial yacht. So for an hour they draw far away from asphalt streets and the treadmill of daily labor.

Edward A. Filene was more fortunate in that at one time he did possess a boat, and for half his life he might have possessed a yacht. He did in fact visit far places and cross seas of which the men and boys around the basin only dreamed. But the advantage, he knew, was slight. As far as the things he really wished to accomplish were concerned, he was no better off.

His dreams were wider and more complex than theirs, but they remained dreams ever beyond his power to realize. A small boy with a toy boat dreaming of Bermuda and a philosopher with an idea dreaming of Utopia are equally landbound. With what he has in hand, neither can possibly reach the realm of his desire. Many men realizing their impotence are content to lay dreams aside forever and look contemptuously upon such persons as model yachtsmen and Edward A. Filene. They are old men at forty and spiritually dead men at fifty. They may continue to walk around until they are ninety, but as far as their minds and spirits are concerned, *rigor mortis* set in the moment they became content to remain at home in imagination as well as in body.

Filene was not of their number. He had no more hope of accomplishing all that he desired than a model yachtsman has of sailing on his twelve-inch boat. But neither would he turn his back upon sky and sea to live out his days comfortably and dully in short and narrow Otis Place; at least he could sit by his window and look out into vast spaces, and even when he was dead, he did not wish his ashes entombed where dead men lie but scattered upon the water by which the dreamers congregate. The wish may have seemed odd to his contemporaries, but in fact it was consistent with his whole career.

Since he offered no other explanation, it is not unreasonable to adopt this one, for the wish was no passing whim but was expressed emphatically enough to make his executors feel that they ought to respect it.

II

"If I go out of a hotel room and leave an electric light burning," said Filene in a self-analytical mood one day, "and I think of it before I get on an elevator, I know if I go down in that elevator I will come back and turn that light out." *

---

* Conversation with Charles Wood, recorded in Mr. Wood's notes made at the time.

It is a highly revelatory sentence. Completely understood, it tells more about the man than is to be learned from many of his most carefully prepared speeches and magazine articles, although to him it meant nothing significant. To him it was merely evidence of the ineradicable character of childhood impressions.

"The first thing my father taught us," he said, "was that any man who wastes things like gas and electric light, because he does not directly have to pay for them, is a fool, because finally he has to pay a share of that total waste, and, more than that, he is not a good citizen."

But in this instance the childhood impression was powerfully reinforced by a lifetime of observation and thought. Waste was bitter upon his tongue, because to it he attributed a large part of the tragedy of human existence. The waste that counted, though, was not the waste of gas and electricity, nor even of other goods and money, but the waste of human life in labor expended to no purpose and pain endured without necessity.

The fearful climax of this waste came, of course, in 1914 with the outbreak of the First World War. It was not mere blood that appalled him. Filene was a humanitarian but never a sentimentalist. Soldiers have to be killed if a war is to be won, and nothing is to be gained by wringing one's hands over it. Filene was as ready as any military man to accept the calculated risk without being paralyzed by shock when predicted losses materialized.

What racked him were the stupendous losses in nonmaterial things. Science, art, and philosophy suffered far more than the loss of the Louvain Library and the killing of uncounted numbers of brilliant young men. They lost a large part of their dominance over the minds of men in all countries, even those not directly involved in the war, and naked force resumed the throne of final arbiter.

In Paris he was one of a group of Americans, business and professional men, summoned by Ambassador Herrick to assist him in coping with the overwhelming problems dumped upon the embassy by the outbreak of war. Filene participated in the meeting that passed upon the question of whether or not to evacuate American civilians remaining in the city as the Germans approached.

Today it may seem strange that there should have been any difficulty about that decision; today we should take them out, or at least the women and children, without a moment's hesitation. But we have lived through thirty years of carnage that has never ceased entirely, although at times it has subsided into relatively little wars fought in China, or in Abyssinia, or in the jungles of South America. Today we assume as a matter of course that the approach of an enemy army means the indiscriminate butchery of noncombatants without regard to age, sex, or physical condition.

But Filene and his colleagues lived in a different age, and for them the decision was a hard one. In 1914 they had no adequate realization of the fact that the world had reverted to the mode of warfare practiced by Genghis Khan, of whom it was said that where his horse's hooves had trod, the grass never grew again. In 1914 they still clung to the delusion embodied in that contradiction in terms "civilized warfare," and they assumed that the slaughter of civilians attending military operations would be restricted to the irreducible minimum imposed by chance. Unrestricted submarine war, the occupation of Belgium, and the Zeppelin raids were still to come, not to mention such hellish things as Rotterdam, Coventry, Warsaw, Lidice, Oswiecim, and Hiroshima. It is our thirty years' education in ferocity that makes it seem strange to us that anyone should hesitate to remove women and children at the first suggestion of an invasion.

But in 1914 deliberate butchery, especially of neutrals, was unthinkable, yet there was, even in the estimation of those men, a very considerable danger to anyone remaining in Paris. Flying shells make no distinctions, and already the Germans were threatening to bombard the city. But the French army was still unbroken, and the government was maintaining that Paris would never fall. For the Americans to evacuate therefore would be tantamount to a proclamation that in their opinion the government was either lying or stupid, and that would inevitably shake the morale of the French civilian population.

The question before the group at the embassy then was should they risk their own lives and, what was worse, the lives of many other Americans who could not leave without their help rather than inflict further discouragement upon the hard-pressed French? They voted to take the risk, Filene assenting. They then split up the work that had to be done, and it fell to his share to arrange the best shelters he could for Americans in case of bombardment and to mark all American property. He had large posters printed and ready and had gained an intimate acquaintance with all the cellars in the neighborhood of the embassy before the first battle of the Marne rendered his precautions unnecessary.

He also acquired a tremendous admiration for Myron Timothy Herrick as a man who could keep his head in a tight place, and his respect for the Ambassador lasted the rest of his life.

Back in America he cherished no illusions as to what was to come. The cataclysm was too prodigious to allow hope that we might escape being drawn in. He went to the President and told him so. According to his own account years later, he found Woodrow Wilson little disposed to argue the point but utterly convinced of his own duty to refuse to admit that war was inevitable until it was thrust upon him. Filene had supported Wilson in 1912 and continued to support him, regardless of his own conviction that the hope of maintaining neutrality was illusory. Indeed he conceded the point that the head of the state is under an obligation to work for peace no matter how many advisers tell him that war is inevitable, and for that reason he refused to join the chorus of criticism of Wilson's voluminous note writing.

He also joined William H. Taft, Elihu Root, and—ironically as it sounds today—Henry Cabot Lodge in their League to Enforce Peace movement.

By 1915 he was deeply involved. Events in Europe had moved so rapidly that it was clear to informed Americans that our only hope of keeping out lay in vigorous action either to halt the war or to limit its scope. Purely passive neutrality was no longer possible, whatever the President might say for the sake of the record.

Idealists reacted to this pretty much in accordance with their experience of the world. Men whose lives had been largely confined to their libraries came forward with schemes of many varieties but all smelling of the lamp, and men whose lives had been confined to this country were susceptible to these schemes. A notable example was Henry Ford, a business genius certainly, but one who had never been anywhere and never seen anything beyond the limits of America and not very much of America.

Because Ford's experience of the outside world was so largely confined to what he had heard and read, instead of what he had seen, when he heard and read the notions of the ivory-tower dwellers, he was persuaded by them, and they trapped him into the peace-ship adventure. He chartered a neutral vessel, the Swedish *Oscar II*, and loaded it with a cargo of talkers and writers who were to persuade the warring nations to "get the boys out of the trenches by Christmas." This rank negation of all reality brought nothing but ridicule upon the man responsible. The bitterness engendered by this ridicule probably had much to do with Ford's later aberrations, such as his crusade against the Jews and his absurd outbursts against book learning, culminating in his assertion on the witness stand under oath that he believed history to be "bunk."

A man who knew Europe, not only its chancelleries but its working-class districts, not only the fashionable world that inhabited its spas but the peasantry that cultivated its fields and vineyards, was not deceived into thinking that talk could end the war. Filene, much as he admired Ford's business genius, knew that he had gone badly astray in this affair, yet he knew even better than Ford how terrible was the necessity of doing something to chain the dragon of war. The League to Enforce Peace might be no more successful in the end, yet to Filene's way of thinking there was a core of reality in the word enforce. He preferred the rule of reason always, but he had no uncontrollable phobia against backing reason with cold steel if it became necessary. That is to say, he was pacific but not a pacifist.

As a protagonist of the League to Enforce Peace he proceeded at once to attack the greatest obstacle in its way, to wit, the lack of funds. It was generally agreed that to get anywhere the league would have to have a fund of at least two hundred and fifty thousand dollars, and neither Taft, Root, nor Lodge knew much about raising such a fund. But Filene did. He had no doubt that the best fund raiser in the country was Charles Ward, whom he had known in Boston, and he set out to get in touch with him. But he found that Ward was in St. Louis in the midst of a campaign to raise a million dollars for some local charity. In a telephone conversation Ward protested that he could not possibly leave St. Louis, because he was under contract to finish the campaign there, and it would collapse if he left.

Filene stressed the international importance of the League to Enforce Peace and Ward's civic duty to promote it. He asked Ward if he would come east provided the St. Louis campaign were satisfactorily adjusted, and Ward said he would. Thereupon Filene called half a dozen rich men of his acquaintance in St. Louis, explained the situation, and said they would simply have to guarantee the remainder of Ward's campaign in St. Louis and release him. They protested but eventually agreed, whereupon Filene called Ward again and told him to report in Washington immediately.

"But he played me a dirty trick," said Filene with a grin, in recounting the incident years afterward.* "He said that if he were to raise two hundred fifty thousand dollars in so short a time, he could not hope for success unless he started with ten per cent of the amount. Therefore he was putting down Edward A. Filene for twenty-five thousand dollars."

But he did not depend altogether upon Ward. He went after personal acquaintances on his own responsibility. An instance that he recalled was that of Charles M. Schwab, the steel magnate. He demanded a contribution from Schwab and was offered five hundred dollars, which he dismissed with contempt.

"Have you brought me here to rob me?" complained Schwab.

"Yes," said Filene, "in a way you will thank us for the rest of your life. Will you give as much as I gave?"

"You won't catch me that way," said Schwab.

"Well, will you give half as much as I gave?"

"I'll give ten thousand dollars," said Schwab, and that ended it.

The upshot was that at the luncheon the promoters were able to report contributions of two hundred and fifty thousand dollars to the program of the league, and the next day Filene went to the White House. The President admitted that he had read the papers and that he was impressed by the evident seriousness of the men behind the League to Enforce Peace. Filene insisted that Woodrow Wilson agree then and there to attend the projected dinner of the league and to say a word in its favor. That was the famous dinner at which the principal speech in favor of the league was delivered by Henry Cabot Lodge, after which President Wilson said a few words in approval of its program—and Lodge never again appeared publicly in favor of it. This was the beginning, as far as the public knew, of the program that culminated in the formation of the League of Nations.

Naturally Filene was tremendously interested in the great

* In an interview with Charles Wood, recorded in the Wood manuscripts.

adventure. It was based on the assumption that men are capable of subordinating their prejudices to their reason in international as well as in domestic relations. In 1918 and for some years thereafter Filene remained unshaken in this faith—indeed he never yielded it altogether.

Yet he was better prepared for the difficulties that appeared in the way than were many others. His business experience had given him wide knowledge of how difficult it is to persuade men to act in their own interest. He was as convinced as Machiavelli that self-interest is the great motive power of human action, but he was conscious of the fact that vast numbers of men have no idea what constitutes their self-interest.

His own employees had proved that to him. The Filene Cooperative Association, which he had organized to open the way for workers in the store eventually to take it over, had been used by the employees merely to eliminate a certain number of annoyances and to secure somewhat more comfortable working conditions, nothing more. By slow degrees Filene came to realize that, no matter what they might say, at heart they didn't want his store and quite literally wouldn't have it as a gift if any considerable burden of responsibility went with the gift.

This had shaken him, but by the early twenties he had come to realize that it was true. Therefore he was never as optimistic about the immediate success of the League of Nations as were some others with less experience in dealing with men. This is probably the reason why he never became one of the "tired liberals" who finally turned upon Wilson with a venom not matched by Lodge or Borah or Fall. Filene worked harder and longer than a great many of those who quit; presumably he was as tired as any, but his fatigue was never embittered by the disappointment of expectations that were silly from the start. He had hopes, unbounded hopes, but he kept his expectations rigidly restricted.

However this is speculative, and the reader should accept it with great caution, for its implications are large. One of them is that practical experience in management, while it may make a man cautious in estimating the moral and intellectual capacity of the average man, does not necessarily make him cynical. If the manager's own intelligence is sufficiently active and wide ranging, the undeniable sloth and inertia of the average man may be, to the manager, not an insurmountable obstacle but merely one of the factors in his problem, to be taken into account certainly but simply as time and distance must also be taken into account. They too are irremovable, but they are not insurmountable.

No really able leader, whether he be an army commander, a statesman, a merchant, or a manufacturer, falls into despair because his objective is distant in time or in space, but after 1920 a discouraging number of liberals did lose hope when they found that the masses were psychologically much further behind them than they had thought. Filene did not, and it may be because he was braced for the disappointment by the relative failure of one of his most cherished schemes.

III

The Filene Co-operative Association was not a complete failure. If the party of the first part was disappointed, the party of the second part found its record quite satisfactory. As far as the outside world was concerned it seemed remarkable, so much so that in 1930 Mary La Dame, in her study of the store,* devoted a large part of her book to the operations of the association. Without doubt, it prevented any amount of labor trouble and contributed largely to the satisfaction of the employees. There is no question that the FCA was one thing that made Filene's a good place in which to work.

It would seem logical, then, to suppose that the appropriate place for a discussion of this venture would be in an earlier chapter—that relating to Filene, the merchant, or Filene, the

* Mary La Dame, *The Filene Store*. Russell Sage Foundation, New York, 1930.

citizen, or at latest in that relating to Filene, the patriot, rather than here in the discussion of the internationalist.

But the FCA was the work of many hands, affecting many people in many different ways, and this book has to do with one only, Edward A. Filene. What the FCA did to the other partners, to the store, to the employees, to the city of Boston, and to labor relations in general is another story, which has been told repeatedly. Even on Edward A. Filene its effect was multiple; it took certain problems off his hands, created others, certainly cost him money but probably added to his profits in the long run, both added to and subtracted from his anxieties, irritated him at times and soothed him at times. But its most important effect by far was in modifying his conception of leadership, and that conception steadily increased in importance as the field in which it was exercised grew larger. The largest field in which it operated is therefore the proper place for its consideration.

The Filene Co-operative Association was not a creation; it was a growth. It originated, or so Mary La Dame supposes, in William Filene's habit of conferring with his employees in a group from time to time and in his wife's human interest in the girls who worked in the store. It was Mrs. Filene who made her husband furnish a room in which the girls might rest and who undertook to see to it that they had proper lunches—the beginning of the employees' restaurant. The sons therefore found an informal organization already in existence when they took over the business.

But as the business expanded and the number of employees multiplied, the original personal relationship grew difficult to maintain. It began to assume more and more the aspect of an impersonal philanthropy and less and less true co-operation. Both the Filenes were firm in the conviction that philanthropy is not business and that the two do not mix satisfactorily. So about 1898 they determined that responsibility must be assumed by the employees. As Edward A. Filene put it at an association dinner in 1904:

> After many experiments arising from a desire on our part to do the right thing for our employes, after many experiments with lunchrooms and other types of what is called welfare work, we finally came to the point where we had to acknowledge our work had been a failure. My brother and I, in talking the matter over, and having grown wise by our defeats, were obliged to acknowledge we had not done our work in a way suitable to the environment in which we were trying to do it. It is worth while, in viewing the work from our present democratic standpoint, to acknowledge that in the beginning we had tried to do the work for our people under well-meant but still despotically benevolent principles. But grown wiser and more democratic by our failures, we agreed to do nothing for our people, but to help them with all our minds and strength to do everything for themselves.*

This describes nothing more than a mutual-benefit association, and the FCA has discharged that function, but its original purpose was very much larger. The Filene brothers hoped to develop among their employees leadership capable of participating actively in the management of the business, and Edward A. Filene, at least, confidently expected them eventually to acquire ownership. Some progress was made toward these ends. At one time the employees elected four of the eleven directors of the corporation, but in 1929, excluding executives, less than 1 per cent of the common stock was held by some 150 employees.

On the other hand the work of the FCA in determining hours and working conditions was markedly successful. As regards wages, its influence is not so easily traced, because it had al-

---

* Quoted by La Dame, *op. cit.*, 119-120.

ways been the policy of Filene's to pay wages a little above the general level. At the time of the Sage Foundation study, wages represented about 60 per cent of all operating costs, which management considered rather high, but the theory was that the way to reduce the proportionate cost was to hire more efficient employees not cheaper ones.

Employees were given an absolute right through the FCA to enact store rules. Management had a veto, but the veto could be overridden by a two-thirds vote of all members after two meetings at which management might present its case, not to the officers but directly to the members of the association. This was by no means a dead letter. Vetoes were overridden more than once, especially on such matters as closing the store for holidays and refusing night openings in the week before Christmas. In all these cases management acquiesced, and in some cases the outcome was that competing stores, instead of enjoying an advantage, were forced to follow the lead of Filene's.

In general the employees used the association to improve the conditions of their daily labor, for the most part in a reasonable manner that did no permanent harm to the business—certainly no irreparable damage—for throughout this period the business flourished prodigiously. But toward acquiring authority on the highest level and eventual ownership nothing was accomplished.

The Sage Foundation study attributes this failure entirely to two factors, both the fault of management. The plan of acquiring stock ownership, it says, was not carefully worked out in the beginning, and in the end management changed its mind about the whole project. This means that Lincoln Filene, Frost, and Kirstein changed their minds about the desirability of the scheme; Edward A. Filene continued to think it desirable, but even he had to admit that it was not working out in practice.

He did not concede however that its failure was due to lack of precision in its terms. That could have been corrected at any time had there been any resolute demand for its correction. It wasn't lack of precision; it was lack of interest that killed the scheme. The employees simply didn't want the store.

Why indeed should they? The majority of the employees were women, a large proportion of them young women, whose thoughts turned toward marriage not merchandising as a career. Even among the men there were many who were repelled by the thought of responsibility more than they were attracted by the thought of power.

Filene didn't understand this at the time, and he never came to understand it completely, but he was forced to admit that the condition existed, and as long as it existed not much could be done along the lines he had planned to follow. He was a born leader and the mentality of a born follower was beyond his comprehension, and, not comprehending, he was frequently contemptuous of it. But he never held facts in contempt, and it was a fact that most people were like that. He must therefore bear it in mind, and he bore it in mind, whether the issue in which he was involved was a new rule for Filene's store or the Covenant of the League of Nations.

His error was the error to which every man alive is prone, the error of forgetting that one man's meat is another man's poison. In the "Boston 1915" movement he had subscribed to, if he had not written, a summation of the minimum return that an American able and willing to do a good day's work has a right to expect, but it was hard, perhaps it was impossible, for him to believe that that minimum was near the maximum of many people's desire. Authority was sweet to him; it was inconceivable that it could be bitter to any man.

This was an error, but it is not certain that it was a weakness. Cherishing this error, he assumed that it was ignorance or misinformation that betrayed people into rejecting what was to their own best interest. Ignorance can be removed and misinformation corrected. It was all a matter of education, which is to say a matter of time. If the time required proved to be longer than he had expected, that would be disappointing but not catastrophic. A successful leader must have endurance.

Whatever the path by which he reached it, this was certainly his position in the dark days right after the League of Nations had been waylaid and murdered by petty politics. Let those who would abandon the field and repair to the Wailing Wall; a liberal he was and a liberal he remained, even though liberalism at the moment was obviously a wreck and a ruin. Radicalism, to which some of his late comrades in arms resorted, attracted him not at all, for he attributed the late defeat to a simple miscalculation of the strength of the foe not to any inherent weakness in the cause itself. Hence he had no need to take up any other cause.

If the defeat of the larger purposes of the FCA contributed to this certainty, then that defeat was far from being a net loss. It could have done so, for it set Filene somewhat apart from those liberals who gave up after the League of Nations fight and re-enlisted, some under the banner of radicalism, others under that of reaction.

They quit because they had no confidence in a long slow program of education and explanation. Mankind had Moses and the prophets under the names of Woodrow Wilson and the Covenant; if men would not believe them, would they believe though one rose from the dead? Liberals little experienced in dealing with the common people did not think so and despaired.

So might Filene if he had not had before his own eyes, under his very nose, an illustration of the way in which people may sometimes decline to act in their own interest. Were not his own employees doing exactly that? Yet there was nothing basically wrong with them. They merely needed more light. Why then assume that there was a deadly sickness infecting the world because it acted pretty much like the Filene employees? Filene refused to do it. He went down with the wreck, and he remained a Wilson man when that was a term of ridicule in "advanced" circles.

He who couldn't go away leaving a light burning in a hotel room couldn't go away leaving a world burning behind him. He had no romantic dreams of building a new hotel or a new world, for the existing ones could be rendered habitable and even comfortable provided men would do the reasonable thing, and he was unshaken in his belief that they could be brought to see reason.

IV

In the year 1907 Filene made a trip around the world on a cruise ship, but at Bombay he left the vessel and at no small risk hired an automobile and chauffeur to drive him across the country to Calcutta. Forty years later a motor drive of twelve hundred miles across India was an arduous trip; considering what automobiles and roads were when Filene made it, perilous is by no means too strong a word to apply.

However, it was the only way to see India quickly. The cities that were ports of call for tourist ships were not India any more than Southampton is England, or Le Havre, France, and the big express trains that were available gave no better opportunity of seeing the country than express trains do elsewhere. The motor car on the other hand brought one into intimate contact with the countryside—in 1912 a contact even more intimate than today since there were no superhighways tempting the driver to great speed.

The traveler found adventures in plenty although he does not record that human enemies offered to molest him; but heat, dust, bumpy roads, uncomfortable lodgings, and questionable food exacted fairly stiff payment for his close-range view of India. He took pride in having made that trip, not without reason for it was formidable.

What makes it worth mention here though is neither the

fortitude it required, nor the wealth of information about the people and government of India that it yielded, but the motive that drove him to it. In Bombay he encountered an Englishman who had voluntarily reduced his own rank and pay in order to further an idea. A man who would do that always interested Filene, no matter who or what he was, but this man was doubly interesting, because it was a business idea. He had been governor of a province, a position that Filene described as almost royal in both pay and prerogatives, yet he had resigned to take a position at a smaller salary and with no rank whatever in order that he might further the credit-union movement.

Filene had heard of credit unions, but there is no evidence that he knew much about them until he met this enthusiast in India, and the Englishman, being a genuine enthusiast, offered to instruct him not by telling him but by showing him, which was the way Filene preferred to learn. So together they set off on a jaunt through the subcontinent.

It was probably the most colorful event in the Bostonian's career. They had a Mohammedan chauffeur whose faith in kismet was sublime, especially when engine trouble developed. If the car stopped, the driver was content to wait with infinite patience for Allah to provide, and it took the combined energies of the passengers, reinforced by whoever happened to be passing, to induce him to go to work on the machinery, yet somehow they pounded through.

They penetrated districts in which an automobile had never been seen, and people supposed it to be a god. The Englishman made good use of this error when they came to a bridgeless river. It was the dry season and the river consisted of a mere trickle of water in an immensely wide bed, but the bed was sandy, and the car had not power enough to plow through. So the Englishman secured a long rope, which he attached to the front axle, and then announced to the natives that anyone wishing to acquire merit with the god in the machine might do so merely by pulling on the rope, so the equipage went triumphantly through—the first genuine miracle in his experience, said Filene dryly.

They invaded districts in which the word poverty took on a significance like nothing in the previous experience of the American traveler. The poorest slum in Boston was opulent by comparison with some of the remote villages through which "the god in the machine" snorted and bumped his way. The Englishman told him of families that had been in debt from generation to generation. It usually began with the expenses of a wedding or a funeral, paid for with money borrowed from a moneylender at extortionate interest rates. At such rates before one loan was paid off another wedding or funeral would require a new loan. Yet interest rates had to be high, for defaults were numerous. Everyone was losing, yet there seemed to be no way out.

But the British agents found one. Investigation convinced them that defaults were usually attributable not to intentional dishonesty but to death or to some calamity such as a crop failure or the loss of livestock through accident or disease. They therefore persuaded groups of villagers, sometimes enlarged to take in practically all of them, to become jointly responsible for their individual debts. Using this means of spreading the risk, they were able to obtain money at reasonable rates, and when the interest rate was reduced to reason, the villagers began to pay out.

The American was fascinated. All his life he had been struggling with the problems of credit in his own business, and he had read the economists and monetary theorists with close attention. He knew John Law and Robert Owen, as well as Adam Smith and David Ricardo. He was acquainted with the records both of Lloyds of London and of the American wildcat banks.

But there was a direct simplicity about this Anglo-Indian work that impressed him. It was a scheme devised to relieve a local situation, and there is no evidence that the men who administered it knew much if anything about economic theory. What they did know was that the people in their particular village were reasonably honest. Most of them would pay their debts if they could, but under the conditions existing they couldn't.

On the other hand they knew that there were people willing to lend money at moderate rates provided they had a reasonable chance of getting it back. They may never have heard the words venture capital, but they knew that there were people willing to lend and people willing to pay; what stood in the way was the hazard that the conditions of Indian life imposed upon the individual borrower. They could not reduce that hazard appreciably, but they could spread its effects so thinly that they would not be disastrous to any individual. They did it in the most direct and simplest way by persuading a number of honest men to guarantee each other's credit. This did not add one dollar to the physical resources of the community, but it mobilized its moral resources and added them to the physical. The result was that it relieved the situation and restored the village to solvency.

At the moment Filene did nothing about it, but it stuck in his mind, and the more he considered it, the more it impressed him. Years were to pass before he was to proceed to any overt act based upon it, and when he did it was upon a plan so greatly modified and elaborated that it was hardly recognizable as the Indian idea. Nevertheless this was the beginning of the American credit unions, now flourishing all over the United States and conducting transactions involving sums that would stagger the villagers in the heart of India.

But as far as the development of Filene's thinking was concerned, this was only half of it. Everyone understands how he was impressed by the way the village had been drawn out of hopeless poverty and misery and converted into a decent place in which to live. Filene's sympathy for the villagers is taken

for granted and applauded, and his admiration of the British
agents is readily understood.

What is frequently ignored is the fact that he thought about
the moneylenders too. He was bound to, because they presented
in miniature and simplified to the limit the problem that was
peculiarly his own. He had solved the problem of how to get
rich, but he found as difficult as ever the problem of how to
stay rich. In that village the moneylenders were regarded as
rich men; in relation to the village some of them were probably
as rich as Filene was in relation to Boston. But at the moment
when the British agents evolved their idea they were getting
poorer not richer; the moneylenders' problem may have been
less urgent, but it was no less threatening than that of the villagers on whom they preyed.

Any fool knows that the way to stay rich is to avoid wasting
one's substance. But what was the moneylenders' substance?
They assumed, as did the villagers, that it was the coined silver
in their strongboxes, and they were making frantic efforts to
avoid wasting that. The extortionate interest they charged was
their means of avoiding waste of their money. Yet the money
was diminishing.

Here was a vivid illustration of the principle that Filene had
already thought out in part and which he was to spend the
rest of his life expounding. The moneylenders' real wealth was
not their own money but the prosperity of the village from
which they drew their incomes. Whatever they did to reduce
that prosperity was wasting their substance and making them
poorer.

It was the same in Boston. For years he had been preaching
that the most valuable assets of Filene's were not to be found in
its inventories, nor in its bank accounts, but in thousands of
customers with money in their pockets. For Filene's to charge
unreasonable prices would be to do exactly what the moneylenders were doing when they charged extortionate interest—
wasting real wealth for a temporary profit.

If it were true in the Indian village and in the city of Boston, it must be true in the nation and in the group of nations trading with each other that constitutes Western civilization. The time was to come when Edward A. Filene was to be conspicuous among those who advocated what was called a liberal policy in repairing the damage done by a great war. It was a liberal policy, but shortsighted people construed liberal as synonymous with altruistic, which it was not at all. In his view the United States of America, having acquired great wealth, was faced with the problem of staying rich, and he saw no way of solving it save by a policy of carefully guarding the prosperity of the customers. If the customers happened to include a great many defeated enemies, the fact was irrelevant. To keep them in the market was not unselfish; it was merely wise, and if keeping them in the market incidentally benefited them, then they must be benefited not for their own sakes but for ours.

Events since his death have gone far to prove that this policy was somewhat less wise than Filene thought. His accounting was faulty in that it omitted or rated at less than its real importance one factor, to wit, the thinness of the veneer that overlays Neanderthal man and converts him into a man of the twentieth century. Even the experience of the First World War did not give him an adequate conception of the fragility of the covering. Yet it hardly lies in the mouth of the generation that sent delegates to Munich and that passed the American Neutrality Act of 1937 to criticize him. Overoptimism was an exceedingly common error in those days.

The policy of international co-operation in repairing the ravages of war was advocated by countless Americans who took no interest in such projects as the credit unions. People who noted that Filene was interested in both frequently took it for granted that this showed that there were two sides to his character, that of the economic statesman who could apply logical principles to a world situation without regard to the passions released by war and that of the sentimentalist who could not resist assisting his unfortunate fellows in the bonds of hopeless poverty.

But in reality there was no difference at all. Filene's interest in the Dawes plan, the Young plan, and all the other schemes whereby reparations were supposed to be adjusted to Germany's power to pay and his interest in the credit unions both flowed from the same primary source, his interest in maintaining general prosperity as the only safe basis of individual prosperity, whether that of a poor man or of a millionaire. In the restored Indian village the moneylenders also prospered. They no longer drew 80 per cent on loans, but they no longer lost both principal and interest by defaults, so at the end of the year they had more rupees than ever.

To the sentimentalist this is intolerable. The moneylenders who had been grinding the faces of the poor should be punished. To permit them to share in the revived prosperity of all, indeed to take perhaps a larger share than any other individuals, was to defeat the ends of justice from the sentimentalist's standpoint. Sentimentality is notorious for its cruelty.

It would be difficult to defend the assertion that Edward A. Filene was completely devoid of sentimentality. Those who knew him could promptly cite a dozen instances in which it broke out; he was frankly sentimental about children, and perhaps the most convincing evidence of that trait in his make-up was the extreme bitterness he cherished toward former friends who had, as he thought, deserted him. It was not that he was implacable. More than once he was betrayed, blatantly and outrageously, and took it philosophically. There was one instance in particular of a dishonest employee who converted to his own use a considerable sum of the firm's money, but when the man's family made restitution, Filene refused to prosecute. In every case, though, the man whose recreancy he overlooked was one for whom he had never cared much anyhow. The failure in loyalty of a real friend, however, he never forgave, and sometimes he imagined it where it had in fact not occurred. There was sentimentality in that.

But his political and economic liberalism was based on what was to him logical unemotional reasoning. To be sure no man is ever quite a thinking machine, and our ideas of what is logical are more or less untrustworthy, but to the extent that a man can do so, this one based his attitude toward public affairs on what he thought not on what he felt.

In India, for example, he noted with no approval whatever the rigorous social caste system that the British had overlaid upon the previously existing Hindu religious caste system. He disliked it, he regarded it as stupid, and he took pleasure in flouting it. On several occasions he was warned by intelligent cultivated natives that it would not do for him to be seen in public with them, and in such cases he invariably made it a point to be seen. There is no record that it did him any harm with any man for whose opinion he cared a rap, but there can hardly be a doubt that he would have done it at cost of considerable annoyance, simply to register his protest against the system.

But his dislike of this feature of the situation did not unsettle his judgment. If the people who established the credit unions also were given to insulting unoffending Indians, nevertheless the credit unions were good. He saw how his friend, the ex-governor, was sacrificing himself for the benefit of the debt-laden villagers; he saw how faithfully British officials were struggling to maintain public order and decent standards of public justice; he saw how British engineers were sweating their lives away at small salaries building, and building honestly, roads, irrigation systems, sanitary facilities, dams, and hydroelectric plants; he saw British doctors and sanitarians as devoted as any in the world. So he struck a balance and in spite of the caste system decided that it was good for India that the British were there. It was profitable for all concerned, and he was not one to permit sentiment to override profit.

Credit unions were co-operative banking on the community level. The various German reparations schemes were co-operative banking on the international level, but regardless of the level they were both based on the theory that to be lenient with an embarrassed customer is better than to thrust him into bankruptcy and out of the market, better for the lender's own interest. It is also praiseworthy to relieve a sufferer, but Filene insisted that the moral excellence of the attitude is fortuitous; the ruling consideration is that it is profitable in the long run even if it is temporarily expensive.

V

"I am a shopkeeper," said Edward A. Filene not once but repeatedly when people tried to thrust upon him the role of an economist, or a philanthropist, or a social philosopher, or a liberal statesman.

"I am a shopkeeper," he told an audience at the University of California when he was receiving a degree and making a series of lectures.

"I am a shopkeeper from Boston," he told a group of distinguished Frenchmen when he had been sent over from London in one last desperate effort to save the Dawes plan—which by the way he saved, although to no ultimate good.

"I am a shopkeeper," he told Charles Wood when the two were considering the possibility of a biography.

There was nothing in the world of which he was more certain than that his position in the world was that of a retail merchant, and all his ideas and activities must of necessity be based on that.

Yet the time came when many of his contemporaries regarded him as the scourge and destroyer of shopkeepers, and in his will he so arranged things that many of them hold that opinion unto this day. This was because he became interested in the consumer co-operative idea, and one of the foundations he endowed, the Edward A. Filene Good Will Fund, has driven ahead with the program of investigation since his death, and through its subsidiary, Consumer Distribution Corporation, has begun actual experimentation.

It is difficult to trace with precision the development of Edward A. Filene's thought on retail merchandising, partly because it was never completely crystallized. He knew more about retail merchandising than he did about anything else, and for that very reason he was most uncertain about it. To the end of his life his opinion was shifting, and if he had lived another decade, he might have swung into a new direction. Certainly the people who have attempted to translate his ideas into action have had to modify them materially as the result of knowledge gained by experience.

But what Filene altered was his method never his objective. He tried one avenue of approach after another, but always he was striving to reach the same goal. This goal was a reduction of the gap between the cost of production of an article and the price at which it was sold to the consumer. He never wavered in his belief that reduction of this gap is the most important function of the merchant—of the industrialist and the farmer too, as far as that goes—but he was a shopkeeper, therefore he confined himself to the merchant's responsibility. By inference what he said applied to others, but explicitly he argued always from the standpoint of the merchant and usually from that of the retail merchant.

There was nothing of what the French call *mystique* in this. The duty of the retail merchant is to reduce the cost of distribution not because it is noble to help out others but because a decrease in the cost of distribution facilitates the flow of trade, and upon the flow of trade depends the merchant's continuing prosperity.

It follows that a merchant whose methods do not contribute to this end or are destructive of this end is not a merchant at all but a bungler. Filene had no patience with bunglers. He was a profound believer in democracy, but he understood democracy.

He did not confuse it with mob rule, still less with anarchy. There is no evidence in the records that he ever used the word egalitarianism, but he knew the difference between it and democracy.

By democracy he meant the destruction of all artificial barriers that tend to prevent brains and character from rising to the top. It makes no difference whether the barriers are political, social, or economic—if their tendency is to hold down able men and give advantage to the incompetent, they are undemocratic. That applies to some egalitarian ideas as strictly as it does to the law of primogeniture. If a man is elected by majority vote to a position he is not competent to fill, the process may be egalitarian, but it is not democratic.

In the management of a retail store, for example, Filene knew as well as any man alive that brains are required, and not only that, but they must be brains of a particular type. It is easily conceivable that William Shakespeare might have made a horrible mess of Filene's shoe department if he had been its manager. Hence any system that results in setting a poet to selling shoes or a born shoe merchant to writing plays is essentially undemocratic because it sets artificial barriers in the way of talent. So is the law of inheritance. The son of a good shoe merchant is not necessarily a good shoe merchant himself, and the fact that he inherits a business does not make him one. If the fact of his inheritance keeps a better man out of control, that fact is undemocratic.

In the instance of retail merchandising, it was Filene's belief that anything that keeps a merchant from discharging his true function, that of reducing the cost of distribution, sets an artificial barrier in the way of talent and is therefore not to be defended on the ground that it is democratic. It may be egalitarian, but it is not democratic.

Thus when Aaron Shapiro, who had just organized the citrus growers into one of the most successful of producers' co-operatives, endeavored to persuade Filene to head a group of co-operative retail stores, Filene declined when he learned that control was to be exercised by a widely scattered group. He realized that people far removed from the center of operations would have no adequate conception of what was going on and therefore could not possibly act intelligently. With all the good will in the world, they would prevent the managers from acting efficiently, that is to say they would lay an artificial barrier against the exercise of brains and character. To Filene that was not democratic rule; it was simply misrule, and he would have nothing to do with it.

Naturally this gave his critics an excuse to accuse him of insincerity, of being an autocrat at heart. But he saw no inconsistency in believing in both democracy and discipline. To grant the people the right to select their own rulers is by no means to grant them the right to select no rulers, and to select incompetent rulers is next to selecting none at all. This distinction Filene always bore in mind, and the ability to perceive it is what made him genuinely liberal, rather than autocratic on the one hand or anarchic on the other.

His interest in consumer co-operatives was of long standing, but in the beginning it was not materially stronger than the interest he exhibited in every other new idea that was brought to his attention. Only after many years of experimentation with the examination of other ideas did he concentrate on co-operatives.

In the days when he was hypnotized by Henry Ford, he paid relatively little attention to co-operatives. He was cherishing the illusion then that the problem of reducing the cost of distribution could be solved by concentrating on small unit profits on a large volume of business, which he called mass distribution. Fundamentally the idea was sound, but as time passed he discovered that in retail trade obstacles to its attainment existed that Ford had avoided. There was that matter of proprietorship. Ford was owner as well as manager. He managed in the interest of Ford not in that of Tom, Dick, and Harry, who were merely investors never looking beyond the dividend rate.

Little by little Filene apprehended the truth that retail merchandising will never be well conducted until it is conducted by or in behalf of people who are interested in retail merchandising. The problem then was to secure owners with an interest in good conduct of the business as well as in immediate profits.

The problem is complicated by the fact that in the machine age retail merchandising cannot be well conducted unless it is conducted on a large scale, which means heavy capital investment. The actual capital has not been a problem in this country since the turn of the century. Nowhere else in the world are such tremendous sums available for any enterprise that promises a good return. The difficulty was, and is, to secure along with the capital investment a genuine and lasting interest in efficient merchandising that would leave management free to act.

It would be fatuous to claim that Filene ever overcame this difficulty. Perhaps it is insurmountable. But it was his effort to overcome it that gave some people the impression that he was really trying to destroy the retail merchant. He was never careful to eradicate this impression. He was constantly making statements that strengthened it, although they did not mean what people supposed they meant. "The little merchant must go" was a favorite dictum that he stated over and over. What he meant was not that the small man must cease being a merchant but that he must cease being little. The little store has obvious advantages as long as it is managed by a man whose mind isn't little but is keen enough and broad enough to participate in large enterprises.

Filene's first solution was an adaptation of the chain-store idea. Mention has already been made of his concept of chains of chains, that is chains of department stores, each department of which would also be a link in a chain of departments. The insuperable difficulty with that was that it resulted in paralysis of the general manager. To co-ordinate a group of departments that were essentially autonomous would be difficult to the point of impossibility.

Later he toyed with the idea of the independents, that is local stores associated for certain purposes, such as purchasing, but not organically linked. This was more fruitful. As a matter of fact, it has achieved an impressive success in such things as neighborhood groceries and drugstores that have managed to hold their own against the chains in many localities.

Even this however was open to the objection that it accepted small units as the basis of operations, and Filene was convinced that the cost of distribution cannot be cut to the absolute minimum except in establishments of very considerable size, and such establishments involve a large capital investment. Capital in large sums was available but without the interest of the investor in the business; capital with the interest of the investor was available but only in small sums. How to secure much capital with ownership interest was a problem that he never solved; his successors in the foundations he established have been struggling with it ever since and only recently have they begun to hope that they may have found a way out.

Needless to say, in many quarters these activities of Filene aroused astonishment and bitterness. Here was a man who had made a fortune as a retail merchant apparently bent on wiping out retail merchants. Treason to his class could hardly go further. Conservative business found no denunciation too harsh for Filene.

Nor were the conservatives alone in their perturbation. To many liberals also his course seemed perilous. Men of Louis D. Brandeis' turn of mind, men suspicious of bigness, were shocked by Filene's calm disregard of the evil potentialities of the vast organizations he dreamed of creating. "Always making weapons for the enemy," Brandeis' acid comment, expressed their fears precisely.

It would be folly to dismiss these criticisms as of no weight.

Edward A. Filene was not gifted with omniscience, and the consumer co-operative as he envisaged it has not yet been tested under conditions that will demonstrate conclusively what it will or will not do. It is conceivable that both criticisms are valid. Consumer co-operatives certainly threaten the existence of the small shopkeeper as chain stores do. It is possible also that any system big enough to effect a maximum reduction in the cost of distribution would be unworkable on account of its size.

But we shall never know until the thing is tried. Filene set in motion the machinery that may result in giving it a fair trial. If it comes to grief, definitely and unmistakably, then it will be established that in this particular matter he was a reckless plunger, but if it succeeds, then he will be firmly established as a bold pioneer extending the boundaries of the world.

VI

"It is easy to prophesy, if the prophecy is based on figures, not on dreams and delusions," said Edward A. Filene to Charles Wood one day as they were discussing the League to Enforce Peace.

This was in the early thirties when Filene probably had not read *Mein Kampf* and certainly had not believed it was prophecy. It was a milder world, even though it had been shattered by the First World War, a world in which an intelligent man could still believe in figures. It was also the world in which the second batch of hellbroth was being brewed, and Edward A. Filene was prominent among the brewers. It is fashionable now to condemn the liberals of the Long Armistice or, if not damning them outright, at least to deride their puerile thinking, but the condemnation is usually passed without much understanding either of the way they thought or why they thought that way.

Filene, for example, although he held no official position and sought none, was in the very thick of things through the period

—perhaps all the more influential because he had neither rank nor title. In 1917 immediately after our entry into the war, he had gone to see his old friend, Newton D. Baker, secretary of war, and offered his services provided he could serve out of uniform. So did two of his partners, Simpson and Cory, who became dollar-a-year men ("but they drew twenty-five thousand dollars a year in profits from the store which they didn't mention," commented Filene with some asperity years later). Eventually Kirstein went abroad under the auspices of the Army, "and did good work," Filene admitted. Baker tentatively offered Filene a commission, but when it was refused the Secretary accepted the refusal with an alacrity that suggests relief. At any rate he used Filene in this country exclusively, largely in organizing procurement.

After the shooting stopped, he plunged into the fight for the League of Nations and when that was lost undertook to renew his personal contacts in Europe, still convinced that men could be brought to see reason. There were moments when this belief seemed to be justified. For instance, he was in London when the struggle for adoption of the Dawes plan, the scheme worked out by the American, Charles G. Dawes, for the payment and allocation of German reparations, came to an impasse. Neither the French nor the German delegation, it developed, was really representative. The delegates were not in London to make the best bargain they could; they were merely agents of Paris and Berlin, bound by rigid instructions that they dared not disregard. These instructions were so far apart that no agreement was possible. Since Filene was an unofficial bystander, both delegations talked to him freely explaining their helplessness.

"Go back and demand new instructions," he advised them.

"Useless," said the Frenchmen. "If the government gave us new instructions it would be swept out of power tomorrow. Every newspaper in Paris but two is fighting the Dawes plan, and public opinion is so inflamed that the government cannot move."

But, argued Filene, if the Dawes plan failed, the government would fall anyhow, and France would probably fall with it.

"You go tell them," said the delegates. "They would not believe it from us, but they might from you, since you have no official position and therefore nothing at stake."

In the end he went. A dinner was arranged with some two dozen guests, including the most influential newspaper proprietors, bankers, and industrialists, with one or two very high government officials. Filene's presentation of the case was simple. It was the Dawes plan or ruin, and since the government dared not accept the Dawes plan, it was ruin. But it must be understood that the blame rested not on the government but on those who had terrorized it, which included many of the men in that room.

He prophesied from figures. He carefully eschewed dreams, and he thought he eschewed delusions. He did not defend the Dawes plan; he merely pointed out that it was that or nothing, and nothing meant the collapse of the economy of Western Europe, which would inevitably drag down France. He was, of course, telling them nothing that they had not known before; he was merely putting it to them with unprecedented bitterness, all the more bitter because it was completely unemotional. In the end they faced the facts and reluctantly but definitely eased the pressure on the government.

Filene proceeded to Germany, and at Munich in the private house of Kurt Wolff, the industrialist, repeated what he had said at Paris, merely substituting the name of Germany for that of France. The struggle was more stubborn and more prolonged here than it had been in France, but the outcome was the same. Reluctantly the powerful individuals concerned released the pressure, and the government was able to release its delegates. The Dawes plan was accepted.

Filene drew certain inferences from this that confirmed him in his position, but it is questionable that he drew the right inferences. To him it meant that when men have the facts laid

before them they will respond in a reasonable way. But these
men had the facts before them before Filene appeared on the
scene. His intervention did not bring them any additional information, but it did bring them something that enabled them
to reverse their course and act in accordance with the dictates
of reason. The same story that their own reporters and statesmen had been dinning into their ears without effect could cause
them to reverse their attitude when it was told by a foreigner
with no ax to grind.

Twenty-five years later it is easy to see that this is the aspect
of the affair that should have impressed Filene. The men to
whom he talked did react in a reasonable manner but to a quite
unreasonable stimulus. Unquestionably the failure of the liberalism of the Long Armistice is attributable in large measure,
perhaps in the largest measure, to its blindness to this aspect of
the situation. Filene did not perceive, or chose to ignore, the
significant truth that the men to whom he spoke accepted not
the facts but a neutral presentation of the facts. But that was an
emotional not an intellectual response. Facts are facts no matter
who presents them, but the same facts that, presented in one
way, will persuade men to act when presented in another way
only stiffen their opposition.

As the event proved, Filene's labor was wasted along with
that of all the statesmen, economists, and publicists who had
toiled to fabricate the Dawes plan, for it collapsed. A later generation is prone to speak of it scornfully as hopeless from the
start. Yet it was a good plan, logically correct, economically
possible, politically wholesome. It worked creakingly for a
while, and some things were accomplished under it, but its
larger aim, the pacification and rehabilitation of Europe, was
an utter failure.

It failed for exactly the same reason that the Filene Co-operative Association failed in its larger aims. It failed because
nobody really wanted it to succeed in any but its more trivial
aspects. The Filene employees wanted more holidays and bet-

ter working conditions and got them under the FCA, but they did not want the store and never made a real effort to acquire it. The French wanted more coal, and the Germans wanted more loans, and they got them under the Dawes plan. By comparison with the restoration of Europe these were trivial matters, but they loomed large in the minds of the people concerned—much larger than the utopian goal of a continent at peace. The FCA never collapsed entirely, because the employees never pressed a series of demands incompatible with the continued existence of the store, but the French wanted security, and the Germans wanted expansion, and these were incompatible with lasting peace.

The difference was in magnitude not in kind. On a vastly larger scale and in vastly subtler and more complicated ways, the individual nations played the role that the individual employees had played, but more recklessly and therefore more ruinously.

Yet it is a foolhardy man who will assert flatly that Filene was wrong in encouraging the formation of the Filene Co-operative Association. His larger hopes were disappointed, it is true, but not because his plan was a bad one; it was because he understood imperfectly his employees' ways of thinking and credited them with a larger share than they possessed of his own vision and ambition. Vision and ambition are not bad qualities, and as men's experience widens they usually increase. The time may come when such an undertaking as the FCA will succeed brilliantly, for a man may fail as certainly by being ahead of his time as by being behind it.

The liberalism of the Long Armistice failed. That is incontestable. The years between 1939 and 1945 stamped the brand of failure upon it indelibly. Wilson, Briand, Smuts, and those who followed them, including Edward A. Filene, failed; William II, Hitler, Mussolini were "wiser in their generation than the children of light." But it does not follow that the liberalism they professed was wrong. It may have been too right, too enlightened to comprehend how thick was the darkness it strove to penetrate. The failure has just been demonstrated with hideous clarity, hence it occupies men's minds to the exclusion of all else at the moment. Yet it is far from certain that they were wrong in anything except in being ahead of their time, and if that is the case, the future will hold the fact that they made the effort far more remarkable than the fact that the effort failed.

Certainly Filene never succumbed to doubt. Chagrin he felt but not doubt. Woodrow Wilson spoke for him in the famous observation that it is better to fail in a cause that is bound eventually to succeed than to triumph in a cause that is bound eventually to fail.

VII

As all the world knows now, the problem that was most appallingly fumbled in the period of the Long Armistice was the problem of Russia. For seventeen years the government of the United States pursued the one policy that Edward A. Filene always maintained could lead to nothing but trouble, in business, in government, or in the personal life of an individual, the policy of refusing to face the facts.

No doubt the extremists on both sides were wrong, but there was more to be said for either extreme than for the policy we adopted. There was some semblance of logic in the contention that the Soviet Union was a monstrosity of such hideous potentialities that it ought to be destroyed at any cost. There was some semblance of logic in the opposite contention that the Russian system was the hope of mankind. But there was no semblance of logic in officially ignoring the existence of the Communist régime, in hampering it, irritating it, annoying it in a thousand trivial ways without ever striking it a crippling blow. Bear hunting could have been defended with a certain plausibility. Bear training could have been defended after a fashion. But bear baiting was then, as always, a brutal, demoralizing, and highly dangerous sport. Yet it was the choice of the United States.

It was purely a matter of respect for facts not of respect for communism that made Filene deplore this course. Nevertheless, although it made no appeal to him, communism represented a broad field of governmental theory until that time unexplored, and it was not in Filene's nature to object to the testing of any untried theory, especially when someone else was willing to undertake the trouble and expense of making the test.

"If Russia is willing to make this experiment, I don't know of anything that would help the world more," he said in the late twenties when it was still the official policy of this government to ignore everything that Russia did and not to admit even that Russia belonged to the family of nations.

It is significant that he did not argue for the Russians' right to conduct their affairs by any system that, in the words of Jefferson, "to them shall seem most likely to effect their Safety and Happiness." As a believer in the principles of the Declaration of Independence, he would have granted that right without question, but there was what he considered an even stronger argument against any attempt at repression. He believed that the experiment, conducted under conditions that would really test the theory, would be a positive help to the rest of the world.

Again it was not love of the Russians, much less love of the Communists, or altruism of any sort that he brought to the support of his argument. It was enlightened self-interest.

"For definite reaction against that kind of radicalism," he pointed out, nothing "is so sure as the failure of this experiment."

But who could say that the experiment had failed if other governments prevented its completion or so hampered it that the results were inconclusive? That was what they were doing as he spoke, and what this government continued to do up to 1933, by which time the pattern was set. The Russians firmly believed that the rest of the world was willing to destroy them

—had it not been proclaiming that willingness from the house-tops for seventeen years?—and thereafter the Communist leaders had a perfect excuse for everything that went wrong. Capitalist encirclement could account for anything. In 1948 it was still blamed for whatever failed in Russia, and against that adamant conviction the ablest of our diplomatists struggled in vain.

Filene had at least looked into *Das Kapital,* but what was far more important he had talked to people in practically every country in Europe—not merely statesmen and businessmen but little people, people so small that even the newspaper correspondents saw them but rarely and the great lords of the press hardly ever. Through these contacts he had some comprehension of the strength and depth of the impression Marx's half-truths had made. Most of the men who posed as statesmen in Europe had no such comprehension. They would not concede that Marx had propounded even half-truths.

This was never Filene's attitude. "I think if the rest of the world do not adopt some of the experiments of Russia," he said, and then suddenly altered his conclusion, "they are making experiments that are pretty important."

He knew whereof he spoke, because he had taken the trouble to go there and find out. In 1927, at the moment when America was roaring to the top of the great boom that preceded the great bust, when everyone in many commercial houses, from the president of the corporation to the office boy, was giving his main attention to speculating in the stock market, Edward A. Filene took seriously to heart the dictum that President Coolidge had offered the newspaper editors two years before, "The business of America is business." He ignored the stock market and set out to investigate business as it was done in Russia.

The Iron Curtain was not then impenetrable, and Russia gave some indications of desiring friendly intercourse with the Western world. Filene was not only permitted to visit Moscow, he was allowed to select the persons there whom he wished to see.

They were businessmen—that is to say the heads of bureaus and departments engaged for the most part in distribution. He avoided the factories on the ground that he was not an expert in production. He preferred to gain his idea of Russian productivity by examining what was distributed.

He was aware, too, that if he wanted to see production at its highest he would do better to visit Detroit instead of Moscow. If the Russian experiment had anything new to contribute to the world, it would be in the field of distribution, so that was the field he chose to examine.

He found nothing that was new from the ground up, but he did find a new vigor and boldness in the application of many ideas that had been known to the world for many years. He came away convinced that the Russian system was going to last for a long time. He thought it would shift gradually to the right, as in fact it did, but he dismissed as nonsense the countless American predictions of its early collapse.

It seems never to have occurred to him however to consider the Communists as somehow fraudulent because the ideas with which they worked were for the most part old, some very old.

He had said in another connection, "I realize constantly that there are enough ideas lying loose around the world to make heaven on earth if all the good ones could be adopted."

Novelty was not in itself either a virtue or a vice. "The world does not need so much new ideas, as new ideas that are practically applicable to the next step forward in the right direction."

This was of course the heart of his liberalism—to take the next step forward in the right direction. The reactionary who will take no step except backward, the conservative who will take no step at all, and the radical who will take no step except a stride with seven-league boots annoyed him almost equally, for they all seemed equally unwilling to deal with the world as it is.

As far as their philosophy of government was concerned, the Russians were in his view mystics, and he had learned long ago that it is useless to argue with people who profess to see a higher truth than is perceptible to the eyes of ordinary men. For that reason he avoided the propagandists and statesmen in Moscow. There was nothing to be learned from them. But the men who had to keep the trains running, get the freight packed, shipped, delivered, and unpacked were not dealing in intangibles. They were handling facts, hard refractory facts, measurable in ton-miles, in yards, bushels, gallons. A Marxian dictum might mean —usually did mean—one thing to a Russian and something different to Filene, which impeded the exchange of ideas. But a bolt of cloth was a bolt of cloth, and the way a man handled it could not be mistranslated if one stood and watched him handle it.

Since the retail stores in Moscow concealed no military secrets, he was permitted to investigate them without much interference. They fascinated him, because here was the most direct and forthright attack on the problem of mass distribution that had been made anywhere in the world. True the test could not be called conclusive either way, because Russia was afflicted with such a shortage of consumer goods that distribution remained a secondary problem. Still he saw a good deal that raised questions in his mind to which he could find no immediate answer. He needed more data. For that reason he was not merely willing to allow the Russians to work out their experiment without interference; he ardently hoped they would do so for the instruction of the rest of the world.

Naturally this made him a sympathizer with communism in the eyes of Americans whose minds were closed, but that gave him little concern. He had been anathema to people with closed minds for a long time, and one charge more or less brought against him made little difference. He continued to observe and to study. Eight years later he returned to Moscow to check and extend his observations of 1927, but this time he accomplished little, for a bout of pneumonia disabled him and came very close to killing him.

Right to the end the noteworthy thing about Filene was not that he claimed to understand Russia better than anyone else but precisely the opposite. He didn't understand Russia at all. It was the extremists on both sides who claimed to understand that vast and complicated phenomenon and were ready to proceed at once, half of them to destroy it, the other half to embrace it. With less intellectual conceit Filene admitted that he needed more light, a great deal more light, before he could arrive at an intelligent judgment. Light, he was certain, could come only from careful and prolonged study of the facts, and he had not nearly facts enough. The experiment was so vast that the facts about it could not possibly be developed rapidly, nor could the truth be discovered at all as long as outside pressure continued to warp the Russian program from its logical development.

After a fashion this did make him a Russian sympathizer. For one thing he discovered that the news from Russia was frequently unreliable, and he blamed American newspapers bitterly. He laid upon them in fact more blame than was just. Some papers did distort Russian news, even to the extent of complete falsification, and all papers printed a good deal of material that fell far short of the standard of objective truth, but it was not always by their own choice. If the reactionary press had some unscrupulous reporters, the Russians themselves developed liars as adroit and energetic as any in the world. Honest reporters soon discovered it and found that they must be forever on guard respecting any news that came out of Russia. Their efforts to disentangle truth from falsehood were not always successful even when they were quite sincere.

All of this clouded Edward A. Filene's judgment as it did that of everyone else. It would be nonsensical, therefore, to attempt to set him up as one who discovered and proclaimed the correct American policy toward Russia. To begin with, he never discovered any policy. He was uncertain to the end, because he knew the facts were elusive, and without the facts the formation of a sound policy was impossible. The credit due him is simply the negative credit of not making up his mind on fragmentary evidence.

But there was one other element in the situation that deserves emphasis. It was not intellectual but emotional, therefore Filene himself might have been inclined to pooh-pooh it had it been brought to his attention. Yet it was highly important, perhaps of primary importance. This is the simple fact that in facing the Russian problem he was unterrified.

As to whether or not he deserves credit for this, it is hard to say. But it was the fact. He was a liberal democrat to the marrow of his bones. It was inconceivable to him that liberal democracy had anything to fear in fair competition with any other theory of government. His faith was as absolute as Jefferson's in "the impunity with which error may be tolerated where reason is left free to combat it."

It is astonishing how rare that quality is in the American democracy. In the Old Testament Book of Samuel II it is related that when the ark of the covenant was being transported on a cart one Uzzah made up his mind that it was going to fall unless he laid hands on it to steady it. He did so with fatal results. Whatever else Filene may have been, he was no Uzzah; he did not believe that democracy needs to be sustained, or can be sustained, by the abandonment of democratic principles, one of which is that any government resting upon the consent of the governed has just powers. A thousand voices shouted in his ears that the Soviet Union did not rest upon the consent of the governed, but his own investigations had not proved it. On the contrary they strongly indicated that a majority of the Russian people did consent. Therefore he was vigorously opposed to laying hands upon their structure, no matter how rickety it might seem to be. He may have been in error, but if so, he erred because he lacked possession of all the facts, not because he wavered by a hairbreadth from the principles of liberal democracy.

CHAPTER 6

The Technician

I

ONCE AN EMPLOYEE came to Edward A. Filene with the news that he had just made arrangements to purchase a home. If the announcement was made with a trace of smugness, that is no cause for wonder, for home ownership has long been accepted in this country as an evidence of good citizenship. Employers have frequently made vigorous and sometimes expensive efforts to encourage home ownership among their employees. Chambers of commerce, the press, sometimes even the pulpit have constantly proclaimed the virtues and advantages of owning one's home.

So the man was stunned when Filene's reply to the announcement was that in that case the employee's salary would be reduced ten dollars a week since any man working for a weekly wage who bought a house obviously lacked intelligence. The threat was facetious; Filene had no intention of reducing the man's pay, but he did wish to emphasize his skepticism with regard to the home-ownership program.

His reasoning was not at all obscure. Ours is an industrial civilization, which is to say a mobile civilization. Industries are constantly shifting their bases of operation, and industries of any considerable size have many bases. A worker therefore should be in position to follow the good jobs, but if everything he owns is tied up in a house—or, worse and more common, in a small equity in a house—it is difficult for him to move suddenly. Sometimes it is so difficult that he prefers to remain where he is at a worse job that reduces his standard of living.

Unquestionably there is force in this argument, but it is cited here not for its own value but because it illustrates the basic technique by which Filene strove to put his ideas into effect. That was to follow the facts always and everywhere, to follow the facts in the teeth of all theories and theorists, if necessary in flat defiance of what nine tenths of the world considered right and proper.

It was a rugged policy. It conceded nothing to popularity and not much to understanding. It could be followed only by a very resolute man very sure of his premises.

Nor is it to be denied that it is a dangerous policy. Facts are elusive as Filene discovered to his cost over and over again. Let a single important one be missing out of the prodigious number that figure in any large calculation, and the whole scheme is wrecked. Few Americans have engaged in as many abortive projects as did this Boston merchant. He had ample reason for calling himself unsuccessful. Not one man in a million would have survived so many defeats. It would be easy to fill a book larger than this one with accounts of projects in which he took more or less active interest but that came to nothing.

Needless to say this contributed to the bewilderment of his friends and to the merriment of his foes. Filene had a hand in everything. As a rule he spoke from the standpoint of a retail merchant, but that was his only fixed point of reference. His mind darted in every direction in which something caught his interest. He invented a footstool that wouldn't work. He discoursed on railroad reorganization and better dining cars, a new Socialist party, a name for violators of the prohibition law (but he did not attain the dubious distinction of inventing the term scofflaw), low-priced steamship tickets to Europe, city planning, an international newspaper chain, industrial housing, a new kind of school of domestic science, a contest for the best international peace plan, public-school education, crime and punishment, municipal government, and boss rule.

If the footstool failed, another of his inventions not only succeeded but has attracted world-wide attention in recent years. This was the Filene-Finlay simultaneous translator, a system of making multiple translations of an address as it is being delivered. Translators equipped with special telephonic apparatus listen to the address and translate it as it is made for the benefit of listeners equipped with earphones. It received the attention of people of all nations when it was employed during the trals of the German war criminals at Nuremberg. This might have seemed to Filene an ironical kind of success; he devised it for the benefit of the League of Nations and defrayed the cost of installing it at Geneva.

Needless to say, it is not within the capacity of any human mind to follow such multifarious and divergent projects through to a successful conclusion, even when success is possible. Filene didn't follow through and by refusing to do so laid himself open to pointed criticism. But it was never his intention to follow through. He regarded himself as primarily, if not exclusively, an idea man who planned but left the execution of his plans to others.

His technique is illustrated in the making of the multiple translator system. He was not an electrician, much less an electrical engineer, but he knew where such men were to be found. He described the sort of apparatus he wanted and left it to them to construct it for a fee. The technical difficulties were not formidable, but they did require a certain amount of study and experimentation, which a good telephone man could do much more rapidly and competently than an amateur. So Filene left it to the engineers, specifically to Finlay, whose name is on the apparatus, and while they were working it out, he was off on something else.

The same method he applied *mutatis mutandis* to projects that did not involve engineering. He had a keen appreciation of the value of expert help and considerable, but not supreme, skill in using it. His failure to develop the very highest skill in dealing with first-rate people may perhaps be charged against him as a real failing—certainly with much more reason than the frequently repeated assertion that he never saw things through. It has already been pointed out that Filene was extraordinarily adept at selecting young men of great ability; the number that were in his employ at one time or another is startling. But the other side of the medal is the incontestable fact that he lost too many good men. Some he lost by the creditable process of thrusting them into higher positions, but a great many he irritated into quitting his service. If he had known how to retain and to apply to his purposes all the talent that he assembled, he would have been a much greater leader.

His second failure is attributable in part perhaps to the time in which he lived, but in part it was temperamental. He was hypnotized by statistics as deeply as any economist of the Manchester school. He based his prophecies on figures, and sometimes figures do lie.

Note that in spite of the astonishing variety of the projects that enlisted his interest there is a significant omission. There was one great field of human experience that Filene never invaded. It was the field of the arts, and he kept out of it because he sensed that the guides on which he was accustomed to rely, his tables and graphs and charts, are unreliable in that field.

That is to say he intended to keep out, but as a matter of fact he edged somewhat into it whenever he dealt with government, for government is not altogether a science, not nearly as much a science as Filene believed. To a very large extent it is an art, a branch of the art of dramaturgy.

Logicians have ever been disconcerted by their finding that every supremely great ruler is a scientist only up to a point, beyond which he takes on many of the attributes of the medicine man, the primitive dramatist. The great ruler must base his

project on logic to be sure, as the great painter must base his on
the laws of optics. But the ruler, if he is to rank among the supremely great, must do more than reason; he must know how to
weave spells and cast out devils, how to harness the emotions of
great masses of men and apply the power of emotion to the machinery of reason.

This necessity confused Filene, and he never learned how to
meet it. There was no logic in it. It was not subject to statistical
measurement. It supplied no reliable figures. Some people—
both the Roosevelts, for example—seemed to be able to base
their prophecies on it with uncanny success but not Filene. His
responses to aesthetic stimuli were not strong, and his emotional responses were usually although not always under pretty
rigid intellectual control. Therefore a good many experiences
common to far smaller men he did not share, and they puzzled
him. A strain of music, a flaming sunset, a resounding phrase
("All we have to fear is fear itself") had power, sometimes tremendous power. So much was obvious, and he knew it as well
as the next man, but the source of that power was a mystery
that he did not penetrate. So he remained restricted in dealing
with human beings, less effective in many ways than certain
blatant demagogues with not a tithe of Filene's brains and with
no character at all.

There is one weakness with which he is frequently charged
that cannot be denied with assurance, yet which ought not to
be accepted without important reservations. This is the charge
of exhibitionism. There are men in Boston, honest and intelligent men, who are still convinced that Filene was primarily a
publicity hunter, motivated by vanity more than by anything
else, and they can cite evidence to sustain the theory.

But they overlook the fact that Filene was working in the
field of public opinion. He was endeavoring to persuade men in
large numbers, and for such work publicity is an indispensable
implement. He discovered that early in his career. As a retail

merchant he knew the uses of straight advertising, and in the Public Franchise League and the "Boston 1915" movement he learned that publicity is the first requisite of anyone who hopes to persuade the public.

Therefore, if he was a publicity hunter, it was for a much better purpose than to serve his personal vanity at least originally. But it is not to be denied that publicity is a habit-forming drug. It is possible for a man who originally sought it for a legitimate purpose to become habituated to the practice until he seeks it automatically. "The art of publicity is a black art," said Learned Hand, "but it has come to stay; every year adds to its potency and the finality of its judgments." It is of the very essence of the Faustus legend that any black art comes in time to operate upon the sorcerer, and there were times, especially in his later life, when Edward A. Filene took action that seemed to be and perhaps was publicity hunting for publicity's sake. Yet if it were proved to be so, it might still be argued in extenuation that he was in some sense a victim, comparable to those anesthetists who experimented with cocaine when it was first introduced and made themselves drug addicts before they understood the insidious nature of the stuff.

The ways in which Filene sought to apply his theories were so multitudinous and so various that it is not easy to trace any logical pattern among them. But there was a pattern. The confusion is due to the fact that he made innumerable abortive attempts, tested many ideas that quickly proved to be no good, so that to the superficial observer he resembles Leacock's rejected lover who, in a black mood, abandoned the unresponsive fair one, rushed from the house, mounted several horses, and rode off in every direction.

Yet if one ignores these fits and starts and concentrates attention on the larger figures, a consistent pattern emerges and an interesting one. The following pages therefore deliberately omit a great deal that he did in order to trace out the main lines of his endeavor.

II

One of the puzzling aspects of his character is the fact that a man so conspicuously unsuccessful in his own personal relations should have had such high confidence in the effectiveness of close personal relations toward ameliorating the ills that afflict the world. Yet it is true that a great many of the projects in which he engaged, especially in the early days, were based upon the assumption that to bring men together to talk over their differences smooths the road to agreement. This is clear enough in such a matter as the International Chamber of Commerce, which was an organized effort to that end. But it is true, also, of his project, which he pursued with unflagging energy and at considerable cost to himself, to persuade the trans-Atlantic steamship companies to provide cheap accommodations in order that the number of American visitors to Europe might be multiplied many times. He was unquestionably the chief progenitor of "tourist third," which he bedeviled the steamship lines into instituting.

Up to a point his reasoning is clear enough. He had found Europe a fruitful source of ideas. Contact with Europeans of all classes had stimulated his own thinking and clarified his understanding of European attitudes. Therefore he assumed that European travel is good for an American.

This is one project that he did follow through, but curiously it is one that he had not thought through. That European travel is good for an American is not an absolute but a contingent truth. It is possible for an American to collect ideas there, but it is equally possible for him to collect prejudices. Contact with Europeans may stimulate him, but it may do no more than exacerbate his prejudices. In 1914 we were sending abroad some three hundred thousand tourists every summer. They all carried financial profit to Europe, and some of them established there respect and liking for this country, but a great many did nothing of the sort. It is by no means certain that the effect, on

balance, of our tourist activity was to strengthen amicable international relations.

Then, beginning in 1917 and again in 1942, we dispatched
young men to Europe by millions, and anyone who thinks the
net effect of that activity was to buttress friendship is an opti-
mist indeed. Filene did not live to see the second effort, but he
saw the first. He had before his eyes the evidence that the
American Army came back with a healthy liking and respect for
nobody but the enemy and was respected, and even liked, by
no one else. He must have known, too, many American civilians
who went to Europe only to be confirmed in their prejudices
and whose conduct while there confirmed the prejudices of Europeans. When men come together to discuss their differences
the result may be amicable agreement, criminal conspiracy, or
mere vituperation. Filene chose to ignore two of the three possibilities with an optimism that he would have disapproved
sharply in a business deal.

There is of course the possibility that he ignored nothing but
was assuming a calculated risk in the belief that the good results of increased American contact with Europe would out-
weigh the bad. If that were true, he adduced little evidence to
support the theory; the probability is that in this instance he
simply accepted the prevailing opinion without examining it too
closely.

This stands in sharp contrast with his attitude toward home
ownership by wage earners and salaried employees. There he
flatly rejected the prevailing opinion. He admitted that home
ownership encourages thrift and to that extent is valuable, but
he did not concede that this value outweighs, or even balances,
the irremovable disadvantages.

It has been almost forgotten that he attacked this problem
too. He accomplished little, for he soon perceived that it was too
vast for his resources; he could not hope to make even an effective demonstration against it, far less a frontal attack, so he laid
it aside.

His ideas on the subject are interesting however because they reveal Filene in the role of a conservative, in the exact sense of the word. Here was a value, thrift, attached to a policy in other respects destructive of values; the problem then was to conserve the value while eliminating the other features. The joker in the deck is the fact that the mobility of industry, as compared to the immobility of agriculture, requires a commensurate mobility on the part of industrial labor.

To encourage a wage earner to save part of what he earns is incontestably good, and the purchase of a home is one of the strongest persuasions to thrift. Filene accordingly worked on the idea of transferable equities. He envisaged a type of housing so nearly uniform that differences in unit cost would be slight and a titling system that would permit the exchange of an equity in a house at one place for an equity of equal, or nearly equal, size in a similar house in another place. Thus if a worker found it necessary to move, he could pack up his equity as easily as his household goods and carry it along.

The difficulties in the way of this scheme were so tremendous and so complex that Filene made no attempt to carry it far. It came into collision at once with accepted principles of the law of realty, with real-estate dealers, with the housing industry, with existing schemes of taxation, and worst of all with ancient habits of thought on the part of both employers and employees. In addition—and this was perhaps the consideration that really stopped Filene—the money required to try out such a scheme on a scale large enough to make it a real test would run into astronomical figures, far more than Filene had or could hope to collect.

At the same time the idea is interesting as showing the way his mind worked, and, even more important, the way it did not work. Here was a notion that bore the superficial aspect of an idea radical in the extreme but that on examination proves to be not radical, indeed, rather the reverse.

It challenges no single basic principle of the capitalistic sys-

tem. Indeed it carefully respects at least one of its cherished
superstitions, the one that makes lawyers give to land the designation of real property, as if all other forms of property were
illusory. Far from proposing abolition of private ownership of
land, it proposes to make such ownership more difficult to attack by enabling persons to hold land safely who, under present
conditions, must hold it precariously if at all.

Least of all is it open to the charge most frequently brought
against leftist notions, the charge of requiring conditions to
conform to a theory. To the contrary it requires our theory of
private property to conform to the fact. If we are to indulge in
any distinction between reality and illusion in property, then
the fact is that a 10-per-cent equity in a three-thousand-dollar
house is more illusory—in the sense that it is more likely to vanish suddenly and beyond recall—than three hundred dollars
in a savings bank or in a government bond. Filene's hope was to
make the worker's grip on his house firmer, more not less entitled to the designation of real property.

If this were done workers would have a stronger incentive to
become home owners, which is to say capitalists. True certain
risks would remain, but Filene felt no impulse to abolish all
risks. He was interested only in removing that one which, as he
saw it, was so grave that it threatened to drive by far the larger
part of the population into the ranks of landless men, genuine
and permanent proletarians.

As to the validity of this idea no conclusive judgment is possible, nor is any likely to be possible for a long time to come. To
prove or disprove it would require operations so extensive in
space, in time, and in capital investment that they are not likely
to be undertaken soon. But one point it illuminates with great
clarity. The man who originated it was a utopian without
doubt, but he differed from most utopians in that his vision of
the desirable society of the future was not static. He did not
yearn for a perfect and unalterable state of things; he believed
in an approximation of perfection, a continuous progress to-

ward a goal that he did not expect to attain. In his mind indeed the progression was the only attainable goal. Mankind in heaven is matter for the consideration of the next world; in this one, mankind advancing is the race in its highest attainable state.

This idea, so daring that even Filene had not the courage to try to do anything about it, conforms strictly to the basic principles of capitalism, yet to call it conservative would involve a flagrant disregard of the ordinary meaning of terms. To the average mind radical describes anything diverging from the commonly accepted point of view, but in that sense the policy of simply facing the facts is more radical than anything the wildest Communist has ever proposed. For there is no greater crime in a Communist state than to accept a fact that is inconsistent with the party line. It is as flagitious as it is in reactionary American circles to accept a fact inconsistent with the dicta of Adam Smith or with the Republican platform of 1896.

It is characteristic of all the operations of Edward A. Filene that they were based on no party line whatsoever, unless indeed one chooses to call by that name a very old doctrine indeed. "Whenever any form of Government becomes destructive of" the rights of life, liberty, and the pursuit of happiness "it is the Right of the People to alter or to abolish it, and to institute new Government, laying its foundation on such principles and organizing its powers in such form, as to them seem most likely to effect their Safety and Happiness." Under government Filene would have included not merely political institutions, but all those constraints under which men must live in an orderly society. This perhaps is radicalism in its purest form, for to have no more respect for a rule of escheats that is plainly obsolete than for an electric light bulb that is burned out is regarded by certain types of mind as heretical, sacrilegious, and blasphemous, though why, no philosopher has ever been able to explain.

It is a point that must be borne in mind however if one is to understand Filene's method of handling any problem. He was, as has been pointed out repeatedly, no mystic. Perhaps he had never heard of the distinction between noumenon and phenomenon, and if he had he wasn't interested, but he did hold firmly to the belief that there is such a thing as objective truth, at least as regards the ordinary affairs of mundane existence, and he believed that by the employment of reason it was possible for men to approach if not to attain it. He admitted no obligation to respect anything that stood in the way of this approach, whether a principle of the law of realty going back to Domesday Book or a decree of some church council respecting the Substance of the Persons, or a deliverance of Karl Marx in *Das Kapital.* His first principle as a technician was to approach his problem with an open mind. If that is, as not a few of us seem to think, radicalism, then without doubt he was more radical than Stalin even though the aim of his work was to brace and strengthen capitalism.

III

That the open-minded approach is the most effective possible is decidedly questionable, but it is the liberal approach. Nevertheless it constantly involved Filene in disputes with men who were as sincere as he was and who had no doubt whatever that they were liberals. These disputes in turn contributed largely to the current belief that he could get along with nobody, and he always defeated his own ends by his intransigent attitude.

A case in point is the history of the credit-union movement. There is a vague impression in many minds that Edward A. Filene invented this idea, promoted it for a while, and then quarreled with his associates and let them take it away from him, and his critics frequently cite it as typical of Filene's inept and blundering way of handling things.

There is a half-truth in this that will be examined in a later section on Filene's weakness as a technician, but the whole truth puts the project in a very different light.

In the first place Filene never claimed, suggested, or even hinted that he invented the credit union. It has already been explained how it first came to his attention in India, but it wasn't invented there. The Indian credit union was a British adaptation of a German idea that goes back at least as far as 1848 when Friedrich Wilhelm Raiffeisen adapted, in his turn, an idea evolved by Hermann Schulze-Delitesch. Seven years before Filene visited India, the idea—but once more adapted to local conditions—had been brought to North America by Alphonse Desjardins, a Canadian cleric, who set up the first credit union in Quebec in 1900. It was simply one of those good ideas lying loose around the world, which Filene insisted could make this earth a heaven if they were all adopted.

But the credit union like any other form of banking is capable of many very different uses and may be organized in many different forms, yet, as in the construction of tribal lays, "every single one of them is right" if it serves efficiently the most important need of its community.

For instance, the Raiffeisen banks in Germany were organized with the primary purpose of inculcating thrift in classes of the German population that in 1848 were conspicuously thriftless. In India, on the other hand, the desperate poverty of the villagers had already imposed on them a thriftiness unknown and almost unimaginable to Europeans; the need there was for some means of escape from the grip of moneylenders who charged extortionate interest rates. Desjardins in Canada dealt with a population thrifty enough but brought to a low economic level by an unusual exposure to the vagaries of nature on account of the rugged climate and the short growing season. The Raiffeisen banks accordingly differed in organization from the Indian credit unions, while the Canadian organizations were not exact imitations of either.

In the United States Filene realized that credit unions must be prepared to deal with all these problems and yet another peculiar to this country. The United States is not a tight homogeneous nation comparable to Germany or French Canada, not an empire comparable to British India. It is continental in extent, with climates ranging from subarctic to subtropic and with people of every type under heaven. Conditions vary as widely as climate, so the type of credit union admirably adapted to one section may be very much less efficient in another. Among industrial workers, for example, loan sharks might be the most serious menace while in some rural areas crop failure was the great foe. Wastefulness is characteristic of the over-all picture, but there are fairly large communities in the United States as thrifty as any in Europe. Obviously then a credit-union program adapted to the United States must have, first of all, flexibility.

However, there is—or at least Filene thought there was—a function for credit unions to perform in this country that has an importance not attaching to it in any other. That is the function of teaching people with little money the rudiments of financial practice. It is important here because of the fluidity of American economic strata. Nowhere else do so many people move so rapidly from one level to another. Nowhere else does the commercial banking system directly affect so large a proportion of the population. In Europe a peasant may live long and prosper without ever having occasion to handle a bank check; but only in the remotest corners of the United States will you find an American of mature age who has never been paid by check for something at some time.

It follows that at least a slight acquaintance with banking practice is more important to a poor American than to a poor man in any other country. He needs it for his own protection, for no matter how small his transactions, they are pretty sure to involve him with banks in some capacity. He needs it also to enable him to make use of opportunity if it comes, and it comes more frequently to the poor American than to the poor man elsewhere.

In a credit union operated by its members, as the smaller ones usually are—and as all were in the beginning—everyone is compelled to learn something about banking. The members of the committee, who pass on applications for loans and who bear the prime responsibility for collections, of necessity learn what one of the greatest of American bankers, the elder J. Pierpont Morgan, called the most important qualification of a good financier, the ability to judge character. Everyone learns that the very mudsill of the whole credit system is the willingness of the average man to pay what he owes. To teach this to the millions who have little personal contact with bankers and who have never heard of an economist seemed to Filene one of the most important functions of the credit union.

Not at the beginning, perhaps, but before the project had been long under way, he perceived another possibility in co-operative banking. He thought that it might furnish a lubricant to the credit system at the point where its working is stiffest and most laborious, that is to say at the bottom of the economic scale. Every businessman undersands the tremendous importance of a smoothly operating system of finance on the upper levels of business. If the country were restricted to specie payments or payments in currency in all transactions, business would stall within twenty-four hours, and the national economy would be a wreck. All the coin and currency in the United States would be ridiculously inadequate for the payments that are made in an ordinary business day. All but a negligible part of the burden is carried not by money the government turns out but by private paper drawn on banks—checks, drafts, notes, bills of exchange, and so on—which is to say by credit in one form or another.

That is perfectly clear to everyone as it applies to transportation, industry, and commerce in the large. No railroad could operate, no factory could produce, no big department store could do business if the smooth flow of credit suddenly dried up. When it dries up even in part we have an 1873, an 1893, a 1929, years that businessmen recall with shudders and goose flesh.

But it is by no means as clear to everyone that when a million little men need fifty dollars each and can't get it the effect upon the national economy may be much more serious than when a railroad or a steel company needs fifty million dollars and can't get it. Filene with his towering respect for statistics did see it, and he saw in credit unions a means of oiling the economic machinery where it is too often neglected.

These points must be borne in mind if one is to understand the line he took in promoting the credit-union movement. It was an operation highly characteristic of the man, exhibiting both the strength and the weakness of his technical methods as well as his basic philosophy.

As his critics tell it, the story has a maliciously beautiful simplicity. Filene, they say, with the help of public-spirited citizens of Massachusetts, including Felix Vorenberg, Boston merchant, Howard Coonley, Judge A. K. Cohen, Henry S. Dennison, and others, started the credit-union movement, became more and more interested, brought in R. F. Bergengren to help him, and saw it wax mightily. But when Bergengren began to receive widespread public acclaim, Filene grew jealous, fought with Bergengren, was beaten, and withdrew sulking, leaving his associate triumphant on the field.

There is this much truth in it: Filene did start the movement. He did bring in Bergengren. He did fight with him twice. He was beaten once. Bergengren did remain the most powerful influence in the movement while Filene concerned himself with other affairs.

But these indisputable facts do not carry the connotation that some of Filene's critics have put upon them. At the outset Filene found that permissive legislation would be required from the legislature of Massachusetts before credit unions could be set up in the state, because they are a form of banking, and banking was closely regulated. So he first brought down Desjardins from Canada to an important conference with Bank Commissioner Pierre Jay, to give practical advice to his lawyers in drafting the bill and also to appear at hearings before the legislative committee involved. There is no doubt that the Canadian had much to do with framing the legislation and with getting it passed. Filene, far from denying it, advertised the fact that Desjardins had been brought to Massachusetts for that purpose, because his experience in Quebec had made him the best available authority on the subject.

But no idea of this sort ever propagated itself. A man must be found to devote his whole time or the greater part of it to the movement if it is to have any chance of success. Filene found the man in a young lawyer who had attracted his attention when the man was finance commissioner of Lynn. Roy Frederick Bergengren was a large dogged Scandinavian, born at Gloucester and a product of Dartmouth and the Harvard Law School. In handling the fiscal affairs of Lynn and as a member of the Massachusetts Constitutional Convention in 1917 and 1918, he had demonstrated a willingness to allow precedent to yield to fact that persuaded Filene of his ability to examine a new idea without hobbling prejudice—the type of man needed to handle anything as relatively new as credit unions.

Accordingly he employed Bergengren at his own expense to devote his time to the work. The quality of his judgment is illuminated by the simple statement that five years before Filene's death and little more than a dozen years after Bergengren started to work there were 2,200 credit unions in the United States doing a business of $65,000,000 a year.

They fought. The fact is undeniable, and in the two big battles it was no wrist-slapping match either but an all-out combat in which anything went; Filene won the first time, but Bergengren took the return match, and shortly after it Filene did turn his attention to other affairs, practically to the exclusion of the credit-union movement.

But the important point is that in neither case was the quarrel over any petty question of personal credit but over a real divergence of opinion on an important matter of policy.

In the first instance Bergengren wished to carry forward the movement on the national level by means of federal legislation. Filene opposed this, preferring to proceed state by state. Each could bring sound arguments to support his point of view, and each did. Neither convinced the other, but Filene won for the time being, which was what he wanted. In the end federal legislation was enacted but not until the movement was thoroughly established, by which time Filene's objections were largely invalidated.

Bergengren argued that a movement of this kind, to have any appreciable effect, must be widespread. To proceed through forty-eight separate legislative bodies with the possibility of a long battle in each seemed to him an inexcusable waste of time when Congress by one statute could give the credit unions power to operate as effectively as by one statute it had empowered the national banks.

Filene felt that the tremendous diversity of America was the dominant factor in the situation. The needs of a community of farmers in central Maine are not the same as the needs of a community of shrimp fishermen in Louisiana, and even more widely different are their attitudes, habits, and prejudices, while a community of factory workers in Fall River, Massachusetts, differs from both. Filene did not believe that enough was known about these diverse situations to serve as a basis for drafting a national law sure to be adequate in all cases. He did not think that the facts were known, and above all things he opposed acting without first finding the facts. His view prevailed but not without a resounding battle.

The second collision came some years later after the crash

of 1929 had precipitated the country into the Great Depression. Then Filene's mind turned to the possibility of using credit unions to lubricate the economic machinery. Hoover was President and the Reconstruction Finance Corporation was madly pumping money and credit into banks, railroads, and large corporations. Why not, asked Filene, pump some into the bottom of the system? True credit unions were primarily a means of self-help, but in times when the House of Morgan couldn't help itself, why expect people at the bottom of the economic scale to do so? He favored asking the Reconstruction Finance Corporation to put up a hundred million dollars as capital for credit unions to restore purchasing power down where it was worst needed.

Bergengren couldn't see it. To him it meant destroying the vital principle of the whole movement by converting a community enterprise into an agency of the government. To teach people how to help themselves was more important by far in times of depression than at any other time. His view prevailed, but again it was not without a resounding battle.

In the occasion of these wars it is hard to see anything discreditable to either combatant. Possibly they fought more savagely than was strictly necessary, and Filene in particular may have been more waspish than just. But any opinion worth fighting for is worth fighting for as hard as one can.

> Beware
> Of entrance to a quarrel, but, being in,
> Bear't that the opposed may beware of thee,

has ever been regarded as sound advice and he who follows it is a sensible man. In any event, Filene's last word on the subject, spoken when the battles had been over for years, was, "Give Bergengren full credit for doing a wonderful piece of work. He is a first-rate man. He has done a remarkable job." It may be, of course, that the speaker felt that the most re-

markable of Bergengren's feats was whipping Edward A. Filene in a straight-out fight, but the lingering vindictiveness of
which critics have talked is not in evidence here.

IV

The somewhat detailed account of the credit-union movement and its attendant commotions just given might, if passed
without further comment, mislead the reader into believing
that Bergengren was the only, or at least the most formidable,
foe with whom Edward A. Filene strove. Nothing could be
further from the truth; one is tempted indeed to indulge in the
exaggeration of saying that like some medieval knight posted
before a bridge he fought everybody who came along. It was
not that bad, but his career was liberally illuminated with fire-
works, sometimes very spectacular indeed.

The credit-union project was singled out for examination in
part because it was an important one but in part because it illustrates with notable clarity how Filene went about applying
his ideas. This project exhibits both his weakness and his
strength, his faults as well as his virtues. Not once but over and
over again he expressed his conviction that to analyze his
errors is the chief justification of a biography of a businessman,
for young men, by reading the analysis, may avoid some of
the errors.

This was not in the least an endorsement of scandalmonger-
ing. He had in mind the errors that defeat a man's effort to
accomplish his purpose, not mere infractions of propriety or
even of the moral law unless these infractions impeded or defeated the effort. Of course if the subject, like Jim Fiske and
Stanford White, got himself shot in a quarrel over a woman,
his amorous adventures must necessarily play a large part in
the narrative, but otherwise they are of interest only to seekers
of vicarious thrills, not to serious students.

It may be noted in passing that there was very little that the
most assiduous scandalmonger could do with Filene anyhow,

He was no ascetic. He had a certain appreciation of good wines and a rather startling devotion to terrible cigars. In Europe once he ran across a dreadful object, a cigar made up in the shape of a pipe, and was so delighted with it that he not only brought a great quantity back but would not rest until he had persuaded an American cigarmaker to turn them out in this country. He called them "cigapipes" and one of the perils of association with Filene was the risk of having him thrust one of the fearsome things upon one and being compelled to smoke it.

He lived simply and could not understand the passion for ostentation characterisic of the *nouveaux riches*. It annoyed him not merely because he considered it silly but because he regarded it as a wanton and inexcusable exacerbation of social conflict. He never forgot the conduct of a Lynn millowner whose workers struck when Filene was a very young man. Production had been paralyzed for two months, but negotiators got together, and the affair was almost settled when this fool chose to drive down to the plant in a brand-new carriage drawn by four horses and with an extra footman on the box. Somebody hurled a stone, there was an explosion of rioting, and the strike dragged on for many additional weeks to the distress of the whole community.

"Flaunting a red flag in the face of a bull," snorted Filene disgustedly.

Nevertheless, he did not hesitate to gratify his own tastes, and if he lived rather simply, it was because his tastes were simple. He liked good clothes, good food, and a comfortable habitation. If he smoked bad cigars, it was because he liked them, and he scorned to switch to Havana for no better reason than that every other millionaire in Boston bought Cuban tobacco. Yet in general his nonconformity was confined to ideas. In matters to which he was indifferent—which included most of the social conventions—he went along with the crowd contentedly enough.

His relations with women had only a negative effect upon his career, always excepting the strong influence exerted by his mother, which was exercised so quietly that the biographer can be certain of nothing except that it was there. His celibacy of course was a factor of great importance in making him the kind of man he was, but this was a negative influence. There was no doubt whatever of his masculinity, and his relations with various women became close enough to give rise to cynical speculation, but his affairs, if he had any, were conducted so discreetly that scandal never found a real weapon to use against him.

The personal fault with which critics charged him most loudly and confidently was vanity, and the charges cannot be dismissed with a flat denial. Vanity unquestionably did seep into the picture, especially in later years, and it is probable that it sometimes interfered with efficient accomplishment of his purpose. It is therefore the kind of error that he thought should be analyzed in any book claiming to deal with his career.

It was not of course the vanity of a popinjay. Nothing bored him more dreadfully than the flashy sophistication that small and ill-trained minds mistake for distinction. He liked to be recognized but not by headwaiters;* he wished to be mentioned in print but not by gossip columnists; he coveted applause but not that of chorus girls and playboys. It gave him unaffected delight to appear in public with a prime minister, but he had no taste for going about with persons whose prominence was based on notoriety not fame. He might indeed converse long and pleasantly with a prizefighter or a professional buffoon if the man were the best in his line, but that was because of his conviction that the man who is the best of his kind,

---

* Perhaps this statement ought to be slightly modified by the admission that if it were the headwaiter at the Waldorf in New York, the Savoy in London, the Meurice in Paris, or the Adlon in Berlin, that is to say at some place frequented by statesmen and men of large affairs, rather than by café society, a bit of obsequious attention was by no means displeasing to Filene. But is it to any man who will be candid about it?

whether the best brickmason, or the best cotton picker, or the best croupier that ever spun a roulette wheel, always has something to teach a wise man.

In other words, if he had a touch of snobbery, it was intellectual snobbery not the attitude of the cheap-jack who is happy to be the subject of the gabble of fools. To be talked about by persons with some claim to intelligence did please him, perhaps too much, and there may have been times when he indulged that taste to the detriment of his work, but certainly that was not his heaviest handicap in life, and its total effect on his career was probably negligible.

There is little doubt however that it had something to do with Filene's one conspicuous personal extravagance. He who looked with withering scorn on establishments with platoons of liveried flunkies, with first, second, and third chauffeurs, with hierarchies of butlers, housekeepers, footmen, and parlormaids, hired personal attendants of a different type lavishly. These were assistants to work on the various projects that engaged his attention. They were not servants; on the contrary they were carefully chosen for native intelligence and the highest intellectual training attainable, but for all that they were personal attendants, and it gave Filene a serene and high content to have a large number of exceptionally competent men and women at his beck and call.

When the psychological explosion in the store occurred in 1928 one thing for which he battled to the end and which he won was a clause in the contract providing that his personal office staff should not be reduced in number, should be under his exclusive control, and should be paid at least as much as the secretaries, stenographers, and assistants of the other executives. In view of the fact that his antagonists were resolved that none of the important business of the store should go through that office, they raged against this provision, but Filene clung to it with a grim determination that shattered all assaults, and in the end it was so ordered.

Bergengren, Lincoln Steffens, and others were in a different classification. They were employed to do specific jobs and worked more or less independently, but Filene liked to have around him men of ability who could take up any sort of idea that might occur to him, develop it, analyze it, criticize it, and give him an intelligent opinion. Glenn Frank, Ernest M. Hopkins, Charles Merz, Wheeler Sammons, Robert L. Moore, Curtice Hitchcock, and Percy S. Brown were among those who served in this capacity at one time or another—an astonishing list to have served one man and he no statesman, public official, or university president, but merely a businessman in private life.

Among them the most successful in maintaining good relations with his employer was Brown, who remained with Filene a dozen years, but he was an executive and a specialist in personnel problems of long experience before he joined Filene. Next to Brown, the assistant who lasted longest was Charles W. Wood, who never troubled to maintain good personal relations with his employer but who remained in his service on a week-to-week basis, quarreling constantly, for ten years.

Wood was a seasoned and sardonic newspaperman whom Steffens recommended to write a life of Filene while he was still living. It was not to be a ghostwritten autobiography but Wood's own book, yet, since it could not possibly be lucrative, Filene was to finance it. Wood was so skeptical of the whole business that he refused a lump sum for a completed manuscript; instead he demanded a weekly wage so that when Filene lost his temper and fired his biographer, an event that Wood confidently expected within a few weeks, the account would be squared. On those terms he removed from New York to Boston and went to work.

Trouble did develop but not precisely as he had expected. Filene discovered that he had an alert intelligence, an old newspaperman's tremendous fund of general information, and a lucid and graceful English style, therefore he constantly interrupted work on the biography to put Wood on some other job that called for his special talent. Wood protested, but Filene pointed out that he was being paid by the week, so if the book were delayed the loss would be Filene's not his. This was true, so Wood spent several months closely associated with Filene but doing everything in the world except write a book. Then Filene suddenly announced that he was sailing for Europe in three weeks and wanted to see a good part of the manuscript before he left.

Wood picked up his hat and a portable typewriter and fled to a beach cottage, leaving no address. There, free from interruption he turned out half a dozen chapters of the proposed biography. Later he admitted that he never intended to publish what he wrote because, while it was true enough, it lacked any sort of proportion. What he meant to do was to end an intolerable situation, but on that he was grimly determined.

Filene had told him so often that he was weary of hearing it that he expected the book to be completely candid. He declared that he wanted the truth, so Wood let him have it—not the whole truth but the truth about his temperamental handicaps. It was an effort to explain Filene to himself, not to the rest of the world, so it deliberately omitted all that Filene understood perfectly and concentrated on those things that in Wood's opinion he did not know. It was an extraordinary piece of work —shrewdly aimed, brilliantly written, and utterly ruthless. Then Wood, a man of reckless courage, returned to Boston, sat with Filene and Lillian Schoedler, his secretary, in the library at Otis Place, and read it aloud to them. He finished about midnight and left the house intending to start next morning looking for another job.

But he received no notice of dismissal the next day or for a couple of days thereafter, and then he got a telephone call, not from Filene, but from his physician.

"What the hell did you do to E.A?" demanded the doctor wrathfully.

"I?" asked Wood nonplussed. "Nothing. Why, I haven't seen him for three days."

"I know you haven't," returned the doctor unappeased. "He's been in bed, and you put him there. Now you go to see him at once and straighten this out, or I won't answer for the consequences."

So Wood, somewhat subdued but still resolute, called. He informed his victim that if he wrote without mercy he also wrote without malice, and if Mr. Filene did not care to go ahead with the book, neither did he, and they could part then and there with no ill feeling as far as he was concerned. Filene said no, he did not wish to go on with the book, but as for parting, there were other things on which he could use Wood, so he would put him on a yearly salary with a three-year contract if he wished. Not at all, said Wood. He was willing to work for Filene but not on any contractual basis. He would draw his week's wages every Saturday night, so that at the end of any week he could quit, or Filene could discharge him without prejudice. In the end it was so arranged.

"And how long did you stay on that basis?" Wood was asked.

"Ten years," was his reply. (Actually it was a little less.)

Considering the temperaments of the two men, it was probably the only basis on which the connection could have lasted so long. But as matters stood, it worked admirably. Wood was purely and simply the craftsman with no ax of his own to grind. Indifferent to the idea, he was concerned only with its lucid and exact expression, and within a year or two he knew Filene's mind so thoroughly that he required little instruction. Given a subject in any of the old familiar fields, he knew what Filene would say as well as Filene did, and Wood knew how to say it better than Filene could. Naturally scornful critics said, and no doubt some believed, that Wood was the brains of the combination and Filene merely the mouthpiece, but ten years after Filene's death Wood himself was strenuously denying this suggestion. He was not, he said, a ghost writer; he was exactly what he purported to be, a literary assistant.

In any event the Wood episode illustrates Filene's technique. He valued competent assistance and to secure it he was willing to pay in more than money; he would retain in his employ a man who trampled heavily on his own vanity if the fellow knew his job. He had a healthy respect, too, for a man who would stand up and fight if the fight were based on something more than mere pique. He battled with both Bergengren and Wood, but he held them. He had his petty side, but he was big enough not to permit it to deflect him from his purpose.

On the other hand the same episode illustrates his technical weakness. It was an intensity of concentration on the idea at the moment uppermost in his mind that blinded him temporarily to other considerations of equal or greater weight. It is an ironical circumstance that this is a weakness he was fond of denouncing in others. Failure to consider the problem as a whole is, he knew, a common and serious failure of leadership, and his warnings against it were innumerable.

He had a favorite metaphor that he used in this connection. Solving any social problem, he said, is like lifting the sunfish, which must be boosted up all at once or it will come apart. His associates assumed that he meant the jellyfish, as perhaps he did, but he invariably said "sunfish," and it became an office joke. However there is a marine creature called the giant sunfish (*Orthagoriscus mola*), almost as broad as it is long, sometimes attaining a dimension of ten feet and weighing a ton, which fishermen find difficult to handle. It may be that Filene had run across a reference to this somewhere and knew what he was talking about.

In any event, he was always doing what he warned others against attempting, to wit, undertaking to lift the sunfish—or jellyfish—by gripping it at one point. He employed Wood to write a book, a hoisting job requiring care and, above all, the nicest sense of balance, yet he was constantly calling Wood off that job to attend to some detail. He forgot the whole problem in his intense preoccupation with some aspect of it—lifting the sunfish by one side.

As a leader he was technically deficient also in his power of exposition. To some extent he corrected this by his employment of literary assistants, but it was nevertheless a handicap. Everyone who worked with him agrees on the extreme difficulty of getting a coherent explanation from Edward A. Filene. This was strikingly apparent if an interruption, such as a telephone call, occurred in the course of the explanation. Filene would begin to outline an idea, then stop to answer the telephone, yet while he talked perfectly rationally into the instrument, some other part of his mind seemed to continue to work on the idea. So that when he hung up the telephone, he would resume his explanation not where he left off but five minutes beyond that point and be irritated when his hearer claimed that there was a break in the argument.

The more intelligent the man, the more it exasperated him to be suspected of stupidity when the truth was that he had not been given the necessary information. This is certainly one reason and perhaps the chief reason why so many brilliant men quit Filene's service filled with indignation and perplexity.

He was weak also in another point at which he insisted upon the duty of a leader to be strong. There were some facts that he, the insistent fact finder, would not face; one was the Preacher's chilling observation upon the sons of men, "Time and chance happeneth to them all." Filene did not want to grow old and never would admit the fact of age.

Perhaps there is more excuse for him than there is for most of us because mentally he did not grow old. The process of intellectual growth continued in him to the end, and when his physical frame began to lose the suppleness that his mind retained, he resented it with a bitterness that unquestionably clouded his judgment. His last expedition to Europe is a case in point. Two years earlier in 1935, he had been seriously ill in

Moscow. The malady was pneumonia, next to heart disease the greatest remover of people who have passed seventy. He had never entirely recovered from the effects, yet when he returned to Europe, nothing would do but he must go scrambling up into the high Alps to bag a chamois. He got his game all right and triumphantly had himself photographed with his Alpine guide, the chamois lying at their feet. But he came down more tired than a man of nearly seventy-seven should allow himself to become. He proceeded to Paris still decidedly under par, and then, instead of taking the boat train, decided to drive to Le Havre in an open car although it was September and the weather was gloomy. He didn't make it. He was taken ill on the trip, had to return to Paris, and died there on September 26.

Incidentally it was his secretary's car not his. He never owned an automobile except the one that he and Lincoln bought for their mother—incidentally, with a spat over which of the brothers should pay for it. When this car was purchased, Mrs. Filene was frankly getting old, and the automobile was purchased to enable her to take the air with less strenuous exertion than walking. She lived for many years, and her chief pleasure came to be having herself driven about in the afternoons.

Some of his associates hold that Filene's curious refusal to buy a car of his own is explained by his dislike of ostentation, which in this instance betrayed him into being ostentatiously simple, but others hold that it was a subtler thing—that the business of supplying a car to his mother set up in his mind some association between automobiles and aged persons. He did not object to riding in them, even when they were much more unreliable than they later became; his trip across India in 1907 is evidence that he was not at all afraid of them, and he used taxis and hired cars as readily as anyone else. But he may have had an obscure feeling that to own a car would be an admission that he was growing old since that was true in the case of his mother, and he would make no such admission. In any event he died without a car.

Finally his technical efficiency as a leader unquestionably was reduced by the way in which to the very end of his life the petty-minded seller of pins would obtrude his curious psychology upon the philosopher and social statesman. Edward A. Filene, the philanthropist, the great liberal, the millionaire who followed quite literally the scriptural injunction, "Sell what thou hast and give to the poor," was capable of acts of startling meanness.

The bewildering factor in this is that such exhibitions invariably involved some triviality. When Ward held him up for twenty-five thousand dollars for the League to Enforce Peace, he grimaced but submitted with reasonably good humor, but he actually broke up a theater party one night and called the whole thing off because a ticket scalper tried to charge him twenty-five cents more than the customary exaction. He knew that tickets bought from a scalper were usually half a dollar higher than at the box office, and he was willing to pay that, but when the fellow demanded seventy-five cents, he sent his guests home rather than pay.

His office assistants were dismally well aware that getting a five-dollar raise out of Edward A. Filene was like drawing eye-teeth; yet he offered to pay Edouard Herriot ten thousand dollars a year for two years, while he did nothing except learn English, if Herriot would come to America to assist him with his various projects.

Incidentally, this incident gave Filene one of his most treasured souvenirs. In the midst of the Long Armistice during the endless dreary battle over German reparations, he encountered Herriot at a moment when the French statesman was in a particularly black mood. All his life's work had gone for nothing, said the Frenchman bleakly. He had been defeated in the Chamber of Deputies; he had no more influence on the course of events, and France seemed to be worse off, not better, for all his efforts. He was ready to quit and thought seriously of emigrating to the United States.

Promptly Filene made his offer, and momentarily Herriot hesitated, but then he decided somewhat ruefully that he couldn't quit; it would be tantamount to desertion under fire. Come what might, his place was in France, and there he would live out his days. But he was grateful for the offer and somewhat later, when the talk was ended and he rose to go, he drew out one of his official visiting cards and under the embossed line, "Herriot, Mayor of Lyons" he smilingly wrote, "head employee of Mr. Edward A. Filene."

The most startling of all his picayune affairs, though, occurred in connection with Filene's Moscow illness in 1935. One American and half a dozen Russian doctors recognized it as a particularly virulent type of pneumonia, and they agreed that the best man on that type was Meyer of Berlin. Filene was too far gone to be consulted, but Lillian Schoedler, his secretary, laid siege to William C. Bullitt, American ambassador to Russia, who urged the case upon the Soviet government. After much frantic telephoning and arranging of visas, Dr. Meyer was flown to Moscow, took over the case, stayed ten days, and left his assistant until Filene could be moved. Later he presented a bill that Filene considered exorbitant and a long undignified squabble ensued before the matter was settled.

What possessed Filene to contest this bill no one has ever been able to explain. To a man who had already given away millions the amount could not have been of primary importance. The most plausible theory is that this bill touched off associations as disagreeable as those connected with his mother's automobile. Perhaps its payment would have seemed somehow an admission of frailty, a confession that he had been very ill with an old man's disease, and an acknowledgment that time was having its way with him as it does with all men.

Whatever the reason he pursued a course that embarrassed his friends and highly diverted his enemies. The damage to his influence among those who knew the facts far exceeded the amount of the bill. Once more he was guilty of the most serious fault that characterized his method as a leader of liberalism; once more he had made a weapon for the enemy.

V

The culmination of Filene's public activities was the establishment of the Twentieth Century Fund to which he gave the bulk of his fortune and later of the Good Will Fund, subsequently the Edward A. Filene Good Will Fund, to which he bequeathed the rest except for minor bequests to relatives and close associates.

It is a reasonable assumption therefore that these two foundations are the fruition of his thought and activity as a social technician, and examination of them should go far toward determining their founder's place in the pattern of social and economic development in the United States.

If the foundations are truly representative of their founder, the first impression one receives from them is of the kinetic nature of his thought. In the years since his death, both have changed, were expected to change, and will change still further. As was remarked in an earlier section, Filene dreamed of Utopia but not of a static Utopia. He was willing to believe that the wisdom and integrity of future generations would at least equal our own, and he acted on that belief.

Many persons, honestly bewildered by inconclusive reports and conflicting theories concerning these institutions, have demanded, sometimes petulantly, "But what did Filene expect of these foundations? What are they supposed to *do*?"

The answer, in a word, is nothing. But to answer in a word is merely to increase the bewilderment not to dissipate it. A rather more comprehensible if still inadequate answer is that the foundations are not expected or empowered to act, as, for instance, by trying to influence legislation, but by investigation to determine what course of action seems to be most promising and to make that knowledge available to those who may be counted on to act.

Filene came to maturity in a world of such activity as has rarely been matched in human history. The tremendous—in some ways the terrific—expansion of the United States between the Civil War and the First World War was a social, political, and economic phenomenon without precedent and so far without parallel. It was a triumphal march of men of action, the conquerors of a continental wilderness, the brisk challengers of time and space, the shatterers of precedent. The men who built this country after 1865, the railroad-track layers, the telegraph-wire stringers, the industrialists, stockmen, agriculturists who converted a desert into an empire, who marched from sea to sea to "strew bright, bitter cities down the west," were the greatest dust raisers and noisemakers the human race has as yet produced.

Filene was a part of it, and as a young man he exulted in it, but as he matured he became more and more firmly convinced that in all this action there was too much bustle, too much blunder, too many avoidable errors and accidents that could have been foreseen, too much rule of thumb, and too little careful calculation. Energy he valued, but energy expended without purpose he perceived clearly was waste. The demolition of a fine building to make room for a finer was only in part progress; the demolition represented loss, justifiable only if the finer building could have been provided in no other way.

The older he grew, the less inclined he was to rejoice in the triumphs of our civilization and the more inclined to deplore its collisions, retractions, withdrawals, all its multitudinous mistakes. To retrieve one's errors is excellent, but it is better not to err in the first place, yet one can hope to avoid error only by taking thought before acting.

But action, ever larger, ever more sweeping, ever more triumphant action was the ideal of Filene's generation. A thousand men could be found ready to act for one who was willing to think long and carefully about what line action should take. It seemed to Filene therefore that the best contribution he could make to his time was not to add to the bedlam of action but to consider.

This may cause some lifting of the eyebrows among those who remember the almost demonaic energy with which he drove his associates, calling for action, action, and still more action. But it is not a contradiction. The action he called for was usually experimental, and experimental action is a form of consideration. Definitive action he approached warily indeed, and perpetuities, he was quite certain, were always illusions and commonly nonsense. That is why he provided for the eventual distribution of the assets of his own foundations.

Here is in fact the crux of Filene's career, as far as that career has social as distinguished from purely personal and local significance. He was a product of the age of American empire builders, and within his strictly limited field he was one of them. To be sure, William Filene's Sons Company, as a business enterprise, was not to be compared with the transcontinental railroad systems, with the oil trust, the steel trust, the tobacco trust, with the colossal banks, or with the giant automobile companies. Nevertheless, it represented the conversion of a very small enterprise into one of impressive proportions, in which respect it was typical of the age of expansion. Great fortunes accumulate at an accelerating pace. The first million is the hardest, and after the first ten millions a huge fortune can be piled up with astonishing speed—or could before the era of war taxation—by a man who really puts his mind to it. Filene accumulated something between ten and twenty millions, yet for the last twenty-five years of his life he was not primarily interested in making money. There is no reason to doubt that, if he had really bent all his energies to it, within that final quarter century he might have made several times as much as he made in his earlier years, for that is the history of all the vast fortunes of America.

Thus, in view of the relatively early date at which he turned away from money-making, it is reasonable to assume that he was a much bigger businessman than a fortune of less than twenty millions would indicate. Granting that he was no such business genius as Rockefeller, Carnegie, or Ford, still he rates well up in the hierarchy of American business, high enough to be taken as fairly representative of the big men of the period of expansion. At least he could understand them, could appreciate their point of view and comprehend their habits of thought. Conversely they, or some of them, unquestionably shared some of Filene's ideas and subsequent events have proven that a considerable proportion of them have shared some of his anxieties. Filene therefore was more than a successful Boston shopkeeper. To some extent he was representative of one type of American businessman. No doubt he was an extreme example but an example nevertheless, and it is this that makes him worth the attention of the generation following his own.

Before he was fifty his pride in American accomplishment had been blanketed, if not extinguished, by his apprehension regarding American confusion. The collisions, the miscalculations, the cross-purposes, all the effects of the hit-or-miss method preyed upon his mind as something more and worse than the inevitable cost of progress.

There is no evidence that Filene ever paid much attention to mathematical physics, but for all that he had a firm grasp of the fact that the Second Law of Thermodynamics as stated by Eddington, "Randomness (i.e., disorganization) increases with the passage of time," is not quite a universal law. It has one exception, namely life. In a living organism, at least for the duration of its period of growth, organization not randomness increases with the passage of time.

If our social, political, and economic systems are manifestations of life they should exhibit the characteristics of life, one of which is an increase in functional organization. The opposite tendency is a manifestation not of life but of dissolution, whose end is death. Filene became convinced that in all these fields randomness is increasing. Every year the functional organization seemed to be proving less adequate to the demands made upon it. The great majority of businessmen, certainly the majority prior to 1929, assumed that these twinges and shocks were nothing more than growing pains; Filene was filled with an uneasy foreboding that they might be touches of *rigor mortis*.

In this of course he was at one with the Marxists. The difference was that they considered the condition inevitable and had no suggestion except that it be pushed to its logical conclusion with all possible speed, whereas he regarded it as nothing more than the effect of careless thinking, or rather careless lack of thought, which might be remedied by a readjustment of our ideas to conform to readjusted conditions. The first step in this process obviously was to determine exactly what readjustment conditions had undergone or, as he put it in a thousand speeches, articles, and verbal admonitions, "find the facts." The facts once found, he relied on common sense to dictate a readjustment of ideas.

Apparently it never occurred to him to doubt that he had a certain responsibility in the circumstances, and this was perhaps his most characteristically American trait. The predatory tendencies of his generation were so startling that they have almost monopolized attention, and the world has forgotten that a sense of social responsibility did germinate in the era of the exploiters. No doubt some of the rich men of Filene's day were piratical to the end and nothing else, but not all. The privately endowed American universities, the privately endowed hospitals, all the eleemosynary institutions created between 1865 and 1914 with the aid of private donations—a system unmatched for size and magnificence—are evidence that the successful American businessman, knowing that he belonged to the ruling class, was not disposed to deny that rulership entails responsibility. If his attempts to discharge that responsibility were sometimes fumbling, they were nevertheless sincere. It is unquestionably true that ethical standards in the administration of Grant, which is to say during Edward A. Filene's adolescence, touched their lowest ebb, which has encouraged radicals and some conservatives to denounce the leadership of that time as a set of moneygrubbers unrelieved by any sense of obligation to society at large. Yet it is true that when Filene was in middle life an American millionaire who was nothing but a moneygrubber was looked upon by his fellow millionaires as a low type.

Kirstein, for example, who disagreed with practically everything else that Filene believed in, agreed with him on this point. Kirstein's activities in support of charitable and educational programs were by no means pure benevolence, nor did he think they were. He admitted that it was his duty, as a rich man, to work for measures of social amelioration. It was the American way, and for an American millionaire to depart from it declassed him at once.

Hence the mere fact that Filene felt a certain compulsion to do something toward remedying social evils is not enough in itself to differentiate him sharply from other rich Americans of his generation. They all felt it, and most of them responded in one way or another. What gives him a distinctive place a little apart from the group of benefactors of colleges, hospitals, libraries, asylums, and other philanthropic institutions or programs is his philosophic slant. No man ever took more seriously Plato's dictum that "the unexamined life is not worth living." Let others provide for relief, physical and intellectual; he would undertake examination.

The results were much less than he had hoped. He provided for examination, all right, but humanity exhibited a perverse tendency to examine anything and everything except the main issue. He labored prodigiously to bring the businessmen of Boston together to examine the conditions that were hamper-

ing and damaging their city. He found the industrialists pulling against the merchants, and the real-estate men pulling
against both while none thought of the city as a whole, so he
played a large and enthusiastic part in organizing them all in
the Boston Chamber of Commerce. But the result was not always a careful exact study of civic problems. Too often it was
merely an orgy of logrolling, binding merchants, industrialists,
and real-estate men to pull together for the advantage of property interests, in complete disregard of social and cultural and
even of long-term economic values.

He had a similar experience with the United States Chamber of Commerce. One thing Filene confidently expected it to
do was to make a scientific examination of the actual effects of
the protective-tariff system in the expectation that the chamber
would then insist upon a more rational arrangement, but the
only phase of the examination that seemed to interest members was its revelation of means of making that system more
profitable to particular interests, even to the damage of the
national economy as a whole. Each of these organizations
proved to be a powerful engine but an engine of irrationality
rather than of reason. This is what led Brandeis to make his
comment about Filene's forging weapons for the enemy. It was
in part also the basis of Lenin's acidulous inquiry as to whether
Filene thought the workers were fools.

It was all confusing and discouraging to the last degree. If
Filene had been appealing to men on high and holy grounds,
he could have understood their lethargy. Selfishness, he felt
sure, is the prime mover in human affairs. If he had urged
them to act as a religious duty, or as an expression of brotherly
love, or out of respect for the Socratic concept of virtue, he
would have expected little. But he did not. He urged them to
take steps to assure the continuance and increase of their own
profit. When he found that men would refuse to act even in
defense of their purses, the whole foundation of his thinking
was shaken, but over and over again he had it hammered into

him that the vast majority of men do not understand in what direction the greatest attainable profit lies and prefer to secure a small immediate gain even if it means certain loss in the future rather than wait for a larger gain that may be secured with safety.

His experience naturally made him tremendously interested in the New Deal when that vast social and economic experiment was launched. The National Recovery Administration, in particular, aroused his enthusiasm. Here, at last, were the illimitable resources and the vast power required to lift the sunfish all at once, and his dampened enthusiasm flamed up again, flamed higher than it ever had before. True, the NRA represented an incomprehensibly great organization of capital with all the danger of monopolistic greed thereby implied, but did not the act creating it contain also the famous Clause Seven-A, the great charter of labor? Filene plunged into it with great enthusiasm, the greater because he had long been a friend and admirer of Hugh Johnson, the national administrator. He became head of the Massachusetts organization.

But it was a repetition of earlier experiences. He soon found that the NRA wasn't lifting the sunfish. It was a battlefield on which particular interests contended, each for its own advantage, regardless of what damage might be done to the country as a whole.

Filene was slow to accept the truth. Indeed he never admitted that the basic principle of the NRA was wrong. Its failure was undeniable even before the Supreme Court put an end to it on the ground of unconstitutionality, but Filene attributed that failure to faults of organization. The whole thing had been constructed so hastily that no proper adjustment of its parts had been made, and the great cumbrous machine pulled against itself. This was undoubtedly true. The Massachusetts organization, Filene always insisted, worked reasonably well and seemed to have a more than even chance of success until it was thrown into confusion by a series of incomprehensible

and sometimes contradictory orders—in the outlandish jargon
of the times called directives—from Washington. Yet the NRA
was based upon the theory that large numbers of men can be
persuaded to act reasonably, each in his own sphere, which is a
theory of doubtful validity.

The failure of the NRA did not, however, extinguish Filene's
interest in the New Deal as a whole. On the contrary as experiment followed experiment he grew more and more excited.
This is not to say that he accepted everything blindly. On
the contrary, there were many of those experiments that he
thought doomed from the start, and their collapse instead of
discouraging him merely verified his judgment. As a constant
experimenter himself, he was aware that most experiments are
doomed to failure, but the tenth one, which doesn't fail, jus-
tifies the nine that do. If it were not so, all scientific inquiry
would represent a net loss.

The very errors of the New Deal, it seemed to him, constituted additions to knowledge. To learn that a given theory
will not work is to know more than we knew before the experiment was tried, and the notion that the cost of the experimen-
ation was dangerously weakening the national economy he
dismissed with contempt—a judgment that the events of 1941
to 1945 abundantly sustained.

The four years of this adventure that he was permitted to
witness, although they were years of deep economic depression
and of hideous political turmoil, were therefore among the most
exciting and stimulating of his life. Age was creeping upon him,
and in 1935 illness all but finished him, yet it is probably true
that in these years Filene was happier than he had been since
his early youth.

For one thing he found himself accepted by the ruling powers. Few millionaires supported the New Deal, so those that
did were highly valued. Filene found himself thrust into the
forefront of the battle by the national administration. He who
had been accustomed to beg for a hearing was now begged to

speak up, to speak loudly, to speak incessantly. He did. He worked furiously and happily. Naturally he conceived an admiration for President Roosevelt that surpassed all bounds. Here was the statesman for whom Filene had looked in vain all his life. Here was a leader to whose chariot wheels he did not have to be bound, for he bound himself joyfully.

At the end of the campaign of 1936, intellectually the most spectacular presidential campaign in American history—for Willkie's dazzling foray of 1940 was more emotional than intellectual—on the night before election day there was a grand roundup on the radio in which every campaign figure of first-rate importance took his turn on the national network, with the President himself making a fifteen-minute speech at the end. On that memorable program the next to the last speaker, the one immediately before Roosevelt, was Edward A. Filene of Boston. It was the apex of his public career, and perhaps it was the happiest moment of his life.

Long before this high moment, however, Filene had accepted one bitter truth. Like Moses upon Mount Nebo, he had looked into the land of the future in full realization that it was not permitted him to enter it. What he had undertaken was more than he could perform, more than any one man could perform. To persuade men that it is as true in economics as it is in politics that governments derive their just powers from the consent of the governed and that the only stable government is one resting on the consent of the governed is a work calling for the efforts, not of one man, but of thousands, perhaps of generations. It took a thousand years to establish that as a political axiom in the minds of the English-speaking peoples; why hope to establish it as an economic axiom in a day or within one lifetime?

As early as 1919, in fact, Filene had realized that the problem he was struggling to solve would outlast him by many a long day. More than that, he was not even certain that he was going about it in the right way. He was conscious of his own sincerity but by no means so confident of his own wisdom, which incidentally should be sufficient answer to the charges that he was too arrogant ever to accomplish anything lasting.

He determined, therefore, to seek immediately the counsel of independent minds and to arrange matters so that eventually such minds would continue the work long after he had gone. To find people whose intelligence he respected and who, he felt, understood his objective was not easy. Filene had no difficulty in estimating a man's intelligence rapidly, but he had the utmost difficulty in explaining his own ideas, in part because they were in process of development and he did not know himself where they would lead. However, after some search he organized, on March 12, 1919, what he called the Co-operative League, associating with himself his brother, A. Lincoln Filene, Newton D. Baker, then secretary of war, and John H. Fahey, Boston newspaper publisher. He wished to include William H. Dunbar, lawyer, and Mrs. Elizabeth D. Peabody, but apparently they served only momentarily.

Three years later however on March 30, 1922, Dunbar did come in as Lincoln Filene went out. Henry S. Dennison, James G. McDonald, and Bruce O. Bliven were added. Finally on May 10, 1924, these were joined by Max Lowenthal and Roscoe Pound. On that date the name was changed to the Twentieth Century Fund, and it was incorporated.

To this organization, in 1919, Filene donated his common stock in William Filene's Sons Company by means of an irrevocable trust which was dissolved at his death. Later the stock was sold and the proceeds, amounting to some ten millions, became and remain the bulk of the endowment of the fund.

The board was self-perpetuating, and on it Filene had one vote. It was out of the question, therefore, for him to dictate the policy of the fund. In the beginning it did not even conduct studies of its own but used its money to encourage work already started in its field; later, the fund undertook its own studies, a policy that has been followed since.

After some years Filene's personal interest in the Twentieth Century Fund dwindled until during the last year or two of his life he paid little attention to it and concentrated on other things.

The same old story, said his enemies—he couldn't even retain control of his own foundation. As soon as his associates disagreed with his ideas, he fought them, and they proceeded to take his organization from him, leaving him to go out sulking.

As far as the Twentieth Century Fund is concerned, the one surviving member who was with it from the beginning offers flatly contradictory testimony.* He declares that right from the start the board took a completely independent attitude toward any suggestion that was advanced. If one of Filene's did not win the approval of a majority, the board voted it down without hesitation and without the slightest protest from the founder; he continued to give it his interest and attention for years after he had been voted down many times, and eighteen years after its organization he left it the bulk of his fortune.

This criticism was brought sharply to Filene's attention before his death, and his comment on it is interesting. He had helped organize many movements in his time, he said. The Boston City Club, "Boston 1915," the Boston Chamber of Commerce, the International Chamber of Commerce, the credit-union movement, the Twentieth Century Fund, the Good Will Fund covered a period of thirty-odd years. He had been influential in the organization of them all; in some he had practically dictated the form of organization. It would be singular if he had not learned, in all that time, what he wanted and how to frame the organization so that he would be assured of it. Yet from first to last everything with which he had to do had been organized on the same basis, a democratic basis. In other words, with every opportunity to do otherwise, he had invariably arranged things so that it would be possible for a

* John H. Fahey, a trustee from 1919 on, in conversation with the author.

majority of the membership of any organization to throw him
out if it saw fit to do so. Why should he have done that if his
thirst were for power? Why should he resent opposition when
he had carefully arranged to make opposition effective?

There is no more than a partial answer to this. That partial
answer is that when opposition did develop Filene frequently
fought and fought hard, giving bystanders every reason to believe that he was intent on holding control. He was not one to
surrender to a bluff; the opposition had to prove and prove
beyond a doubt that it had the votes before Filene would surrender anything. But this is not inconsistent with a basic willingness to abide by the principle of majority rule, and he did
abide by it, notably in the case of the Twentieth Century Fund.

As a matter of fact, there is an explanation of his gradual
withdrawal of interest from the fund perfectly consistent with
his character, yet not involving any sense of frustration because
he found himself frequently outvoted in board meetings. It is
possible that he withdrew because he found that the Twentieth
Century Fund began to bore him.

He would have denied this vehemently. To admit that he
dropped any worth-while project simply because it palled
might have seemed to him a confession that his was an essentially frivolous mind. His explanation was that the fund was
growing "too documentary." Nevertheless nothing in his life is
plainer than that Filene never was much interested in a going
concern as such. If he could discover something he could do to
it to make it go faster or in a different direction, his interest
promptly flared up, but merely to maintain a steady pace in an
undeviating line was not at all to his taste.

This is conspicuously true of his career as a merchant. Everyone familiar with the facts admits that his contribution to the
store was a constant succession of ideas for alterations, sometimes in the physical property, more often in methods, but always something different, something new, something nobody
had ever tried before, and usually something involving a cer-

tain amount of risk. It was this characteristic that eventually drove his associates beyond the limit of their endurance. They cast him out because even his admittedly great accomplishments did not, they found, compensate them for being kept perpetually on the rack, wondering, and dreading, what "E.A." was going to do next. It must be remembered that not all of his ideas worked. More than once he adopted policies that cost the store losses that Lincoln Filene, Kirstein, and the rest had much ado to make up. These losses were inconsiderable by comparison with the great profits that his workable ideas brought, but they were large enough to keep conservative men harassed and apprehensive.

By 1929 the Twentieth Century Fund was definitely a going concern. Its policies seemed fairly well settled, and its course appeared clear for a good many years ahead. It was simply not possible for Edward A. Filene to maintain much interest in a situation of that kind. He could think of innumerable things to do to alter the policy or the course of the fund, but when he proposed them the other trustees voted them down. Edward A. Filene was in the business world what the self-starter is in an automobile; once the engine is humming steadily, there is nothing for the self-starter to do until the engine stalls or stops for some other reason. This foundation neither stalled nor stopped; so his interest dwindled, and why not? There was ample reason to explain his relative apathy without dragging in the supposition of ungovernable rage or the intolerable rankling of wounded vanity.

VI

Besides, the restless and inquiring mind was intensely preoccupied with other aspects of the economic situation than its factual and statistical basis. Its immediate effects had suddenly become urgent with the urgency of catastrophe.

The panic of 1929 and the subsequent depression were a ghastly justification of Edward A. Filene's lifelong argument

that the spread between cost of production and price to the
consumer had to be narrowed if the national economy were to
continue to function at a high level of efficiency.

The arguments of the sophists "about it and about" filled not
merely volumes but libraries, yet the facts were horridly simple.
In 1929 the productive capacity of the country, including agri-
cultural production, was at a peak never attained before. The
armies had grounded arms eleven years earlier. There had been
no earthquakes, conflagrations, floods, or disastrous crop failures to impoverish the country. Food, raw materials, and manu-
factured goods were all more abundant than ever before. But
not enough people could buy to remove the goods from the
shelves, so the national economy stalled, and ruin, despair,
and at last starvation began to spread through the land.

It was incontestably a crisis in distribution. Production was
all right. Production was greater than it had ever been. Nevertheless ruin was upon us, and the only possible explanation was
that distribution had broken down.

Every economic doctor in the land, and especially every
quack, had his own diagnosis of the trouble, but Edward A. Filene had advanced his thirty years earlier, a prognosis sustained by the crisis, albeit with a dreadful completeness that he
had never contemplated. He said that distribution broke down
because it was too expensive.

The thesis was vigorously repudiated by retail merchants
who pointed out that retail profits the country over average
well under 5 per cent of dollar sales. As a matter of fact, William Filene's Sons was averaging less than 4 per cent, yet it was
regarded an exceptionally prosperous store. But of course it was
far from Filene's thought to identify the cost of distribution
with the retailer's profit. He included in it every item that adds
to the price of an article on its way from farm or factory to
counter. Interest, dividends, and profits, except the producer's
or manufacturer's profit, he included, but also rents, transportation, insurance, breakage, spoilage, and every other cause of

expense from style changes to bad debts. It is all part of the cost of distribution, and that cost, he averred, had been steadily rising from the day he first entered his father's store. In 1929 it had simply become more than the traffic could bear, and economic depression was the inevitable result.

It followed that a reduction in the cost of distribution was the way out and the only way out. It made little difference how that attack was made. If it ran roughshod over the most sacred principles of Adam Smith, he would not be shocked in the least provided it brought results, and if it did not bring results, it was worthless, although it might be blessed by every classical economist ever heard of.

It was abundantly clear, however, that here was a situation calling for more than fact finding or rather fact finding by methods other than the gathering of information and the compilation of statistics. He had already agreed to the principle that the Twentieth Century Fund should confine its efforts to the assembling of relevant data, and that not through its own exertions but by giving support to others. He had not lost faith in the importance of this procedure, and he wished it to continue; at the same time he felt the urge to try something new and different.

Filene had long since developed the conviction that one of the greatest and most inexcusable wastes in our system of distribution is waste of managerial ability. For a highly competent merchant to be managing a two-clerk store, when he was capable of managing well one with seventy-five employees, he regarded as nothing short of an economic crime. But ability of a high order is rare and costly. He knew by experience that one must have ready money available in considerable sums if one is to be in position to hire men capable of managing large enterprises.

Another inevitable expense of distribution is the cost of the capital tied up in the process. Capital is indispensable, and its cost must be paid, one way or another. But it seemed to Filene that it was not inevitable that its cost should be paid to a relatively small number of investors; was not some arrangement possible by which it might be paid in small amounts to a large number of consumers, to be added to their purchasing power?

By some such steps he argued himself into the belief that the consumers' co-operative offered the most promising available means of making a real attack upon the cost of distribution, and into that project he threw himself with an energy that resulted in the formation of the Consumer Distribution Corporation.

To merchants with more conventional minds this was the ultimate outrage. Here was a man using the money he had made as a retail merchant to support a program that envisaged the eventual extinction of retail merchants! Could treason to one's class go further? Criticism of Filene increased not only in volume but in shrillness.

To Filene this criticism made no sense whatever. It was not he who offered a threat, even a remote one, to the retail merchant. It was the inexorable march of events. He felt indeed that he was offering the competent merchant a way of escape by striving to inaugurate a system under which a highly competent merchandising man might have an opportunity to develop his powers to their fullest capacity as manager of a larger store than he could hope to set up for himself.

As for the man who is a born enterpriser, who can never be content to work as a salaried manager, Filene did not believe he would suffer any serious disadvantage if the bulk of distribution were carried on in large co-ordinated establishments. There would always be specialty shops, carrying luxury goods and novelties, in which a man with a small capital could demonstrate his capacity as an independent. Class distribution did not in Filene's opinion constitute a threat to the national economy and therefore to the capitalistic system, so he perceived no reason for interfering with it.

Such arguments were largely wasted breath of course. Re-

sentful merchants like other businessmen persisted in identi-
fying capitalism with the way in which they had learned to do
business, and a man who questioned one was questioning the
other. Consumer co-operatives were an attack on the prevailing method of doing business; therefore they were socialistic,
probably communistic, and certainly anticapitalistic. It was an
illustration of the age-old tendency of men to identify institutions—the state, the church, the law, the school—with
themselves. Merchants who laughed at the Sun King's gran-
diloquent assertion, "I am the state," had no hesitation in proclaiming, in act if not in word, "I am capitalism"; for they were
so doing in assuming that whatever inconvenienced them was
an attack on capitalism.

In this particular instance however their agitation was, to say
the least, premature. Filene planned the Consumer Distribution Corporation as an instrumentality through which the
theory of the consumer co-operative might be tested in thor-
ough-going fashion, but he did not live to see any really effective test made. Indeed he had been dead nearly ten years
before the corporation was in position to make an experiment of
sufficient magnitude to supply anything more than fragmentary data.

Five years of war account for part of the delay but not all of
it by any means. Filene and his agents discovered in this problem difficulties more formidable by far than those that stood in
the way of, for example, co-operative banking in the credit unions. Consumer co-operatives, and fairly successful ones, are
not unknown in this country, but they are far from common,
and for the most part they are restricted to very limited fields.
They were not reliable as models for co-operative department
stores handling all necessities.

The mere scale of the sort of operation contemplated by Filene altered its nature. The one item of capital illustrates the
point. Every financier knows that the problem of raising a mil-

lion dollars differs from the problem of raising a thousand dollars in more than size. The whole method of going about it is different. Again the problem of raising a large sum from any available source is quite different from raising an equal amount in small individual subscriptions. But a co-operative is not a co-operative unless it is owned by the members, at least in large part.

Added to this was the equally difficult problem of securing competent management. A big business enterprise must have a big businessman at its head, and of all people, really big businessmen are least inclined to devote their energies to new and uncertain enterprises.

All this—and a thousand smaller but thorny problems—served to make the progress of the consumer co-operative project slow and difficult even when it was backed by Filene's money and energy. He died before it had been brought to anything resembling fruition.

But it is nevertheless an illustration of his technique. He started things, put them in competent hands, and then turned to something else. In this instance he organized another foundation, the Good Will Fund, to conduct the research, making it sole owner of the Consumer Distribution Corporation, the active agency that conducts the experiments. To the Good Will Fund he left the residue of his fortune not given to the Twentieth Century Fund, a total of something like two million dollars, half of it in the form of the assets of the Consumer Distribution Corporation. After his death his associates altered the setup slightly. They organized a new foundation to which the assets of the Good Will Fund were transferred and out of respect to the donor's memory did what he refused to do—added his name to it. The new foundation, the one now operative, is the Edward A. Filene Good Will Fund.

Through the two foundations, therefore, Filene's ideas are still effective. Fact finding goes ahead, and its necessary corollary, experimental action, goes ahead. As a social technician he was by no means beyond criticism, but he did work rather effectively to defeat time and chance and to give his thinking a degree of permanence not always attained by students of civilization.

CHAPTER 7

The Prophet

<<<<<<<<<<<<<<<<<<<<<<<<<<<<<<<<<<<<<<<<<<<<<<<<<<<<<<<

I

WHAT MOVED Edward A. Filene to desire that his ashes be scattered upon the surface of the Charles River Basin is beyond conjecture, but he did, and the skeptical realist whose favorite maxim was, "There are no miracles," came to an earthly end like that of the great mystic, Mahatma Gandhi, who believed that everything is a miracle. The ceremonies, however, were necessarily different, as different as Boston is from Allahabad, where Gandhi's son made the disposal according to the elaborate Hindu ritual and in the presence of wailing thousands.

When the funerary urn arrived in Boston one of Filene's friends, uncertain of the correct procedure, consulted a city official, asking where to apply for the permit he assumed to be necessary.

"Don't apply," advised the realistic official after considering the matter. "The request is unprecedented, therefore it will upset any city office you may approach. If you went to the Bureau of Vital Statistics, for instance, they would certainly refer you to the Health Department, which would feel constrained to consult the police, who would certainly lay the matter before the park authorities. In the meantime the newspapers would get hold of it, all the crackpots in town would write letters to the editor, and there would be a flood of the very sort of publicity that Filene would have hated. Just go ahead and do it,

attracting as little attention as possible, and if anyone says anything, argue about it afterward."

So it happened that a small group of Filene's intimates
waited until the toy yachtsmen had gone home at the end of
the day and then went quietly out into the darkness and scattered the ashes upon the river. Rumor has it that a police launch
was put at their disposal and that a high police official was
aboard, but what was done was done unofficially and appears
in no record.

At first glance any sort of parallel between Edward A. Filene
and Mohandas K. Gandhi may seem utterly impossible and
the similarity of their obsequies a grotesque accident. But the
truth is that below the superficialities the Eastern mystic and
the Western realist were not as far apart as many people suppose, and the symbolism of complete withdrawal from the
world is as appropriate to the one as to the other.

They were at any rate alike in being free of the particular sort
of vanity that tormented Shelley's King Ozymandias, and the
pharaoh whom the Greeks called Cheops. They did not believe
that pyramids and colossi can give a man the sort of fame worth
having. Neither wished to have a mausoleum or a column
raised over his mortal remains. Neither cared to leave as relics
anything tangible or ponderable. They aspired to build, indeed, but with ideas not with brick and stone. If their ideas
prove durable, their memory will be preserved safely enough; if
not, masonry or sculpture would be but an ironical tribute to
their fame.

The epigrammatist called Filene a cross between a pack peddler and the prophet Isaiah. Perhaps what the man who turned
the phrase had in mind was no more than that Isaiah talked a
great deal and thunderously, but the comparison is valid further if one gives to the Son of whom Isaiah spoke the significance, not of an individual messiah, but of humanity. In that
case much of the old Hebrew's sonorous poetry expresses pretty
adequately Filene's thought: "All we like sheep have gone

astray; we have turned every one to his own way; and the Lord hath laid on him the iniquity of us all." Understand by "him" not the Son of David but the common man, and there is nothing in the passage that Filene would have denied.

He did not willingly speak much of religion, but only because he thought most of the talk on that subject is empty, not because he was afraid of discussing it. In 1934 he was pressed to make a contribution to a symposium on "Religion—Today and Tomorrow," and he spoke briefly but pointedly. "To me, religion is first of all belief—not a list of beliefs," he said. "It is a drive toward ultimate good—not a conclusion concerning ultimate good." Gandhi might have commented that there is nothing in that inconsistent with the basic philosophy of Hinduism, and Thomas Aquinas could have incorporated it in the *Summa* without difficulty. What it meant was, of course, that Filene's was a religion without theology, just as his politics was democratic without partisanship, and his economics capitalistic without authoritarianism. He was, in sum, very nearly a free spirit, and it is as such that his significance, or lack of it, in the future will be determined.

II

But careless use has attached to the term free spirit many connotations that are false and misleading. One should therefore employ it with caution and never without an explanation of what it is not intended to imply.

For one thing, it has nothing to do with careless gaiety and not much with happiness. Edward A. Filene was far from being altogether solemn. He had a keen sense of the ridiculous, and he was capable at times of seeing the ridiculous in himself. This was conspicuously true of his public acts and relations. No one knew better that his activities were frequently—he would have said usually—futile and occasionally absurd. In general he took his work seriously indeed, but he was not incapable of laughing at himself, even in public, as his sardonic references to his own failures demonstrate. He cannot justly be listed among the dreary pomposities that afflict the world.

But he was a long way from being a happy man. In part this was due to the limitation of his sense of humor. It did not cover his personal relations. His quarrels with those for whom he had a genuine affection could frequently have been avoided, and always softened, if he had held toward them the attitude of tolerance he held toward business competitors or frank and open opponents of his various social and economic projects.

In a way his extreme bitterness toward members of his family and close associates with whom he had quarreled was a left-handed compliment to them. The trouble arose from the fact not that he thought too little of them but that he thought too much. He demanded perfection of those he loved, never of those to whom he was indifferent. It is not recorded that Edward A. Filene ever hated a man whom he had regarded from the beginning as a low fellow. His attitude was that if God made him a swine it was foolish to be angry with him for acting swinishly. It might be necessary in the public interest to take a stick and hit him on the snout, but it was not necessary, indeed it was senseless, to hate him and to pursue him vindictively.

But a man to whom Filene had given his affection, one in whom he had found some admirable qualities, he promptly endowed with all other admirable qualities, including a perception that could penetrate all Filene's frequently hazy hopes and aspirations and make possible perfect understanding. Naturally he discovered this superhuman quality in no one, and his sense of humor was not broad enough to enable him to see the absurdity of expecting it. The result was a series of quarrels that not only hampered his influence and detracted from his dignity but gave him intense personal pain.

Another barrier between him and any lasting happiness was the nasty trick nature played him in endowing the seller of pins with an inextinguishable vitality. The cause is plain enough, but knowing the cause does not eliminate the fact. What was a streak of startling meanness in the millionaire had been a virtue in the adolescent suddenly thrust into a position of responsibility. The spectacle of Filene, the successful merchant and celebrated publicist, getting into an elevator and going all the way up to his hotel room to turn out the light he had left burning is absurd, but for seventeen-year-old Filene to make sure that every light in the little store in Lynn was extinguished before the doors were locked was not absurd; it was plain common sense. If he had not fought desperately rather than be cheated out of a quarter in those days, he would never have become a millionaire. But frequent repetition in the early years made the reaction automatic—a conditioned reflex that could not be eliminated when the need for it had passed.

Nevertheless it was an unpleasant characteristic that drove away people whose companionship he might have had to the enrichment of his life. It was no small factor in bringing about the discontent that everyone about him observed as one of the salient features of his existence.

At the same time if both these factors had been eliminated and he had been endowed with the utmost tolerance and freed from every picayune trait, it does not necessarily follow that he would have been a happy man. He would still have been lonely, and loneliness is not ordinarily a contribution to happiness.

Free spirits are inevitably lonely precisely to the extent that they are free. Obviously a man cannot be a pathfinder and yet walk with the crowd, but a mind that is bound and inhibited by precedent and tradition is not free.

Filene was the more unhappy because apparently he never quite understood this condition. Freedom to him was an absolute good. Other men said that they valued it, and he assumed that they meant what they said. It was late in life that he discovered—if indeed he ever did—that, while all Americans, drilled as school children in the doctrines of 1776, proclaim their devotion to freedom, the masses of men are more terrified than attracted by it. Always the advances in human freedom, in this country as in every other, have been won by a few men who have been able to indoctrinate, perhaps at times to intoxicate, the masses. In the nature of the case those few were lonely men.

It is notoriously true of political leaders. Washington, Jefferson, Lincoln, although they all had tremendous adulation, had few really close friends, Lincoln almost none. Filene had seen with his own eyes how lonely Wilson was. Perhaps the gaiety of the second Roosevelt blinded him, as it did many others, to the truth that the genuine intimates, even of that great extrovert, were very few.

What is true of politicians is equally true of any other sort of leader. Since that hypothetical individual who first swallowed an oyster, it is to be doubted that any man in human history has presented an idea that was really and completely new; most that are so called are, like Filene's, merely slight modifications of notions that have been known and discussed for many years. But even so much novelty in thinking sets the thinker apart and usually fills his associates with uneasiness and distrust. There is no calculation in this; it is an inevitable condition of life as we live it.

Filene felt the uneasiness and distrust with which he was regarded. Intellectually he perceived, at least toward the end of his life, that its real basis was not his freedom but others' bondage to old ideas and outworn concepts. Emotionally however he was never quite able to cope with it. He might say, as he frequently did say, that his antagonists were not bad men but good men hampered by out-of-date thinking, yet while that might satisfy his mind, in his heart he probably felt some stirring of the old emotion that poisoned his boyhood when he was afflicted with eczema. He thought he knew what made men look at him curiously, but after all could he be *sure* he was not breaking out in spots? It is not the sort of thing that adds to any man's happiness, but it is familiar enough to everyone who takes even a single stride off the beaten path.

The embarrassment, the discontent, the disappointment, the

perplexity that harassed this man are too plain to be ignored. They were a large part of his experience in the world, therefore we say he was not happy. But in so saying we are, of course, measuring happiness by the yardstick in common use. We are taking no account of the possibility that he enjoyed a profounder content than is reached by some men whose existence is far less troubled and who seem to be gaining far more pleasure out of life.

Yet nothing is more certain than the existence of this deeper content. The daimon of Socrates has been known to many other men, who have found in obedience to the inner urge the only possibility of a tolerable life. Filene might have found plain that cryptic passage in the *Apology*, "If I tell you that I cannot hold my tongue, you will not believe that I am serious; and if I say again that daily to discourse about virtue, and of those other things about which you hear me examining myself and others, is the greatest good of man, and that the unexamined life is not worth living, you are still less likely to believe me." Like the Greek, the American fulfilled his destiny undeterred by censure, misunderstanding, and unhappiness. Socrates encountered death itself with a serenity that has astonished the ages; perhaps the American had some share of that inner content that compensated him for all malaises.

III

Edward A. Filene's significance for the future will be disclosed in the future. It is not within the province of this work to make oracular deliverances on the subject. But he has already made certain contributions that give him a definite place in the development of American political, social, and economic thought.

This is not an assertion that he was an original thinker. He was nothing of the sort. He was a picker-up of what he described as good ideas lying loose around the world. He was con-

stantly startling people, and his critics accused him of being
unable to resist any novelty that came his way. But the things
he advocated were not in fact new; they were startling merely
because they had been hitherto overlooked and neglected. Any
idea is new to the man who encounters it for the first time, and
Filene won the reputation of an advanced thinker simply because most of his hearers had not thought at all about the subjects he presented.

Nor can it be successfully established that he was a notably
sound thinker. He was wrong many times, and even when he
was right in the main, he sometimes clouded his argument by
introducing *non sequiturs* of the most blatant type.

But if it is admitted, as it must be, that he was not original at
all and sound only part of the time, the impact of his ideas upon
the world must be accounted for by some factor in his personality not strictly intellectual. The factor is not far to seek. He
was prophetic.

His concern with the future was singularly consistent. It affected his whole being. One striking evidence of it is the fact
that he never stopped growing in mind and character. The tra-
jectory of his intellectual development was not a curve, as it is
with most men, but a straight line. Filene at seventy-seven,
when he died, was a bigger man than he was at seventy-five,
and at seventy-five he was far bigger than he had been at fifty.
He passed from sight still rising.

This is sufficiently unusual to make him worth attention for
that reason alone. It is not often that a life of seventy-seven
years, a life of great activity and impressive accomplishment, is
nevertheless more of a promise than a fulfillment. Only one
American in fifty attains that age and those who do are usually
finished, as far as any notable contribution to the thought of
their times is concerned. When a Holmes and a Brandeis prove
exceptions to that rule, the world stares in amazement. Filene
is another exception. An extrapolation of his mental develop-

ment makes possible the belief that if he had been given an additional ten years they would have been the greatest decade of his life.

But, despite earlier references to Isaiah, he was distinctly not a Hebrew prophet. In nothing was he more completely American than in the character of his divination, for it was hopeful prophecy, not a forecast of wrath to come. It is entirely possible that it was as useless as the prophecies of Cassandra, but it was not as terrifying; in fact it was not terrifying at all but bursting with typically American optimism.

For it was a reaffirmation of the old faith that America held in the beginning. We have not been deceived, said Filene, we have merely been lethargic. Democracy has not been exhausted as a method of ordering the affairs of men; democracy as yet is largely untried. Capitalism is not outmoded as an economic system; most of the possibilities of capitalism have not even been explored, much less developed. Our failure is not attributable to our having had faith in democracy and capitalism but is due to our having been content with a pseudodemocracy and a half-organized capitalism instead of pushing boldly on to realize all the potentialities of each. We have not gone in the wrong direction; we have only failed to go far enough in the right direction. Such success as we have scored in finding the good life in the past can be, will be, doubled and redoubled in the future where lies the real Golden Age.

Filene, often denounced as a radical, was the great deflater of radicalism, decrying it as unnecessary. Every lure that radicalism holds before the eyes of the less fortunate to induce them to support revolutionary programs Filene examined and showed how it might be attained without revolution, except as material readjustment of our ways of thinking may be called revolution. He trumpeted abroad that the insensate greed that has all but wrecked the world has only to be enlightened by study and observation to become the most powerful of constructive forces. He may have been wrong, but he was impressive.

Finally, he was not a scholar whose world was enclosed by his library walls, nor a writer skilled in the weaving of fantasy, nor a politician with his ear attuned to the growling of the mob. He was a successful businessman who found his ideas in the market place and tested them by the processes habitually used in the business world. He spoke the language of trade and industry, and traders and industrialists recognized it. The theories of a Thorstein Velben, the prophecies of a Bernard Shaw, the promises of a Huey Long are easily shrugged off by businessmen, for what do such people know of a businessman's experience? But a merchant, and one who had made millions in retail merchandising, was different. It was not to be denied that when he spoke men heard the voice of one segment of American business.

This is the essence of his prophecy—an assertion that out of the American business world may come, will come, men whose hard intelligence, forged in the heat of competition, is capable of seeing the larger profit and the greater good behind the confusions of this disorderly world, and whose sense of responsibility will nerve them to grapple with the difficulties and bring order out of the confusion.

It may be a false prophecy. He may have overestimated both the intelligence and the patriotism of his own class. Nevertheless a prophecy it is, and it is what Filene means to the world. His ideas are still part of today's intellectual ferment. The foundations he established are still operating, and it is easily possible that their influence in the future may greatly exceed all they have attained in the past. Even so, they are not and never will be as important as the proclamation by a businessman that one who knows his business, really knows it in all its implications as well as in its immediate necessities, must necessarily be a worker for the common good, must necessarily be a liberal in politics and a supporter of the old moralities in his private life, because nothing else is good business.

This is a proclamation of American business—not of all business, not of the greater part of business, but nevertheless of business. The environment that produced one Filene can produce another. As a matter of fact, it has produced more than one, for Filene was by no means the only social statesman who has come in recent years from the market to the forum. He prophesied boldly that in the not distant future his would be the dominant element, while the shortsighted who live and strive for their individual advantage regardless of the common good will be reduced to a subsidiary role.

It is a glittering prophecy, too much so to be accepted readily by a battered and cynical generation. But it makes its propounder a fascinating figure whom the world will not willingly forget, and if time should prove that it is true even in relatively small part, future generations will regard him as tremendous. Simmias, the bystander, "seeing all these things" can do no less than agree fervently that "fair is the prize, and the hope great."

INDEX

Index

265